Gerhard L. Weinberg

Editor

Hitler's Second Book

The Unpublished Sequel to *Mein Kampf*

by
Adolf Hitler

Translated by Krista Smith

Enigma Books

Enigma Books

580 Eighth Avenue, New York, NY 10018
www.enigmabooks.com

Übersetzung der Orginalausgabe
—veröffentlicht vom Institut für Zeitgeschichte in München—
Hitlers zweites Buch.
Ein Dokument aus dem Jahr 1928.
Eingeleitet und kommentiert von
Gerhard L. Weinberg.
Stuttgart 1961

Überarbeitete Neuauflage erschienen in der Dokumentation
HITLER. REDEN—SCHRIFTEN—ANORDNUNGEN.
Februar 1925 bis Januar 1933
Band II A
**Außenpolitische Standortbestimmung.
Nach der Reichstagswahl.**
Juni – Juli 1928.
Eingeleitet von Gerhard L. Weinberg.
Herausgegeben und kommentiert von
Gerhard L. Weinberg, Christian Hartmann und
Klaus A. Lankheit.
München 1995

Introduction by Gerhard L. Weinberg
Edited and annotated by Gerhard L. Weinberg, 2003

Translated by Krista Smith
First English-language edition
ISBN 1-929631-16-2

Library of Congress Cataloging-in-Publication Data

Hitler, Adolf, 1889-1945.
[Hitlers zweites Buch. English]
Hitler's second book : the unpublished sequel to Mein kampf / Gerhard L. Weinberg, editor ; translated by Krista Smith. — 1st English-language ed.
p. cm.
Includes bibliographical footnotes and index.
ISBN: 1-929631-16-2
1. National socialism. 2. Germany—Politics and government—1918-1933. 3. Germany—Foreign relations—20th century. I. Weinberg, Gerhard L. II. Smith, Krista. III. Hitler, Adolf, 1889-1945. Mein kampf. IV. Title. V. Title: Hitlers zweites Buch.

DD247.H5 A365 2003
943.086—dc21

Contents

Foreword by Gerhard L. Weinberg   vii

Introduction by Gerhard L. Weinberg

   I The Authenticity and History of the Document   xi

  II The Origin of the Book in 1928   xiv

 III The Content of the Book   xxi

 IV Why Was the Manuscript Not Published?   xxiii

  V Why Publish the Text Now?   xxv

Editorial Method   xxvii

Translator's Note   xxix

The Document

Preface   *3*

   I *War and Peace in the Struggle for Survival*   *7*

  II *Fighting, Not Industry, Secures Life*   *16*

 III *Race, Conflict, and Power*   *29*

 IV *Foreign Policy Critique and Proposals*   *38*

  V *The Policies of the NSDAP*   *48*

 VI *From the Unification of the Reich to a Policy of Space*   *51*

 VII *The Misguided Economic and Alliance Policies of the Second Reich*   *58*

VIII *Necessity of Military Power—The Borders of 1914 Not the Goal*   *83*

 IX *Neither Border Policies Nor Economic Policies Nor Pan-Europe*   *99*

  X *No Neutrality*   *119*

 XI *Germany's Political Situation: No Alliance with Russia*   *134*

 XII *Basic Principles of German Foreign Policy*   *153*

XIII The Possible Goals   *155*

XIV Germany and England   *160*

XV Germany and Italy   *175*

XVI -Conclusion   *224*

Appendix I   235

Appendix II   236

Notes   241

Index   289

FOREWORD

by Gerhard L. Weinberg

U ntil 1958 the actual document of what became known as *Hitler's Second Book* remained hidden within the archives of captured German records in Alexandria, Virginia, where I located it. Hitler had dictated the text in 1928 but never had it published. In 1961 the Institute for Contemporary History in Munich published the book with the title, *Hitlers Zweites Buch: Ein Dokument aus dem Jahr 1928* (Hitler's Second Book: A Document of the Year 1928.)

The availability of a reliable English-language text is especially important for English-speaking readers and Americans in particular because beyond the repetition of such themes from Hitler's earlier work, *Mein Kampf*, as the eternal struggle for land, the racial basis of all history, the need for Germany to conquer additional living space, and the endless repetition of the importance of fighting an imaginary Jewish enemy, there are also themes of particular relevance today. There is far more extensive discussion of the United States than can be found elsewhere. It is somewhat more positive than his later remarks, and it culminates in the assertion that a Nazi government of Germany would have as one of its major responsibilities the preparation of the country for war with the United States. This belief of Hitler's may make it easier for Americans to understand why, as soon as the initial rearmament steps of Hitler's government had in his eyes reached the point at which the weapons needed for war with Britain and France were well on the road to full production, he gave orders in 1937 for the development of the inter-continental bombers and super-battleships he considered necessary for war against the United States. And this at a time when the United States Congress was busy passing the so-called "neutrality laws."

There are, furthermore, still those who imagine that Hitler hoped to reverse the losses Germany had incurred through the 1919 Peace Treaty of Versailles. As he constantly asserted in his speeches and explains in detail in this work, that was the last thing Germany needed. In his eyes, the demand for this by other German politicians only showed what utter fools they were. A National Socialist government would never follow such a route; it would fight wars for hundreds of thousands of square kilometers of land, not the little snippets that Germany had lost in 1919 and that would never suffice for the Germans to feed themselves on their own land. And, if Germany was to dominate the globe, obviously, as he points out in this work, the end of each war that he would lead for massive additional land would only provide the basis for the next conflict.

Both in the thinking of some and in Nazi propaganda during the war, there is the notion of Germany as a bulwark against Bolshevik Russia. In Hitler's racial perception of history, however, the Bolshevik Revolution became a racial displacement of the allegedly Germanic ruling elite of the Tsarist regime by a bunch of incompetents now ruling racial inferiors. It was, therefore, a stroke of great good luck for a German government that saw in this the easier opportunity to seize land for settlement in Eastern Europe.

Neither the inter-continental bombers nor the super-battleships were ever built; and the derogatory view that Hitler had of Slavic (and one should say Chinese) people turned out to be grossly mistaken; but a revolution halted in its tracks cannot be understood without attention to the beliefs of those in charge and the goals toward which they thought themselves headed. Those who are interested in understanding one of the major and most evil figures of the twentieth century will find Hitler's exposition of his own views essential.

Since the 1961 German-language edition of this book quickly went out of print and there was new evidence about the manuscript and additional relevant scholarship, the Institute of Contemporary History in Munich decided ten years ago to include the text of the document with a revised introduction by myself, and additional notes provided by members of the Institute staff, Christian Hartmann and Klaus A. Lankheit, as a special volume in its comprehensive edition of Hitler's speeches and writings. The intent to publish, at the time, a carefully translated and edited edition in the English language that would immediately follow the original German one was aborted by the appearance of a pirated edition which appropriated many of my notes but was neither carefully translated nor properly annotated.

In the Foreword of the original German edition I thanked a number of individuals who had helped me at that time. In addition, special thanks are due to Dr. Albrecht Tyrell, who provided me with significant archival information incorporated in the Introduction and to the staff members of the Institute of Contemporary History in Munich. I am very pleased that Enigma Books has decided to publish a carefully prepared English-language edition of this important source. The only extensive work dictated by Adolf Hitler other than *Mein Kampf* is therefore now accessible to those in the English-speaking world.

Although as editor I accept responsibility for the introduction and commentary, the author—Adolf Hitler—is responsible for the content—rambling, repetitive, and highly questionable from both a factual and a moral perspective. Sixty years after World War II it is surely important to show again how directly Hitler's thinking led to the great catastrophe.

—Gerhard L. Weinberg
October 2003

Introduction

by Gerhard L. Weinberg

I

The Authenticity and History of the Document

In view of the appearance of a supposed diary of Adolf Hitler which was exposed as a fake,[1] evidence of the falsification of a number of documents in the volume *Hitler: Sämtliche Aufzeichnungen 1905-1924*,[2] and the numerous forgeries in a book about Hitler's paintings and drawings,[3] it is important first to say something about the authenticity and history of the document being published here.

The first public reference to the existence of an additional book by Adolf Hitler appeared in 1949 in the book by former French officer Albert Zoller, *Adolf Hitler privat: Erlebnisbericht seiner Geheimsekretärin*.[4] According to this account, in 1925 Hitler had started an unpublished book on foreign policy, which he kept secret and mentioned only very rarely. On the basis of this reference, I began to search for the manuscript. The incorrect (as we now know) date recalled by the secretary, who in any case had only worked for Hitler since 1933, is also found in the only indisputable documented mention of the book known to have been made during Hitler's lifetime—a statement made by Hitler himself.

In 1953 Hugh R. Trevor-Roper (subsequently Lord Dacre of
Glanton) published an English edition of Hitler's table talks.[5] In
this edition, under the date of February 17, 1942, a mention of an
additional book by Hitler appeared—a reference, which, for unknown reasons, Gerhard Ritter had omitted from his prior German edition of the text.[6] Later editions of the table talks in German, however, retained this mention. It reads: "In 1925 I wrote in
Mein Kampf (and also in an unpublished work) that world Jewry saw
in Japan an opponent beyond its reach."[7] Here Hitler is no doubt
alluding to statements on this problem in *Mein Kampf*, volume 2 (pp.
723f.), which he dictated to Max Amann in 1925. They were published in 1926 in a special reprint of the thirteenth chapter, under
the title "The South Tyrolean Question and the German Alliance
Problem,"[8] and appeared in December 1926 (with a copyright date
of 1927) in the second volume.[9] In the manuscript published here,
the discussion does not concern Japan in the sense mentioned; however, there is a great deal about "world Jewry." The reference is also
inaccurate. But the origin of the books was fourteen and seventeen
years prior, respectively, and Hitler's known references to the personal testament he had made less than four years earlier are likewise inaccurate in certain key points.[10]

In the meantime, the Institute of Contemporary History in
Munich also heard about the reported existence of another book.
This news came from Erich Lauer in May 1951. Lauer had published a series of Eher-Verlag songbooks and had been shown the
manuscript of a book by Hitler when he was there during World
War II. Josef Berg, the man who showed it to him, reported on the
manuscript in detail to the Institute in September 1958.[11] Berg had
been a colleague of Max Amann's since the early twenties in the
central publishing house of the NSDAP, Franz Eher Nachfolger.[12]
In January 1935, Berg assumed control of the book publishing division at Eher, and thus of the manuscript. He claimed that Hitler
dictated the manuscript to Amann, and that in addition to the copy
in the Eher-Verlag safe, a second copy of the text existed, which

was supposedly stored at the Obersalzberg. Both claims would be confirmed with the discovery of the manuscript.[13]

When the Institute of Contemporary History asked me, on the basis of this information, about the whereabouts of the manuscript, I had already searched for it in the German files then located in Alexandria, Virginia, where they were being microfilmed jointly by the American Historical Association and American authorities prior to being returned to the Federal Republic. In the summer of 1958 I located a document that had been laid aside as a draft of *Mein Kampf*, and succeeded in identifying it as the sought-after manuscript. It was then released for research. Enclosed with the document was a confiscation memo, which is included as an appendix to this publication. According to this report, the document was seized by an American officer in May 1945 from the Eher-Verlag; it was handed over by Joseph Berg with the claim that it was a work written by Hitler more than fifteen years earlier. Shortly after the seizure, a microfilm was made for an English authority; the original was brought with other files to the United States. In the Record Center in Alexandria it was filed under EAP 105/40. Later, it was transferred to the German Federal Archive where it is filed as BA, N 1128 (Hitler), volume 21.

In 1961 the manuscript, for which I provided an introduction and notes, was published for the first time in the "Quellen und Darstellungen zur Zeitgeschichte" (Sources and Representations of Contemporary History) series put out by the Institute of Contemporary History. Two years later a French translation followed, without an introduction; some of my notes were included, but without any reference to their author.[14] An English version, hastily rushed to market, was characterized by one reviewer as "in many respects a burlesque imitation of the Weinberg edition."[15] The reviewer's prophecy, that "its appearance in such poor translation with inadequate editorial framework unfortunately precludes a trustworthy scholarly edition in English," was borne out in the following decades.

When the present 1961 German publication was announced in Germany, Albert Speer noted in his diary that Baldur von Schirach and Rudolf Hess viewed the whole thing as a fraud, but he himself remembered that Hitler, at the time of the construction of the Berghof, had "accepted a hundred thousand mark advance" from the Eher-Verlag "for a manuscript that he—for reasons of foreign policy—did not yet wish to see published."[16]

Immediately after the first publication, the scholarly community assessed the document as genuine. Major articles about the book accepted the authenticity as certain.[17] As far as the editor is aware, no scholar has disputed the authenticity of the document or the identification of Hitler as the author.

Several years after the first publication of the *Second Book*, the German scholar Albrecht Tyrell discovered—in the Central State Archive of Lower Saxony (Niedersächsischen Hauptstaatsarchiv Hannover)—a letter signed by Rudolf Hess in Hitler's chancellery in Munich, dated June 26, 1928. Hess responded to a request for an appointment for Bernhard Rust with the reply that "Herr Hitler is likely to be in Berlin for several days at the beginning of July. A visit by *Pg.* [National Socialist party member] Rust can hardly be considered earlier, as Herr Hitler will probably be away from Munich until his trip to Berlin, in order to write his book."[18] This document proves not only that Hess knew at that time about Hitler's work on another book—the second volume of *Mein Kampf* had already appeared—but also confirms the date suggested for the manuscript's origin in the introduction of the first publication.[19] The history of the document can thus be considered certain.

II

The Origin of the Book in 1928

T he content of the book fits well with the late June and early July 1928 time frame mentioned in the letter from Rudolf Hess. All of the current political events referred to in the manuscript fall within the specified period. The many attacks on the still living Gustav Stresemann (e.g., pp. 85 and 247), the comment on the occupied left bank of the Rhine (p. 170), and the lack of a reference to the Young Plan (p. 258) point to the years 1927 to 1929. In the preface, Hitler speaks of the two years since the 1926 publication of the chapter on the South Tyrolean question from the second volume of *Mein Kampf*. In another passage (note 385), Hitler refers to the destruction of the Bismarck Tower in Bromberg at the beginning of May 1928 as an event that took place "in the last few months."[20] The book contains various references to the opera *Jonny Strikes Up* (pp. 238-241), which was staged in Munich in 1928 and attacked by the National Socialists. In one passage (p. 238), Hitler speaks about the alleged losses of the party in the first five months of the year, using the same words as in a speech on July 13, 1928.[21] Hitler also cites (pp. 258ff.) an article appearing "today" in the *Münchener Neuesten Nachrichten*; this article appeared in the June 26, 1928, edition.

The date thus confirmed twice—by the letter from Hess and the references in the text—corresponds with the events of the summer of 1928. These circumstances also provide good evidence for Hitler's decision to dictate another book; at the same time, they explain the book's focus on foreign policy questions, especially the South Tyrolean problem. And his decision not to publish the text is probably also related to this.

In the years prior to 1928, Hitler had dealt numerous times with foreign policy questions. Because these concerns—particularly the strained relations with Italy due to the South Tyrolean question—are the focal point of this work, it is necessary in addressing the issue to take a step back.

Hitler had already considered the issue of a future National Socialist foreign policy before the putsch attempt in November 1923, and in this context he had emphasized that German-Italian relations were particularly important.[22] He had by then already decided on an alliance with Italy; his conclusion, which he drew on November 14, 1922, stated: "For this purpose, Germany must make a clear and concise renunciation of the Germans in South Tyrol."[23] It is unlikely that this decision was in some way related to Mussolini's financial support of the NSDAP, as was later claimed.

At the end of World War I, Italy had been allowed by the peace treaty with Austria to annex the Austrian province of Tyrol up to the Brenner Pass in the Alps. This change placed under Italian control both those inhabitants in the southernmost portion of the transferred land who were predominantly of Italian cultural background and those closer to the new border who were of German background. In the discourse and political debates of the time, this issue was generally referred to as the "South Tyrol Question."

After the failed putsch attempt, Hitler began composing *Mein Kampf* while in prison. The first volume, published in 1925, contained some statements on foreign policy, but these issues were not addressed in greater depth until the second volume, which appeared in 1926. The content cannot be reviewed here. Hitler's position on the South Tyrolean question was already felt to be contestable at the time. The German-speaking population of South Tyrol, in terms of its cultural life, was probably the most besieged in Europe at that time; under these circumstances it was hardly surprising that those who considered themselves particularly nationalistic pointed to this.[24]

Under these circumstances and in line with his aggressive instinct, Hitler, as mentioned, published the chapter on this topic[25] as a special reprint, with a preface dated February 12, 1926. In the preface to this pamphlet, titled "The South Tyrolean Question and the German Alliance Problem," Hitler complained that except with reference to the Locarno Pact, the press reported only on South Tyrol. Hitler viewed this interest in South Tyrol as merely a pretext for agitating against the "phenomenal genius" Mussolini—an assumption that he repeats many times in this manuscript. To counter the disparagement of Mussolini, he decided to distribute the relevant part of his work as a special pamphlet.[26]

The following year—1927—Alfred Rosenberg's work *Der Zukunftsweg einer deutschen Aussenpolitik* (The Future Direction of German Foreign Policy) appeared.[27]

The ideas are, on the whole, the same as those found in *Mein Kampf*, especially the incessantly recurring claim, here greatly elaborated, that "Lebensraum" must be won in Eastern Europe.[28] France and Poland are the enemies of Germany; England and Italy, in contrast, are "not affected" (p. 59) by this ethnic imperialism. The statements about Italy emphasize that Mussolini, although he had not yet turned against the Jews, had indeed recognized the danger of Freemasonry and was fighting it. That was why the South Tyrolean question provided a welcome cause for agitation against Mussolini, who had been poorly counseled in the handling of this issue. Italy must seek its future in North Africa and on the Adriatic, and therefore must proceed against France and Yugoslavia. That would draw Italy toward Germany as well, allow the South Tyrolean question to disappear, and show at the same time that it would not be in Italy's interest to obstruct the union of Austria with Germany (pp. 86-97).

On March 30, 1927, Hitler made markedly positive statements about Mussolini and his "imperialistic" policy, making it clear that an alliance between Germany and Italy should not be allowed to break down over the issue of South Tyrol.[29] This defense of Mussolini led to an attack on Hitler in an open letter from the "Deutsch-völkischen Arbeitsgemeinschaft für Südtirol" (Ethnic German Consortium for South Tyrol).[30] This open letter was reprinted by the "Bund Deutscher Aufbau" (German Development League) during the election campaign of 1930 in a small pamphlet of "secret documents"—a pamphlet that was placed on the official "list of harmful and undesirable writings" after Hitler's appointment as chancellor.[31] In the late twenties, however, Hitler could not ignore the question so easily.

The South Tyrolean question was also in the forefront of German public awareness in 1928. In February, public opinion—particularly in Austria—was aroused when the Italian language was introduced into religious education in South Tyrol. After a pointed speech by Austrian Chancellor Ignaz Seipel, Mussolini was quick to respond and temporarily recalled the envoy Giacinto Auriti from Vienna. From March onward, a heated press campaign focused on the South

Tyrolean question; both the German public and the press participated actively until the conflict was resolved in early July by Seipel's retreat, which calmed the situation. The Nazi Party newspaper *Völkischer Beobachter* could not keep entirely quiet about these somewhat awkward developments for the NSDAP. When the conflict began, the *Völkischer Beobachter* reported on it quite matter-of-factly (on January 20 and February 24 and 25), while trying at the same time to downplay the events (see the *Reisebrief* [Travel Report] from Italy in the January 17 issue of the *Völkischer Beobachter*). On March 3, Rosenberg weighed in with an article "Vienna and Rome": Everything was a pretext for Jews and Marxists to agitate against Italy. On March 6, Rosenberg assessed Mussolini's March 4 speech somewhat more negatively. He believed Mussolini had been "poorly counseled" and that his sharp words had played into the hands of his and Germany's enemies. The next day, Rosenberg's editorial already took a completely different tone again. Under the headline "The Marxist Swindle of South Tyrol," he claimed that the international press agencies had misrepresented Mussolini's speech; the issue was really only those agitators against Italy who saw in the German people of South Tyrol a means of fighting against Mussolini. Similar articles appeared in the following weeks (for example, on March 9 and 14), and on April 11 Rosenberg commented approvingly on the recommendation by a Dr. Eduard Melkus, of Vienna, of a German-Italian-Hungarian alliance which would end the South Tyrolean agitation through the subsequent facilitation of the annexation of Austria by Germany and through Italian concessions in South Tyrol.

Meanwhile, campaigning had begun in Germany for the May 20, 1928, Reichstag elections. Gustav Stresemann was running in Bavaria, where Hitler attacked him in a speech on April 17 in Munich.[32] Under the title "Stresemann: The Candidate by France's Grace," he played the well-known melody in the usual key for his enthusiastic adherents. Politics are the battle for the basis from which to feed the people; Germany's lack of Lebensraum cannot be solved by industry and should not be counterbalanced by emigration. France is the hereditary enemy. Stresemann would follow the wishes of France and lead Germany to its doom. Then Hitler explained the agitation against him, using the South Tyrolean question as an example: "It's exactly the same game as with South Tyrol: a huge hue and cry, but if an Andreas Hofer stands up, he should take care that he doesn't come to Germany on his flight, or he will be arrested and extradited."[33] When Stresemann spoke on April 25 at a Munich election meeting, he was shouted down by National Socialists.[34] Hitler's later election speeches followed the usual pattern: Lebensraum, not industry, internationalism, or pacifism, but fighting, power, purity of blood, personal qualities, and so on.[35]

In the final days of the election campaign, however, the South Tyrolean question was brought up against the National Socialists. These attacks peaked with the "Adolf Hitler Unmasked" placards that appeared on election day—May 20—in Munich, printed by the Social Democratic Party. The posters included claims about alleged financial support by Mussolini for Hitler and Franz Ritter von Epp (top candidate of the NSDAP) in exchange for their agitation in favor of the relinquishment of South Tyrol. Hitler and Epp took legal action.[36] A long and thrilling trial followed[37]—though not until 1929–1930—in which a certain Werner Abel, who would be killed in Dachau in 1935, appeared as chief witness. We do not need to examine the reliability of Abel's statements here. In any case, Hitler wanted to respond to the attacks immediately. He had already spoken about the South Tyrolean question on May 19 in Munich,[38] in words very similar to those found in this manuscript. It was not the National Socialists but the Jews and Marxists who had betrayed South Tyrol. Italy and Germany must go together. The borders of 1914 are not at all a reasonable goal for a new war. A pro-South Tyrol heckler was thrown out. At the same time, a meeting of the NSDAP was announced for May 23, 1928, in the Bürgerbräukeller; at this meeting Hitler would comment at length on the slander regarding South Tyrol.

In this speech, Hitler repeated many of the thoughts already stated in *Mein Kampf*.[39] He claimed that the Marxists and the Jews were Germany's enemies and were fighting Italy as the only authoritarian state. Similarly, Japan was also attacked as a troublemaker in the Far East. Looking back, he claimed that the Social Democrats had betrayed South Tyrol; they had no concern for the Germans in Alsace, the Sudetenland, and so on—they only protested about the Germans in South Tyrol, no doubt out of fear that a nationalist movement might prevail in Germany as well. As always, Hitler rejected the borders of 1914 as an inadequate goal over which a war should not be fought. "I believe I would have enough energy to lead our people to where it must shed its blood; not for a border adjustment, however, but rather *for salvation in the distant future*, so that so much ground and land can be gained that the blood lost can be given back to posterity many times over." Everything must be based on preparation for war against France. "If Satan were to come today and offer himself as an ally against France, I would give him my hand…" Apparently, though, Hitler did not wish to wait for Satan, as he explained that Italy and perhaps England would be interested in a war against France. The South Tyroleans, however, should serve as a bridge between Italy and Germany until the two could take up arms together for the war against France.[40]

In July the conflict over the South Tyrolean question eased temporarily. This respite was welcomed by the National Socialists because it diminished the anti-Italian agitation;[41] it also provided the opportunity for an attack on Seipel.[42] Rudolf Hess concluded the discussion of this theme with an article on July 27, "Hitler, South Tyrol, and the Extreme Right-Wing Press." Employing the usual arguments, he repudiated the attacks of the far right as well as the mainstream press against Hitler. Hitler himself did not speak publicly for several weeks after May 23.[43] Only on July 6 did he speak briefly at a Munich recruitment gathering for the SA.[44] His first major speech after May 23, however, was the Berlin speech on foreign policy on July 13. This speech contained lengthy passages whose content—and sometimes even the wording—corresponds with that of this document.[45]

This short overview of the political events of the first half of 1928 allows us to identify Hitler's motives for composing the present manuscript. The overall content is so interrelated that a lengthy interruption in the dictation is highly unlikely. But because Hitler would hardly have had time for such an endeavor during the election campaign, it can be assumed that he did not begin the book until after the election of May 20. In this election, the National Socialists obtained 840,000 votes and 12 Reichstag seats out of 30,738,000 valid votes and 401 seats. Although the National Socialists celebrated the results as a victory,[46] the figures show that it would still take some time before a very large share of the electorate would embrace the swastika. The implication was clear: at least part of the blame lay with the party's foreign policy line. When Hitler analyzed the results of the election, he had to think about the final days of the campaign—and thus about the South Tyrolean question. This explains why, in the preface to the text, he mentions the "South Tyrolean pamphlet," and states that it has become "increasingly clear" to him "over the course of the last two years" that that document already presupposed National Socialist perceptions on the part of the reader. He now wished to repeat the necessary fundamental demonstration of the correctness of his views, "as the attacks of the opposition have not only strengthened in the last few years, but have also mobilized to a certain degree the large camp of the indifferent." It can therefore be accepted with certainty that Hitler dictated this book in the last weeks of June and the first week of July 1928.[47]

III

The Content of the Book

If one regards the book as a whole, Hitler's well-known primary themes—with all their variations—are immediately recognizable. In history he sees only the struggle for Lebensraum, based on the rules of racial determinism. The last great conflict, the Great War, was not started in time by Germany and was then lost because of a stab in the back. He (like many others) rejects the idea that the German army was defeated militarily, as this does not fit with the way he wishes to view the world. For the same reason, he will not admit that the structure Bismarck gave the Reich—a structure in which party politicians were systematically prevented from attaining responsible positions—precluded the rise of a great popular leader, whereas in England and France the parliamentary process brought such men into positions of leadership. In the same way that delusions cloud the view of history, they also block a clear view into the future. Based on the mistaken view that in 1914 England instigated and fought the war for economic reasons, the equally false belief logically follows that Germany's renunciation of a major role in international trade would bring England onto Germany's side in the next war. Because the "Nordic" element was the only state-forming element in Russia, and this element had been destroyed by the Bolshevik revolution, the surviving Slavs would ostensibly be unable to build a state, and so on.

In the present and the future, Hitler sees and proclaims the fight against the Jews and for the acquisition of territory in the East.[48] These were his primary ideas throughout his life. Nevertheless, it may be noticeable that in this manuscript the Jewish question appears to hold relatively less significance than the Lebensraum question. However, it is well known what a central role the Jewish question played for him—and not only in *Mein Kampf*; the issue also recurs continually in his statements from the twenties.[49] Following this same theme, Hitler declared to the generals on February 3, 1933, the purpose of the new Wehrmacht that was to be built up: "Conquering new Lebensraum in the East and ruthlessly Germanizing it."[50] One can in any case never overlook the fact that the annihilation of the Jews was included as an integral element of the territorial and Germanizing issue. At the end of his life, Hitler referred again to the combination of these themes as justified in retrospect and valid for the future.[51]

The present manuscript contributes to the primary themes and emphasizes (particularly in chapter IX) the necessity of a future major conflict with the United States—which, incidentally, is assessed much more positively than in other instances.[52] Naturally, the South Tyrolean question takes up an especially large amount of space. The issue is not addressed without ambiguity; Hitler shakes off South Tyrol as not "worthwhile," while at the same time mentioning the suffering of the people as frequently as possible. In the course of later developments, the South Tyroleans—as far as we know today—were the first ethnic German group that he was prepared to resettle in 1937.[53] Initially, he wanted to resettle them in Germany or occupied Poland. Later, they were to be transplanted to the Crimea.[54] On July 1, 1943, Hitler explained to the Eastern Front army group commanders that his stance on the South Tyrolean question had been "initially...actually not tactics but...genuine conviction."[55] Three months later, with the creation of the "Alpenvorland (Foothills of the Alps) Operation Zone," out of the northern part of German-occupied Italy, he engineered Germany's annexation of South Tyrol. One could hardly be mistaken in the assumption that for Hitler the South Tyroleans, like all other people, were simply a means to an end: the unrestrained struggle for unlimited power.

IV

Why Was the Manuscript Not Published?

The existence of the document naturally raises the question of why the Eher-Verlag did not publish it. It is evident from the text itself that a book was intended, not a secret paper, and Hess referred to it as such in his above-cited letter. It is also clear that after the dictation no editing, revision, or correction took place, as happened with the volumes of *Mein Kampf.* The first version of the manuscript was laid aside and was not prepared for printing, either immediately or later.[56] There is no conclusive evidence as to why the entire book never appeared; however, some obvious suggestions can be offered as possible reasons.

It is very likely that Amann recommended refraining from publication, at least temporarily, due to the events of the summer of 1928. As head of the Eher-Verlag, he knew that *Mein Kampf* was very difficult to sell that year in particular; it was the worst year since the appearance of the first volume—the royalty register notes only 3,015 copies sold.[57] A new book by Hitler would immediately have begun competing with *Mein Kampf*. Right at this time when the party was forced, for financial reasons, to cancel its annual rally; could the party's own publishing house be expected or asked to publish a book that would make sales of the slow moving second volume of *Mein Kampf* almost impossible? Max Amann was later always praised by his wartime comrade Hitler as being a particularly good businessman.[58] Perhaps Amann, who was familiar with the content of both the old and new books, dissuaded Hitler from publishing the work, at least at that particular point.

A further reason for the failure to publish could lie in the fact that within a short time significant revisions of the manuscript would have been unavoidable. From the summer of 1929 onward, the NSDAP was engaged in fighting against the Young Plan for resettling the issue of reparations and ending the occupation (which was naturally not mentioned in the manuscript). Stresemann, who appeared in the manuscript as a key enemy, died in October 1929. Then political and economic events followed in rapid succession. Under these circumstances, Hitler would hardly have found time for the necessary revision of the manuscript.

Other considerations may also have contributed to the conclusion that publication was inopportune. In 1928 Alfred Hugenberg became head of the German National People's Party (Deutschnationale Volkspartei). An equally fierce and dim-witted enemy of the republic, he allied himself with Hitler the following year and, in the context of the referendum against the Young Plan, supported the rise of the NSDAP in opposing the Young Plan. At this time, the manuscript's effusions against the bourgeois politicians made little sense. It is of interest in this regard that precisely then—and indeed out of similar concerns—one of the few substantive changes in the text of *Mein Kampf* was made; an insult directed at the German bourgeoisie was deleted.[59]

In his foreword to the first edition of this manuscript, Hans Rothfels also mentioned the possibility that foreign policy considerations might have influenced Hitler's decision not to publish the work. The already mentioned remark by Speer also cites "foreign policy reasons" for Hitler's failure to publish.[60] The open endorsement of a new war to conquer huge areas and the continually recurring disavowal of the 1914 borders as the goal of German policy could have made Hitler, particularly in the first years after 1933, see a publication of his "foreign policy position" as inopportune.

The aforementioned considerations—based on a careful examination of the situation at the time and the content of the document— offer several possible answers to the question of why the manuscript was not published during Hitler's lifetime, but without being able to fully resolve it.

V

The Importance of the Text

In the introduction to the first publication of this manuscript, I rejected the criticism that the document could add fuel to the fire of neo-Nazism. Those who, even today, are still deceived by Hitler's delusions will not find much in the way of stimulus in this reading. Little occasion will be found for glorification in the numerous repetitions. So wherein lies the positive merit of publishing the English translation of the manuscript?

The text constitutes an important source for the years when Hitler was trying to take power by providing an undisguised view of Hitler's ideology as well as his person. Few people have influenced the modern world in such an incisive manner as he. The twists and turns of his philosophy can be followed elsewhere as well, but here they appear before the reader uncorrected and unedited by Hitler. The document offers little beyond his assessment of the United States that is fundamentally new, but for precisely that reason it attests to the lack of any real development in Hitler's worldview between the writing of *Mein Kampf* and the seizure of power in Germany in 1933. At a time when most saw his movement as unimportant or ignored it (after the elections which brought him just under 3 percent of the vote), Hitler dictated to his former wartime companion a book that repeats many of the thoughts he voiced frequently in those years, as if he were making a speech. The study of this material provides a significant contribution to the understanding of Hitler the person in the struggle for power in Germany, and provides major clues to his later policies as Reich chancellor.[61]

Therein also lies the present significance of this book. Much has been forgotten in recent years; the problems of today demand our attention, and the sources of the misfortune are thus often overlooked. But these sources lie not only in the person of Hitler but also in the fact that for years a man expressed in public speech perceptions and convictions like those developed in this book, that thousands paid admission to hear him, and that millions gave him their votes. And then fought hard for more than five years to keep him in power. In truth, Germany and the rest of the world have not yet come close to coming to terms with Hitler as a person, as leader of a great nation, and as a symbol. If, as Shakespeare said, "The evil that men do lives after them; The good is often interred with their bones…," then Hitler's grave is empty, but the effects of the atrocities continue to be felt. Only a deeper understanding of evil can help humanity cope morally with these consequences; may this edition contribute to that process.

Editorial Method

The text is published here in full and the sections are presented in the original order. Transposed letters and other obvious typist's errors, including spelling and punctuation, have been corrected. The characteristically uneven syntax and style of the author, however, have been retained. The paragraph breaks correspond to those in the original. Words abbreviated because of the speed of dictation have been spelled out. If corrections contained in the manuscript reflect some variation in train of thought or phrasing, the relevant deletion is given in brackets next to the final version of the text. Missing words, or mistakes that distort the meaning, have been added or corrected in brackets and italics where it seemed necessary. Passages that are unintelligible or formulated in a highly idiosyncratic manner are identified with [*sic*].

The arrangement of the chapters corresponds to the original. The first pages were also designated as the preface in the original; from that point on, the chapters were divided only with lines. The chapter numbers and titles were added by the editor and thus appear in square brackets and italics. No other changes have been made to the style or structure. The document published as Appendix I was included with the original manuscript in Alexandria, Virginia. The notes are intended primarily as aides to understanding. In addition to the strictly text-critical notes, factual notes offer brief pieces of information on specifically mentioned events, numbers, references, or persons. These notes can serve neither as a correction of Hitler's central ideas nor as a comparison with the policies he later implemented; rather, they may assist in understanding the time in which the document originated. This edition itself cannot resolve the intellectual debate regarding Hitler, but it can substantially encourage it.

TRANSLATOR'S NOTE

The text of *Hitler's Second Book* presented an interesting translation challenge. Translators always face the temptation to polish and "improve" writing that may not be perfectly clear and correct in the original, and in this case the temptation was all the stronger because the original manuscript was an unedited draft.

The intent in publishing this work, however, is not simply to communicate the content in a concise and accurate manner, but to help illuminate the character and ideas of a significant twentieth-century figure. Thus, to maintain a reasonable degree of authenticity and to increase the value of the text as a historical source, it was essential to preserve as much as possible of the original style—including excessive wordiness, ambiguous pronoun references, mid-sentence changes in verb tense, and the occasional barely intelligible fragment.

Although Hitler could certainly be eloquent at times, he could also be repetitive and rambling. And although German sentences naturally tend to be longer and more complex than English sentences, the ideas articulated in this manuscript are often expressed in a particularly convoluted manner. Complicated sentences sometimes had to be broken up or restructured for the sake of clarity, and redundancy was involuntarily eliminated on occasion if the meaning of two different German terms could only reasonably be conveyed by the same English word. The editor has checked the translation against the original text.

Difficult choices had to be made in the effort to strike a balance between staying true to the original and making the text understandable to an English-speaking audience, but hopefully this translation will adequately convey the essence of the original manuscript and thus contribute to a better understanding of a critical time in European and world history.

Krista Smith
Bassano del Grappa, Italy
January 2003

The Document

PREFACE

I n August 1925, while writing the second volume of *Mein Kampf*, I set out—briefly, due to the circumstances—the basic ideas of a German National Socialist foreign policy.[62] In the context of this work, I addressed in particular the South Tyrolean problem, which was the occasion for attacks against the movement that were as fierce as they were unjustified [*sic*]. In 1926 I felt compelled to publish this part of the second volume as a special reprint.[63] I did not believe that doing this would convert those enemies who saw the South Tyrolean agitation as a welcome means of fighting against the hated National Socialist movement in general. These people cannot be disabused, because for them the question of truth or error, right or wrong, is absolutely irrelevant. If an issue appears capable of being used to further their interests—in some cases partisan political interests and in some cases even highly personal interests—the truth or validity of such a matter is completely disregarded by these people. They do this particularly if they can thereby damage the general ascent of our people, because the men who ruined Germany at the time of the collapse[64] are the nation's current rulers, and their attitude has not changed at all since then. Just as they coldheartedly sacrificed Germany for doctrinaire partisan notions or their own advantage back then, so today they hate anyone who opposes their interests, even if he offers a thousand times over the basis for a German reascendancy. Even more. As soon as they think they see a certain name [*sic*] working to uplift our people again, they take care to oppose anything that might come from such a name. The most useful proposals, even self-evident suggestions, are then boycotted, simply because they come from someone who seems to be associated with general thoughts that they believe—based on their partisan political and personal views—they are supposed to fight. To try to convert such people is [impossible] futile.

Thus, when I published my South Tyrol pamphlet in 1926, I naturally did not believe for one second that I would be able to influence those who, as a result of their general philosophical and political attitudes, already saw me as the most menacing enemy. But I did have the hope then that at least some of the opponents of our National Socialist foreign policy who were not already malicious at the outset would first examine our views and only afterward judge them. Without doubt, this did indeed happen on numerous occasions. Today, I can point with satisfaction to the fact that a large number of men, including those in public political life, have undergone a revision in their attitude toward German foreign policy. And even if they didn't see themselves able to take up our position [*sic*], they at least acknowledged the honorable intentions that guide us. It has become increasingly clear to me over the course of the last two years that my writing from that time was indeed based upon a presupposition of general National Socialist views. The fact that many do not follow is due less to bad intentions than to a certain incapacity. At that time it was not possible, within the tightly drawn limits, to provide a truly fundamental justification of our National Socialist foreign policy views. Today I feel compelled to make up for that. In the last few years the attacks of our opponents have not only become stronger, but they have also mobilized to a certain extent the large camp of the indifferent. The agitation that has been systematically carried out against Italy in the last five years is gradually threatening to bear fruit, destroying and killing the last hopes of a German resurgence.

So today, as is frequently the case with regard to other issues, the National Socialist movement, in its foreign policy positions, stands totally alone and isolated among the German people and in political life. To the attacks of the general internal enemies of our people and fatherland are added the proverbial stupidity and incompetence of the bourgeois national parties, the laziness of the masses, and, as a particularly strong ally, cowardice. We can observe that cowardice today in all those who are fundamentally incapable of putting up a resistance to the Marxist plague and who therefore consider themselves fortunate to be able to speak out on a matter that is less dangerous than the fight against Marxism but that nevertheless looks and sounds similar. By raising their South Tyrolean cry today, they appear to serve the interests of the national struggle, while on the contrary they are avoiding every real fight against the worst internal enemies of the German nation. For these defenders of the fatherland, nation, and in some cases for the racists, it is in any case considerably easier to let loose their war cries in Vienna and Munich under benevolent encouragement and in association with Marxist betrayers of the people and the nation than to challenge these enemies themselves in a serious fight. So, just as many things today have become little more than appearances, so too the entire nationalistic fuss of these people has long since become only an outward appearance—but one that satisfies them and that a large share of the people do not see through.

The National Socialist movement fights against this powerful coalition—which tried from various perspectives to make the South Tyrolean question the linchpin of German foreign policy—by steadfastly advocating an alliance with Italy in opposition to the prevailing Francophile tendency.[65] The movement emphasizes, in opposition to general public opinion in Germany, that South Tyrol cannot and should not in any way be an obstacle to this policy. This view, however, is the cause of our current foreign policy isolation and being attacked, and it will however later be the cause of the revitalization of the German nation.

I am writing this work in order to justify and explain these deeply held views in detail. Although I care little about being understood by the enemies of the German people, I feel a duty to endeavor to [make understandable] present and demonstrate the National Socialists' ideas of a true German foreign policy to the elements of our population that are nationally minded and merely poorly informed or poorly led. I know that many of them will, after honest examination of the views presented here, [reconsider] abandon their previous opinions and find their way into the ranks of the German nation's National Socialist freedom movement. They will thereby strengthen the power that will one day bring about the conflict with those who are unteachable because their own personal or party interests—rather than the happiness of their people—determine their thoughts and actions.

[CHAPTER I]

[War and Peace in the Struggle for Survival]

P olitics is history in the making. History itself represents the progression of a people's struggle for survival. I use the phrase "struggle for survival" intentionally here, because in reality every struggle for daily bread, whether in war or peace, is a never-ending battle against thousands and thousands of obstacles, just as life itself is a never-ending battle against death. Human beings know no more than any other creature in the world why they live, but life is filled with the longing to preserve it. The most primitive creature [could without the] knows only the instinct of self-preservation; for higher beings this carries over to wife and child, and for those higher still to the entire species. But when man—not infrequently, it seems—renounces his own self-preservation instinct for the benefit of the species, he is still doing it the highest service. Because not infrequently it is this renunciation of the individual that grants life to the collective whole, and thus yet again to the individual. Hence the sudden courage of the mother defending her young and the heroism of the man protecting his people. The magnitude of

the self-preservation instinct corresponds to the two most powerful motivations in life: hunger and love. While the [fulfillment] satisfaction of the eternal hunger guarantees self-preservation, the
gratification of love secures its furtherance. In truth, these two impulses are the rulers of life. And even if the fleshless esthete protests against such a claim a thousand times, the fact of his existence already refutes his protest. Whatever is made of flesh and blood
can never escape the laws that condition its development. As soon
as the human intellect believes itself to be above that, that real substance that is the bearer of the spirit is destroyed.

But that which is true for individual human beings is also true
for peoples. A people, collectively, is only a large number of more
or less equal individual beings. Its strength lies in the quality of the
individuals who form it and in the type and extent of the unifor-
mity of these qualities. The same laws that determine the life of
the individual, and to which it is subject, are therefore valid for the
people. Self-preservation and continuity are the major impulses for
any kind of behavior, as long as such a body can lay claim to healthiness. But these general laws of life have the same effects in the relations among peoples as among individuals.

If the self-preservation instinct and its two goals of self-preservation and continuity represent the most basic force for every
creature on this earth, but the possibility of satisfaction is limited,
then the logical result is struggle, in all its forms, for the possibility
of preserving this life—in other words, satisfying the self-preservation instinct.

The types of creatures on the earth are countless, and on an individual level their self-preservation instinct as well as the longing
for procreation is always unlimited; however, the space in which this
entire life process plays itself out is limited. It is the surface area of a
precisely measured sphere on which billions and billions of individual
beings struggle for life and succession. In the limitation of this living
space lies the compulsion for the struggle for survival, and the struggle
for survival, in turn, contains the precondition for evolution.

The history of the world in the ages when humans did not yet exist was initially a representation of geological occurrences. The clash of natural forces with each other, the formation of a habitable surface on this planet, the separation of water and land, the formation of the mountains, the plains, and the seas. That [was] is the history of the world during this time. Later, with the emergence of organic life, human interest focuses on the appearance and disappearance of its thousandfold forms. Man himself finally becomes visible very late, and from that point on he begins to understand the term "world history" as referring primarily to the history of his own development—in other words, the representation of his own evolution. This development is characterized by the never-ending battle of humans against animals and also against humans themselves. Finally, out of the unclear tangle of individual beings, formations rise—families, tribes, peoples, states. The portrayal of their genesis and dissolution alone is the replication of an eternal struggle for survival.

But if politics is history in the making and history itself is the representation of the struggle of men and peoples for self-preservation and continuity, then politics is in truth the implementation of a people's struggle for survival. [So] But politics is not just the struggle of a people for its survival as such; rather, for us humans it is the art of the implementation of this struggle.

Because history represents the previous struggles of the various peoples for survival, and at the same time is the concrete rendering of particular policies, it is also the most suitable teacher for our own political actions.

If the highest duty of politics is the preservation and continuation of the life of a people, then [consequently the life of a people is always at stake] this life is the eternal stake for which it fights and struggles and of and about which judgment will be made. Its duty is therefore the preservation of [that] a substance of flesh and blood. Its success is enabling this preservation. Its failure is the destruction, the loss of this substance. But politics is always the leader of the struggle for survival—its organizer—and regardless of how it is formally designated, [such a] its effectiveness will determine the life or death of a people.

One must be clear about this, because the two concepts of a peace policy or a war policy thus immediately become meaningless. Because the stake that is struggled for through politics is always life, the result in the case of failure or success is always the same, regardless of the political means used to try to achieve the preservation of the life a people. A peace policy that fails leads to the destruction of a people—that is, to the obliteration of its flesh and blood substance—just the same as a war policy that fails. The people's extinction is caused by a robbing of the prerequisites of life [*sic*], just as much in one case as in the other. Those peoples were not extinguished on the battlefield; rather, lost battles removed the means of sustaining life, or, better, led to these means being taken away or put the people in a position where they were no longer able to prevent it.

The losses resulting directly from war cannot be compared at all to the losses caused by the bad and unhealthy life of a people.[66] Silent hunger and bad behavior kill more in ten years than would be killed in a thousand years of war. The most horrible war is the one that appears the most peaceful to humanity today: the peaceful economic war. It is precisely this war whose end result leads to sacrifices that far surpass the sacrifices of the Great War. Because it affects not only the living but, above all, takes the unborn. While war kills at most a fraction of the present population, the economic war murders the future. A single year of reduced fertility in Europe kills more people than all those who fell in all European wars from the French Revolution to the present, including the Great War. But this is the result of a peaceful economic policy that has overpopulated Europe without allowing a number of nations the possibility of healthy further development.

In general, the following must also be said on this subject:

As soon as a people forgets that the duty of politics is to preserve its existence by all means and in all possible ways, and politics are instead subjected to a certain mode of action, this destroys the inherent significance of this art of leading a people in its struggle with destiny for freedom and bread.

A policy that is fundamentally bellicose will be able to keep a people away from numerous vices and varieties of sickness; however, it will not be able to prevent a change in the people's inner quality over the course of many centuries. War, when it makes a continual appearance, brings an inherent danger that is all the more prevalent the more unequal the racial components from which the community is composed. This was already true in antiquity for all known states, and it is also true today, especially for all European states. The nature of war, through a thousand individual processes, leads to a racial selection within a people; this means a disproportionate destruction of the best elements. In innumerable individual instances, the appeal to courage and valor is answered by the best and most valuable racial elements repeatedly volunteering for special assignments or being systematically brought together through the organization of special formations. Military leadership has always been dominated by the idea of forming special legions and elite troops of regimental guards and assault battalions. Persian palace guards, elite Alexandrian troops, Roman praetorian legions, advance guards[67] of mercenary units, Guards Regiments of Napoleon and Frederick the Great, assault battalions, submarine crews, and airmen in the Great War—all owe their formation to the same idea and the same need: to select the most capable men out of a multitude of people and bring them together in special formations for certain especially difficult assignments. Because guard units originate not as parade troops but as combat troops. The great recognition that such an organization receives leads to the development of a distinct esprit de corps, which, however, can subsequently grow stiff and end up as mere formality. But it is not uncommon that such formations suffer the heaviest casualties. In other words, out of a multitude of men, the most able are selected and sent to war in concentrated masses. Thus, a people's dead include a disproportionate share of the best men, while, conversely, the absolute worst men are to a large extent preserved. The extremely idealistic [*sic*] men who are ready to sacrifice their own lives for the benefit of the community stand in contrast to those pathetic egoists who see the preservation of their own strictly personal existence as the highest duty of this life. The hero dies, the criminal [remains alive] survives. This seems obvious in a heroic time and in particular to an idealistic youth. And this is good, because it is evidence of a people's still-existing worth. The realistic statesman, however, must view this fact with concern and take it into consideration, because what can easily be gotten over in one war will in one hundred wars gradually bleed a people of its best, most valuable elements. One can achieve victories this way, but in the end there will no longer be a people there worthy of these victories. The pitifulness of the people in ensuing ages, as many do not understand, is not infrequently the result of the successes of the previous ages.

Therefore, a wise political leadership will not see war as the purpose of a people's existence, but only a means to preserve this existence. These leaders must be taught up until manhood that the population entrusted to them must be managed extremely conscientiously. They must not be afraid to risk the highest casualties when necessary for the continued existence of the people, but they must always consider that peace will have to replace this blood. Wars that are fought for objectives that by their very nature cannot ensure the replacement of the lost blood are an offense against the people and a sin against the future of the people.

Never-ending wars can become a terrible danger for a people which has such unequal elements in its racial composition that only part can be considered state-sustaining and particularly culturally creative. The culture of the European peoples is based on a foundation created by the influence of Nordic blood over the course of thousands of years. As soon as the last remains of this Nordic blood are eliminated, the face of European culture will change; the worth of the states will diminish in relation to the declining worth of the peoples.

A policy that is fundamentally peaceful will, in contrast, initially enable the preservation of those with the best bloodlines; however, in the end it will create a people of such weakness that it must one day collapse—as soon as the people's prerequisites for existence appear threatened. Then, rather than fighting for their daily bread, these people will prefer to reduce the quantity of their bread or, more likely, reduce their numbers, either through peaceful emigration or reduced fertility, in order to avoid extreme deprivation. In that way, however, the fundamentally peaceful policy becomes a scourge for the people. Because what is caused in the one case by constant war is caused in the other by emigration—which, through a hundred thousand individual life catastrophes gradually robs a people of its best bloodlines. It is sad to know that our collective political wisdom, to the degree that it does not see emigration as an actual advantage, at most regrets the decreasing numbers of our people, or, in the most favorable case, speaks of a "cultural fertilizer" that is given to other states. What is not recognized is the most difficult [*sic*]. Because emigration does not take place according to region or takes place by age group, but rather according to the capriciousness of fate, it always pulls out of the population the boldest and bravest, the most resolute, most defiant members of a community. The farm boy who emigrated to America 150 years ago was the most determined and boldest in his village, just like the worker who goes to Argentina today. The coward and weakling would rather die at home than summon the courage to earn his bread in unknown places. Regardless of whether need, calamity, or political pressure or religious coercion weighs on the people, it is always the healthiest and most robust who are able to offer the greatest resistance. The weakling will always give in first [*sic*]. His survival is no more beneficial for the victor than those who remain behind are for the motherland. Thus it is not uncommon for the initiative of the mother states to be transferred to the colonial possessions, because there, through completely natural means, a collection of the highest human value has been assembled. But the

positive gain for the new land is therefore a loss for the motherland. When, over the course of centuries, a people loses its best,
most robust, and most natural forces via emigration, it will find it
difficult in critical times to summon the inner strength to oppose
fate with the necessary resistance. It would then prefer to resort to
a reduced birth rate. Here as well it is not the numerical loss that is
decisive, but rather the terrible fact that through a reduction in the
birth rate, those who are potentially the most valuable members of
a community are destroyed at the start. Because the greatness and
future of a people is determined by its collective abilities for high
achievement in all areas. But these are personal qualities that do
not appear to be tied to the birthright of the firstborn. If one were
to strike out from our German cultural life, from our science—yes,
from our entire existence—everything accomplished by men who
were not firstborn, Germany would hardly even be at the level of a
Balkan state. The German people would no longer possess any claim
to being valued as a cultured people. And then it must [*be*] considered that in the case of those firstborn men who still accomplished
great things for their people, one must first check whether there
were any nonfirstborn among their ancestors. Because if there is
[one man who] just one break in the firstborn line in his family tree,
then that man also belongs among those who would not have existed if our ancestors had always held to this principle. In the life
of a people, however, there are no vices of the past that are [would
be] virtues for the present.

A fundamentally peaceful policy which subsequently causes a
people to bleed to death through emigration and reduced fertility
is even more disastrous to a degree that [*a*] people is made up of
unequal racial elements. Because here as well emigration will pull
out primarily the racially superior members of the community, while
through the reduced birthrate in the homeland those who have
worked their way up to higher social levels as a result of their racial
worth are also affected first. Gradually then, they will be replen-
ished from the broad mass of weakened, lesser-value individuals,

and after centuries this will lead to a lowering of the overall absolute worth of the people. By then, such a people will have long lost any real vital strength.

Thus, a policy that is fundamentally peaceful will be just as damaging and disastrous as a policy that only knows war as the single weapon.

Policies must fight about the life and for the life of the people, and to do so they must always choose their weapons in such a way as to serve this life in the highest sense. Because one does not make policies in order to be able to die; rather, one may[68] only sometimes allow men to die in order that the people can live. The goal is the preservation of life and not heroic death or, [also] least of all, cowardly resignation.

[CHAPTER II]

[Fighting, Not Industry, Secures Life]

A people's struggle for survival is determined primarily by the following fact:

Regardless of a people's level of culture, the struggle for daily bread is at the top of all vital necessities. Brilliant leadership can, of course, make a people focus on major goals, distracting it more from material things in order to serve grand spiritual ideals. Generally, strictly material interests will increase to the degree that ideal spiritual viewpoints are disappearing. The more primitive a person is in his spiritual life, the more animalistic he becomes, until in the end he sees obtaining nourishment as the only purpose of life. Thus, a people can indeed endure a certain decrease in material goods as long as supporting ideals are provided as a substitute. But to ensure that these ideals do not lead to the ruin of a people, they must never take place one-sidedly, at the expense of material nourishment, when the health of the community appears threatened by it. Because a famished people will either physically collapse under the effects of malnutrition or will have to bring about a change in its situation.

But physical collapse leads sooner or later to spiritual collapse, and then all ideals vanish as well. Therefore, ideals are healthy and appropriate as long as they help to reinforce a people's inner and collective strength, so that these forces can contribute in carrying out the struggle for survival. Ideals that do not serve that purpose, even if they appear a thousand times beautiful outwardly, are nevertheless evil, because they gradually distance a people from the reality of life.

But the bread that a people needs in order to live is determined by the Lebensraum that is available to it. A healthy people, at least, will always attempt to satisfy its needs from its own territory and land. Every other situation is sick and dangerous, even if it enables the nourishment of a people for centuries. International trade, international industry, tourism, and so on and so forth, are all transient solutions for the nourishment of a people. They are dependent on factors that are in part outside the discretion and in part outside the strength of a people. The most secure basis for the existence of a people has always been its own territory and land.

But now the following must be considered:

The size of a people is a variable factor. It will be a rising one in the case of a healthy people. Yes, the increase alone can secure the future of a people, as far as can be judged. But that means the demand for essential resources is a growing one. The so-called domestic increase in production is in most cases only sufficient to satisfy the growing demands of the people, but certainly not the growing number. This is particularly true for the European nations. In the last few centuries, especially very recently, the needs of the European peoples have grown so rapidly that the increase in European crop yields that could be achieved from year to year (in the best case) could hardly keep pace with the rise of the collective requirements for necessities. The growth in population could only be compensated by growth—expansion—of the Lebensraum. Now, however, a people's number is variable, but the land is a constant. That is to say, population growth is such a natural and therefore self-evident process that it is not seen as exceptional. The expansion of the land, however, is limited by the general property distribution of the world and [*any change in it*] is deemed a particularly revolutionary act and an exceptional process; thus, the ease with which a population can be fed[69] stands in opposition to the exceptional difficulty of territorial alteration.

And yet the management of the relationship between the population and the land area is of the utmost importance for the existence of a people. Yes, one can say for the sake of expedience that a people's entire struggle for survival in reality consists only of securing the necessary territory and land as a general precondition for feeding the growing population. Because as the population continues to grow while the territory and land itself remains the same, tensions must gradually appear. These strains will initially emerge as a shortage that can be counterbalanced for a certain time by greater industriousness, more ingenious production methods, or special thriftiness, but one day all of these means will prove inadequate. The leaders of the people's struggle for survival then have the duty thoroughly to eliminate this unbearable relationship—in other words, to reestablish an acceptable ratio between population and land area.

Now, in the life of a people there are several ways to correct the imbalance between population and land area. The most natural is the adaptation of the territory from time to time to fit the growing population. This necessitates decisions for battle and the willingness to risk lives. This sacrifice is also the only one that can be justified to a people. Because the necessary space for further growth will thereby be won, the human life lost on the battlefield will automatically be replaced many times over. Thus, from the distress of war grows the bread of freedom. The sword breaks the path for the plow, and if one wishes to speak of human rights, then in this one case war has served the highest right: it gave land to a people that wishes to cultivate it industriously and honestly and which can in the future provide daily sustenance for its children. This earth is not allocated to anyone, nor is it bestowed on anyone as a gift; however, it is given as destiny's grant to those people who [possess] have the courage in their hearts to [conquer] take possession of it, the strength to preserve it, and the diligence to till it.

Therefore, every healthy native people sees nothing sinful in the acquisition of land, but rather something natural. The modern pacifist, however, who repudiates this most holy right, must first be reproached with the fact that he is then nourishing at least himself from the wrongs of the past. Furthermore, there is no place on this earth destined to be a people's residence forever, because the laws of nature impelled humanity for millennia to eternal wandering. And finally, the current territorial distribution of the earth was not brought about by a higher power but by men themselves. I can never view a solution as being valid in perpetuity when it was produced by men as then ... by destiny under her own protection and sanctified as the law of the future. So, as the surface of the earth appears forever subject to geologic transformations, and organic life—in continuous change—allows forms to disappear in order to invent new ones, in the same way the boundaries of human dwellings face constant change. As much as some peoples at certain times had an interest in defining the existing territorial distribution as unalterable and binding for all future generations, because it corresponded with their interests, other peoples in such a situation were able to see only something entirely human—which at that moment was to their disadvantage and therefore must be changed using all possible applications of human strength. Anyone who wishes to permanently banish this struggle from the earth might end the fighting between men, but he would thereby also eliminate the highest driving force for their development, just as when in civic life he wishes to perpetuate forever the wealth of certain people or the size of certain businesses and would for that purpose halt the free play of market forces—competition. The result would be a catastrophe for a people.

The world's current territorial distribution [*sic*] is so one-sidedly in the favor of certain individual peoples that they must have an understandable interest in not allowing the present distribution to be changed any further.[70] But these peoples' excessive wealth of land stands in contrast with the poverty of others who, despite the most diligent industriousness, are not able to produce their daily bread. With what higher rights can one confront them when they also lay a claim to an area that can secure their nourishment?

No. The first right in this world is the right to life, provided one has the strength for it. But a strong people will always find a way, based on this right, to fit its land to its population.

As soon as a people, whether out of weakness or poor leadership, is no longer able by expanding its territory to eliminate the imbalance between its increased population and its insufficient land, it will inevitably seek other ways. It will then fit the population to the land.

In general, nature herself undertakes the first adjustment of the population to the inadequate supply of arable land. Hardship and misery are her assistants in this. They can so decimate a people that further population growth practically ceases. The consequences of this natural adjustment of the population to the land are not always the same. Initially, a fierce battle for survival begins among the people, which only the strongest and most resistant individuals can live through. High infant mortality on the one hand and great longevity on the other are the primary indicators of a period like this in which there is little consideration for the individual life. Because in this situation everything weak is carried away by hardship and sickness, and only the healthiest remain alive, a sort of natural selection takes place. It is very possible for a people in this process to be subject to a numerical decline but yet retain—even enhance— its inner quality. But such a process cannot last too long, or hardship may cause the reverse to happen. In peoples whose racial makeup is of uneven quality, ongoing food shortages can in the end lead to a dull acquiescence to hardship, a gradual erosion of resilience, and a slow degeneration instead of a selection furthered by struggle. This is certainly the case as soon as man ceases to value an increase in population and resolves to reduce the birth rate in order to manage the perpetual hardship. Because in doing so he immediately takes the opposite path from that pursued by nature. While nature, out of the multitude of creatures that are born, spares the few healthiest and most robust in the struggle for survival, man reduces the number of births but then tries to preserve the lives of all those who are born, regardless of their true value and inner quality.[71] His humanity is simply the servant of his weakness, and therefore in truth the most terrible annihilator of his existence. If man wanted to reduce his numbers without the dire consequences resulting from a reduced birth rate, he would then have to place no controls on the number of births but limit the number allowed to live. The Spartans were once capable of such a wise measure,[72] but not our current dishonest, sentimental, bourgeois-patriotic crowd. The subjugation of 350,000 Helots[73] by 6,000 Spartans was only possible because of the racial superiority of the Spartans.[74] This, however, was the result of systematic racial preservation, so we see in the Spartan state the first racialist state. The abandonment of sick, frail, deformed children—in other words, their destruction—demonstrated greater human dignity and was in reality a thousand times more humane than the pathetic insanity of our time, which attempts to preserve the lives of the sickest subjects—at any price—while taking the lives of a hundred thousand healthy children through a decrease in the birth rate or through abortifacient agents,[75] subsequently breeding a race of degenerates burdened with illness.

So in general it may be said that the reduction of the population through hardship and human aid brings about an approximate adjustment to the inadequate Lebensraum, although the quality of the existing human material continues to decline, and in the end becomes depraved.

The second attempt to fit the population to the land involves emigration, which if it does not take place according to bloodlines also leads to a debasement of the remaining human material.

A reduction in the birth rate eliminates those with superior qualities, while emigration destroys the average quality of the people.

Now, there are two other means by which a people can attempt to equalize the imbalance between population and land area. The first involves increasing the internal productivity of the land, which in itself has nothing to do with so-called internal colonization. The second involves increasing the production of goods and converting the internal economy into an export economy.

The idea of increasing the productivity of the land within the now established boundaries is very old.[76] The history of human agriculture is one of continual progress, continual improvement, and therefore rising output. If the first component of this progress was in the area of improvements in cultivation methods and cultivation activity, then the second component is in the area of artificial improvement of the soil quality through the addition of absent or inadequate nutrients. This line leads from the ancient hoe to the modern steam plow, from barn manure to today's artificial fertilizers. Without doubt, the productive capacity of the land has increased infinitely. But, just as certainly, there is a limit to this. Especially when one considers that the standard of living of cultured peoples is a general standard that is not determined by a people's quantity of individual goods; rather, it is subject to the assessment of the surrounding nations and, vice versa, [jointly determined] established by their condition. Today's European dreams of a standard of living that is derived just as much from the possibilities of Europe as from the actual circumstances in America. Through modern technology and the communication it enables, international relations between peoples have become so effortless and intimate that the European—often without realizing it— takes the circumstances of the American life as the benchmark for his own life. He forgets, however, that on the American continent the relation between population and size of land is infinitely more favorable than the analogous relations of the European peoples to their territories. Regardless of how Italy or, say, Germany carries out the internal colonization of its land, and regardless of how it raises the productivity of the land through increased scientific and methodological activity, the disproportionate population in relation to the land—as measured by the proportion of the population of the American union in relation to the territory of the union—remains. And if through the most diligent industriousness Germany or Italy were in a position to increase its population, then in the American union it could just increase many times more. And when, at last, further increase is impossible in these two European countries, then the American union could still grow for centuries before reaching the proportion that we have already today [*sic*].

In particular, the anticipated effects of internal colonization are based on a false premise.[77] The idea that internal colonization can bring about a significant increase in the productivity of the land is mistaken. Regardless of how in Germany, for example, the land is allocated—whether it is divided into large or small farms or into small plots for settlers—the fact remains that there are an average of 136 people per square kilometer of land.[78] This proportion is unhealthy. It is not possible to feed our people on this basis and under these conditions, and it would only cause confusion if the rallying cry of internal colonization were introduced to the masses, because they would then latch on to the hope that a means of eliminating the current hardship had been found. But that would not be the case, because the need is not the result of some incorrect allocation of the land, but rather the effect of the altogether insufficient amount of space that is available to our people today.

Thus increasing the productivity of the land can bring relief in the life of a people for a certain time, but in the long term this will never eliminate the requirement to again adjust the people's insufficient Lebensraum to fit the growing population. Internal colonization itself can, at best, provide improvements only in the sense of social rationality and justice. It is irrelevant to the overall sustenance of a people. For the foreign-policy orientation of a nation, however, it is not infrequently damaging, as it raises hopes that can distance a people from thinking realistically. Ordinary decent citizens will then really believe that they can obtain their daily bread at home through industriousness, diligence, and fair land distribution, rather than recognizing that a people's strength must be gathered to win new Lebensraum.[79]

Industry—which especially today is seen by many as the rescuer saving them from hardship and anxiety, hunger and distress—can indeed under certain conditions provide a people with survival possibilities beyond those offered by its own land and territory. However, this is based on a number of preconditions, which I must very briefly mention here.

The point of this type of industry lies in a people producing more of certain necessities than it needs for its own requirements, selling this excess outside its own national community, and with the resulting revenues purchasing the foodstuffs and also raw materials that it lacks. Thus, however, this type of industry is not simply a question of production, but also—at least just as much—a question of sales. People speak, particularly at present, of an increase in production, but completely forget that such an increase has value only if there is a buyer. Within the economic life cycle of a people, an increase in production will be rewarding only insofar as it increases the quantity of goods that are available to the individual. Theoretically, every increase in a people's industrial production should lead to a decrease in the price of goods and therefore to higher consumption, consequently bringing a greater quantity of goods into the possession of individual community members. In practice, however, this does not change the reality of insufficient food production for the people resulting from inadequate land. Because although one can increase—even many times over—certain types of industrial production, one cannot do the same for food production. When a people suffers from this type of shortage, a solution can only be found if a portion of the excess industrial production is allowed to flow outward in order to bring in foodstuffs from the outside to make up for what is unavailable at home. But for this purpose, an increase in production has the desired result only if a buyer—an external buyer—is found. But thus the question of sales opportunities then becomes paramount for us.

Today's international market is not unlimited. The number of industrially active nations has steadily increased. Almost all European peoples suffer from an inadequate and unsatisfactory relation between the size of their territory and their population and therefore depend on international exports. Recently the American union has also joined in, and Japan in the East. Competition for the limited market is naturally beginning, and it will become even fiercer as the number of industrially active nations increases and as the markets constrict. Because while on the one hand the number of peoples competing in the world market increases, the market itself will gradually become smaller, in part as a result of other nations self-industrializing by their own strength, and in part through a system of subsidiary ventures that will be established more and more frequently in such nations, based on pure capitalistic interests. The following should be considered in this regard: the German people, for example, has an active interest in building ships in German shipyards to [*sic*] China, because that will provide sustenance to a certain number of our people who would not be able to obtain it from our own no longer adequate land and territory. The German people has no interest, however, in, say, a German financial group or a German shipyard establishing a so-called subsidiary shipyard in Shanghai to build ships for China with Chinese workers and foreign steel, even if the company itself obtains a certain return from it in the form of interest or dividends. On the contrary—because the result of that would only be that a German financial group would earn profits of so many millions, but German national economy would be deprived of many times that sum through lost sales.[80]

The more purely capitalistic interests now begin to shape today's economy, and the more financial and exchange viewpoints in particular achieve deciding influence here, the broader the grasp of this system of subsidiary establishments will become. This process will [suddenly] artificially cause the industrialization of previous market outlets and reduce the export opportunities of the European mother nations in particular. Today some can still smile about these future developments, but as they continue to progress in thirty years people will moan about their results in Europe.

As the sales difficulties grow, the competition for the remaining markets will become even fiercer. If the first weapons in this fight are the pricing and the quality of the goods, which competitors try to force their rivals to lower [*sic*], the last weapon in this situation as well is the sword. The so-called peaceful economic conquering of the world could only take place if the earth consisted of agrarian peoples and only a single industrially active people existed. But because all the major peoples are industrial peoples today, the so-called peaceful economic conquering of the world is nothing more than combat by means that will remain peaceful as long as the stronger peoples believe they will be able to win by using them—in other words, actually being able to kill the others through peaceful industry. Because that is the real result of a victory of one people over another by means of peaceful economic activity. In this manner the one people obtains the possibility of life, and the other people is thereby deprived of it. Here as well, the stakes are always the substance of flesh and blood, which we call a people.

However, if a truly strong people does not believe it can defeat another through peaceful economic means, or if an economically weaker people does not want to allow itself to be destroyed by an economically stronger one (by gradually losing the ability to feed itself), then [it will reach for the sword] in both cases the fog of peaceful economic phrases is suddenly lifted and war—the continuation of politics by other means[81]—takes its place.

The danger of industrial activity in the narrow sense lies in the fact that a people can too easily lapse into believing that it can completely shape its own destiny through industry, and that this then moves up from a secondary to a primary position. In the end it is even viewed as state forming, and it robs the people of those virtues and characteristics that alone can preserve the existence of peoples and states on this earth.[82]

But a particular danger of the so-called peaceful economic policy of a people lies in the fact that it initially enables an increase in the population that in the end will no longer be in proportion to the productivity of the people's own land and territory. Not infrequently, this crowding of too many people into an inadequate Lebensraum also leads to difficult social problems. People are now gathered into work centers that do not resemble cultural sites so much as abscesses on the body of the people—places where all evils, vices, and sicknesses appear to unite.[83] They are above all hotbeds of blood-mixing and bastardization, usually ensuring the degeneration of the race and resulting in that purulent herd in which the maggots of the international Jewish community flourish and cause the ultimate decay of the people.

But it is precisely in this way that a decline is introduced, because now the inner strength of such a people disappears quickly, and all racial, moral, and ethical qualities are destroyed; ideals are lost, thus eliminating in the end the prerequisite needed in order for a people to take on the final consequences in the struggle for the world market. The peoples, weakened into a dissolute pacifism, will no longer be ready to fight and accept casualties in the struggle to sell their goods. As soon as a stronger power mobilizes the real forces of political power rather than peaceful economic activity, these peoples will collapse. Then they will be reaping the rewards of their own misconduct. They are overpopulated, and now, as a result of losing all the real prerequisites, they no longer have any possibility of adequately feeding their oversize population; they have no strength to break the chains of the enemy and no inner quality to bear their destiny with dignity. They once believed they could renounce force and still live, thanks to their peaceful economic activities. Destiny will teach them that a people can ultimately only be preserved when population and Lebensraum are in a certain natural and healthy relation to each other. Also, this relation must be reviewed from time to time, and to the degree that it shifts into imbalance to the detriment of space, it must be restored to the advantage of the population.

To do so, however, a people needs weapons, because land acquisition is always linked to the use of force.

But if the duty of politics is to carry out a people's struggle for survival, and the struggle for survival consists essentially of securing the necessary land to feed the population, but this whole process is a question of the use of force, then the following concluding definition results:

Politics is the art of carrying out a people's struggle for survival—for its earthly existence.

[Domestic] Foreign policy is the art of securing for a people the necessary quantity and quality of Lebensraum.

Domestic policy is the art of preserving the [strength content] commitment of strength—in terms of the people's racial quality and numbers—necessary to do this.

[CHAPTER III]

[Race, Conflict, and Power]

I [want] would like immediately at this point take issue with the bourgeois view that the concept of power usually means only a nation's supply of weapons, and to a limited degree perhaps also the army as an organization. If the view of these people were correct—if a people's power really does lie in its store of weapons and its army—then a people that lost its army and weapons, through whatever circumstances, would be finished forever. But these bourgeois politicians hardly believe that themselves. Even just by doubting this they admit that weapons and the army organization are things that can be replaced and therefore are not of primary significance; rather, there is something that stands above them and that [is] at least the source of their power. And it is true. Weapons and army formations can be destroyed and are replaceable. As great as their significance may be at the moment, it is limited when viewed over longer periods of time. The decisive factor in the life of a people is the will to preserve itself and the vital strength that is available to do so. Weapons can rust, Formations [sic] can become outmoded, but the will itself can always renew both and shape a people in whatever form the moment of need requires. The fact that we Germans had to hand over our weapons[84] is in my opinion of very limited significance from the material point of view. And that is the only thing that our bourgeois politicians see. At most, the oppressive aspect of our weapons handover lies in the accompanying circumstances under which it took place, in our attitude, which made it possible, and in the pathetic manner of implementation that we experienced.[85] The destruction of our army organization is much more profound. But even there the primary misfortune is not to be seen in the elimination of the organization as the bearer of our weapons supply, but much more in the abolition of an institution that educated our people into manhood—an institution such as no other state in the world possessed and indeed no other people needed as much as we Germans did. The contribution of our old army to the creation of a disciplined people capable of outstanding achievement in all areas is immeasurable [*sic*]. Our people, which because of its internal racial fragmentation seriously lacks the characteristic that, for example, distinguishes for example the English—cohesive unity in times of danger—obtained this quality (which is natural, instinctual, and deep-seated in other peoples) at least in part through army training. People who love to speak of socialism do not understand that the most socialistic organization of all was the German people's army. Thus also the fierce hatred of the typically capitalist-minded Jewry against an organization in which money does not equate with status, dignity, or honor; rather, achievement—and the honor accorded those who belong to [an organization] with certain achievements—is valued more than the possession of property and wealth.[86] A concept which, to the Jews, appears as strange is it is dangerous and which, if it were to become universally adopted by a people, would provide immunity against all further Jewish dangers. If, for example, an officer's rank could be purchased in the army, this would be understandable to the Jews. What is incomprehensible—and even sinister—to them is an organization that honors a man who either possesses no property at all or whose income is only a fraction of that of another who is not at all honored or valued within the organization.[87] And therein lay the greatest strength of this old incomparable institution, which, however, did unfortunately begin to face the threat of erosion during the last thirty years of peace. As soon as it became the fashion for individual officers, especially those of noble descent, to mate with department-store Jewesses, a danger arose for the old army that would one day have become evil had it continued to develop further. In any case, in the time of Emperor Wilhelm I[88] there was no sympathy [shown] left for such goings-on. Yet, all things considered, the German army at the turn of the century was still the greatest organization in the world and its effectiveness was more than beneficial for our German people. The breeding ground of German discipline, German efficiency, even disposition, open courage, bold recklessness, tenacious perseverance, and unyielding honesty. The sense of honor of an entire profession gradually and imperceptibly became the common property of an entire people.[89]

The destruction of this organization by the Treaty of Versailles was all the worse for our German people because it finally gave our internal enemies free rein to carry out their worst intentions; but our incompetent bourgeoisie, lacking all resourcefulness and the capacity for improvisation, was unable to find even the most primitive substitute.

Our German people did admittedly lose weapons and weapon bearers. But this has happened countless times in the history of various peoples, without those peoples collapsing. On the contrary: Nothing is easier to replace than weapon loss, and every form of organization can be recreated or renewed. What is irreplaceable is the corrupted blood of a people—the destroyed inner quality.

Against today's bourgeois view that our people are unarmed because of the peace treaty of Versailles, I can only argue that our real defenselessness lies in our pacifist-democratic contamination, as well as in the internationalism that destroys and poisons our people's most significant sources of strength. Because the source of a people's entire power lies not in its store of weapons or its army organization, but in its inner quality—represented by the racial significance or racial value of a people, by the presence of superior individual personal qualities, and by a healthy attitude toward the idea of self-preservation.

When we as National Socialists go before the public with this view of a people's real strength, we know that public opinion stands entirely against us today. But this is the deepest meaning of our new doctrine, which, as a worldview, separates us from the others.

If we start from the premise that all peoples are not the same, then the peoples' intrinsic value is not the same either. If the value of all peoples is not equal, then every people has, aside from its collective numerical value, also a certain specific value that is distinctive and that cannot be completely the same as that of any other people. The effects of this particular value can be very different and can occur in very different areas, but together they provide a benchmark for the overall valuation of a people. The ultimate expression of this overall valuation is the historical cultural image of a people, in which the sum of all the rays of its genetic qualities— or the racial qualities united in it—are reflected.

But this special value of a people is not in any way simply an esthetic cultural value; rather, it is a general existential life value. Because it builds the life of a people—it forms it and shapes it and also provides all those strengths that a people must mobilize in order to overcome life's obstacles. Any cultural act is in reality the defeat— from the human viewpoint—of a previously existing barbarism, every cultural creation [thus] a contribution to the advancement of man beyond his previously drawn boundaries and a strengthening of the position of these people; thus, strength for the claim to life also truly lies in the so-called cultural value of a people. Therefore, the greater the inner strength of a people in this area, the stronger the countless possibilities to stake a claim to life in all areas of the struggle for survival. The higher the racial worth of a people, the greater its overall value, [through] which, in conflict and in the struggle with other peoples, it must then mobilize for the benefit of its life.

The significance of this racial value of a people will, however, only be completely effective if this quality is recognized, duly valued, and appreciated by a people. Peoples that do not understand this value, or for lack of natural instinct no longer feel it, then begin immediately to lose it. The mixing of blood and the decline of the race are, then, the results that in the beginning are not infrequently introduced by a so-called *Ausländerei* [love for foreign things]—in reality an under-appreciation of one's own cultural value in comparison to that of foreign peoples. As soon as a people no longer values [its] the genetically conditioned [expression] cultural expression of the life of its own soul,[90] or even begins to be ashamed of it and turn to foreign ways of life, it renounces the power that lies in the harmony of its blood and the cultural life that springs from it. Such a people will be torn, uncertain in its assessment of the world and of its pronouncements; it will lose the recognition of and feel for its own expediencies, and instead descend into the confusion of international perceptions and views and the cultural chaos that springs from them. Then the Jew can move in, in every form, and this master of international poison concoction and racial debasement will not rest until he has completely uprooted and thereby corrupted such a people. The end, then, is the loss of a certain uniform racial value and thus the final decay.

Therefore, every existing racial value of a people is ineffective— if not downright endangered—if the people does not consciously remember it and cultivate it with the utmost diligence, base its collective hopes in the first place upon it, and build on it.

For this reason, the internationalist disposition can be viewed as the deadly enemy of this value. Instead, the commitment to one's own people's value must be in line with and determine the collective life and behavior of a people.

As much as the true *Ewigkeitsfaktor* [perpetuating factor of] the size and significance of a people is to be sought in the quality of the people, this value in itself will, as a whole, be relatively ineffective if the initially slumbering energies and talents of the people do not find an awakener.

Because just as humanity as a whole does not have a uniform average value, but rather appears to be composed of various racial values, the individual personal qualities found within a people are likewise unequal. Every act of a people, in whatever field it might be, is the result of the creative achievement of an individual. No hardship exists whose elimination is to be found only in the wish of those affected, if this general wish does not find its fulfillment in the actions of the individual chosen by the people for this task. Majorities have never accomplished creative achievements. Majorities have never given humanity inventions. The individual person is always the instigator of human progress. Now, a people with a certain inner racial value—provided this value is visible at all in its cultural or other achievements—must possess personal qualities to begin with, because without their appearance and creative activity, the cultural image of such a people would never emerge, and thus there would be no possibility of drawing conclusions about the inner value of such a people. When I speak about the inner racial value of a people, I assess this value based on the sum total of the people's visible achievements, thus acknowledging at the same time the presence of the particular personal qualities that represent the racial value of a people and create its cultural image. As much as racial value and personal qualities seem to be intertwined—because a racially worthless people cannot draw significant creative individuals from this source, and, vice versa, it is impossible to affirm racial value without the presence of creative individuals and their achievements—a people can, however, through the formal design of its systems, the community, or the state, nurture or at least facilitate (or even impede) the development of these personal qualities.

As soon as a people instates the majority as rulers of public life—in other words, institutes today's western concept of democracy—it destroys not only the significance of individual thought but blocks the effectiveness of personal qualities. It prevents through the formal construct of its life the emergence and work of individual creative persons.

This is the double curse of the currently prevailing democratic parliamentary system: It is not only incapable itself of attaining creative achievements, but it also prevents the rise and therefore the work of men who somehow tower threateningly above [*the*] average level. Because the majority has always found most threatening the individual who reaches above the average measure of stupidity, inadequacy, cowardice, and also arrogance. Added to this is the fact that in a democracy it is practically inscribed in law that inferior persons must become the leaders. As a result, this system, applied consistently to any institution, debases the entire leadership—to the extent that one can even still speak of such a concept. This is based on the lack of accountability that is part of the essence of democracy. Majorities are elusive phenomena—too elusive to be somehow saddled with responsibility. The leaders they install are in reality only executors of the will of the majority. Their task is therefore not so much to produce brilliant plans or ideas to be implemented with the support of the existing administrative apparatus, but to assemble the particular majorities necessary for the execution of certain intentions. In doing so, however, the majorities conform themselves less to the intentions than the intentions conform themselves to the majorities. But regardless of the results of such action, there is no one who can be held accountable. This is all the more true because every decision actually reached is the result of countless compromises, which are evident in the character and content of the decision. Who can then be held responsible for it?

As soon as strictly personally defined responsibility is eliminated, then the most compelling reason for the establishment of a strong leadership ceases to apply. If one were to compare the army [institution] organization, which is based on the highest degree of individual authority and responsibility, with our democratic civilian institutions, in terms of the results of their respective leadership training, one would be appalled. On the one side is an organization made up of capable men who are as courageous as they are ready to accept responsibility, and on the other are unaccountable incompetents. For four and a half years the German army organization resisted the largest enemy coalition of all time. The demoralized civilian democratic internal leadership broke down literally at the first blow from a few hundred rabble and deserters.[91]

The paucity of genuinely great leading minds among the German people finds its simplest explanation in the dissolute degeneration of the democratic parliamentary system that is slowly eroding our entire public life that we see in front of us.

The peoples must decide. Either they want majorities or minds. The two together can never agree. But the great things on this earth have thus far always been created by minds, and, frankly, what they created was then [*sic*] usually destroyed again by majorities.

So a people can, on the basis of its overall racial value, justifiably hope that it will be able to give life to true minds. However, it must then also, in the design of its body politic, seek those forms that do not artificially, even methodically, block the impact of such minds and build a wall of stupidity against them—in short, prevent them from achieving effectiveness.

Otherwise, one of a people's most powerful sources of strength is lost.

[As the third element of the inner strength of a people, we have education in self-assertion.]

The third element in a people's strength is a healthy natural self-preservation drive. From this, numerous heroic virtues result which alone allow a people to take up the struggle for survival. No state leadership will be able to achieve great successes if the people whose interests it must represent is too cowardly and too pathetic to mobilize itself on behalf of these interests. Indeed, no state leadership will be able to expect a people to possess heroism if the leadership itself has not educated the people for heroism. Just as internationalism damages and thereby weakens the existing racial value, and just as democracy destroys personal qualities, so pacifism disables the natural powers of a people's self-preservation.

These three factors—the people's value itself, the personal qualities present, and a healthy self-preservation drive—are the sources of strength from which a wise and enterprising domestic policy can always pull the weapons necessary for a people's self-assertion. Then army institutions and technical armament issues will always find the appropriate means to support a people in the difficult fight for freedom and daily bread.

If the internal political leadership of a people loses sight of this viewpoint or believes it needs to arm itself only in terms of physical matériel, then it can achieve as many short-term successes as it wants, but the future does not belong to such a people. Therefore, the task of all truly great legislators and statesmen of this earth was never the limited preparation for a war but rather the unlimited inner development and education of a people, so that its future, according to all human reasoning, appears secured almost by law. Then wars also lose their character of individual more-or-less-violent surprises and arrange themselves into a natural—even self-evident—system within the thorough, well-founded, long-lasting development of a people.

That the present state leadership pays this view little heed is in part due to the essence of democracy (to which they themselves owe their existence), but in part also to the fact that the state has become a purely formal mechanism that appears to them as an end in itself; they no longer feel the need to align themselves with the interests of a given people at all. People and state have become two separate concepts. It will be the task of the National Socialist movement to bring about, for Germany, a fundamental change in this regard.

[CHAPTER *IV*]

[Foreign Policy Critique and Proposals]

I f, therefore, the task of domestic policy—in addition to satisfying the so-called issues of the day, of course—is to toughen
and strengthen the body politic by methodically nurturing and promoting its inner value, then the task of foreign policy is to shield
and back this formative work externally and to assist in creating
and securing the collective necessities of life. A healthy foreign policy
must thus always maintain as its ultimate, immovable goal the acquisition of the fundamental means of sustenance for a people.
Domestic policy must secure the inner strength of a people for its
foreign policy assertion. Foreign policy must secure the life of a
people for its domestic policy development. Domestic and foreign
policy are therefore not only tightly connected, but they must also
operate in a complementary manner. The fact that throughout most
of human history, both domestic and foreign policy have held to
other principles, however, does not demonstrate the correctness of
such an approach, but has only supplied evidence of the faultiness
of such conduct. Countless peoples and states have perished, as

warning examples for us, because they did not follow the above-cited elementary principles. It is noteworthy how little man thinks during his life about the possibility of death. [How little as an individual] How little he adjusts the details of his life according to the experiences—with which he is in principle familiar—of the countless people who went before. It is always only the exceptions who consider this and by virtue of the force of their character attempt to impose on their fellow men laws based on the experiences of the past. It is noteworthy that numerous sanitary measures that benefit a people as a whole but are individually inconvenient must be forced upon the general public through the autocratic weight of individual persons, but immediately die away when the authority of the individual is replaced by the mass delusion of democracy. The average person has the most fear of death and in reality thinks most rarely about it. The prominent one occupies himself with it most persistently but nevertheless fears it the least. The one lives blindly from day to day, sinning away, only to sink down before the grim reaper. The other carefully observes his approach but then looks him in the eye, calm and composed.

In the life of the people it is exactly the same. It is often disturbing to see how little people are willing to learn from history, how foolishly unconcerned they walk away from their experiences, and how thoughtlessly they sin without considering that precisely because of their sins so many peoples and states have already perished and even disappeared from the earth. How little they concern themselves with the fact that—even in the short time period into which we have historical insight—states and peoples of almost gargantuan proportions have arisen, only to disappear without a trace two thousand years later; world powers have dominated civilizations that are now heard about only in myths; and vast cities have fallen into ruins, with hardly enough rubble remaining even to indicate their location to current generations. But almost beyond imagination are the worries, hardships, and troubles of the millions and millions of individuals who, as living substance, were once the actors and victims in these events. Unknown men, unknown soldiers of history. And how indifferent the present really is. How unfounded its eternal optimism and how pernicious its intentional ignorance, its inability to see, and its unwillingness to learn. If one were to depend on the broad masses, then the experience of the child playing with fire, not knowing what it is, would be repeated on the largest scale. Thus, for those who feel called to educate a people, it is their task to learn from history and to apply their knowledge practically without regard to the understanding, comprehension, ignorance, or even repudiation of the masses. The greatness of a man is all the more significant the greater his courage to use his superior insight—in opposition to the generally prevailing but ruinous view—to lead to overall victory. His victory will appear all the greater the stronger the opposition that had to be overcome and the more hopeless the fight seemed initially.

The National Socialist movement would have no right to consider itself a truly great phenomenon in the life of the German people if it did not summon the courage [*to*] learn from the experiences of the past and impose on the German people the laws of life that it represents, despite all opposition. As vigorous as its internal reformation work may be, the movement must not forget that there will never be a true long-term revitalization of our people unless our foreign policy measures succeed in securing the collective means of sustenance for our people. Thus it has become, in the truest sense of the word, a fighter for freedom and bread.[92] "Freedom and bread" is the simplest and [*in*] reality the greatest foreign-policy rallying cry that exists for a people. The freedom to organize and regulate the life of a people according to its own interests, and the bread that this people needs to live.

Today, if I appear as a critic of the past and present foreign-policy leadership of our people, then I am aware that the mistakes I see today have also been seen by others. What perhaps differentiates me from these others is simply the fact that [in one case] in most cases these assessments are simply critical perceptions without practical consequences, whereas I attempt—from my insight into the failures and mistakes of German domestic and foreign policy—to derive recommendations for change and improvement and to establish an instrument by which these changes and improvements can someday be implemented.

The foreign policy of the Wilhelminian period, for example, was seen by more than a few in Germany as disastrous in many cases and was characterized accordingly. From the circles of the Pan-German League in particular came countless warnings which, in the truest sense of the word, were vindicated.[93] I myself can imagine the tragedy that befell all of these voices of warning—seeing how and why a people is being destroyed without being able to help. In the last decades of the disastrous prewar foreign policy, the German parliament (i.e., democracy) was not powerful enough to determine the heads of the political leadership of the Reich. This was still an imperial right whose formal existence one did not yet dare to question. But the influence of democracy had nevertheless become so strong that a certain direction already seemed prescribed for the emperor's decisions. This had calamitous effects because now a national voice of warning could on the one hand no longer count on holding a responsible position (against the pronounced tendency of democracy), and on the other hand he could not, out of general patriotic beliefs, battle his majesty the emperor with the last weapon of the opposition. The idea of a march on Rome[94] would have been absurd in prewar Germany. Thus the national opposition found itself in the worst possible situation. Democracy had not yet prevailed but stood in raging conflict with the monarchical concept of a state. The monarchical state itself responded to democracy's challenge not with the decisiveness of destruction but rather with continued concessions. At that time, anyone who took a position against one of the two institutions risked being attacked by both. Anyone who, based on national interest, opposed a decision of the Kaiser was both ostracized by the patriots and scolded by the democrats. Anyone who expressed opposition to democracy was fought by the democrats and abandoned by the patriots. Yes, he risked being ignominiously [sacrificed] betrayed by the German government in the sad hope that such a sacrifice would gain the approval of Jehovah and, for a time, muzzle the pack of Jewish media. The way the circumstances were at that time, it was not possible—against the will of democracy or against the will of h[is] maj[esty] the emperor—to hold a responsible position in the Reich leadership and thereby change the course of foreign policy. This led to a situation in which objections against German foreign policy could be raised only on paper, and therefore the longer the critiques that emerged the more they had to adopt journalistic characteristics. The result, however, was that because of the lack of practical feasibility, progressively less value was placed on positive suggestions, whereas the purely critical observations gave rise to countless exhibits [*sic*] which one would be more likely to submit in their entirety when one hoped thereby to bring down the responsible bad regime. However, the critics of that time did not achieve this. It was not the government of that time that was overthrown; rather, it was the German Reich and therefore the German people that collapsed. What was predicted decades before had now arrived. One cannot think without deep sympathy of the men who were damned by fate to predict a collapse for twenty years and now—without being heard and therefore without being able to help—to have to witness the most tragic catastrophe of their people.

Aged, grieving, and embittered, yet filled with the idea that they must help, they tried after the downfall of the imperial government to assert their influence in the renewal of our people. But, for a number of reasons, this was all futile.

When the revolution broke the imperial scepter and installed democracy on the throne, the critics of that time had no weapon to overthrow democracy, just as they were earlier unable to influence the imperial regime.[95] In their decades of activity, they focused so much on a purely literary treatment of the problem that they now not only lacked the real means of power to give expression to their opinion on a situation that reacted only to the cry on the street, but they had also lost the ability to organize an expression of power that—if it was to be effective—had to be more than a wave of written protest. They all saw in the old parties the seed and the cause of the fall of the Reich. In their sense of inner purity, they had to dismiss the impertinence that they now wanted to play party politics themselves. But yet they could essentially only implement their ideas if there was the possibility of allowing them to be represented by a large number. Even if they wanted to demolish the parties a thousand times, they still had first to form the party that saw the destruction of the parties as its task. The fact that it never came to that was due also to the following: The more these men were forced to express their political opposition through purely journalistic means, the more their opposition became a critique that covered[96] the numerous weaknesses of the current system and illuminated the defectiveness of the individual foreign policy measures; however, because there was no possibility of personal responsibility, positive proposals were neglected, and in political life there are naturally no actions that do not possess a dark as well as a bright side. There is no foreign policy combination that can ever be viewed as completely satisfactory. The critic who, as things stood then, saw his primary task as the elimination of a government generally recognized to be incompetent, had no reason (except when useful for the critical assessment of the actions of this government) to provide positive recommendations that, due to concerns that were also inherent to these ideas, could just as easily have been subjected to critical examination. The critic never wants to weaken the impact of his critique by submitting proposals that could themselves be subject to criticism. But gradually the purely critical thinking of the representatives of the national opposition at that time became so ingrained that even today they observe and deal with domestic and foreign policy only in a critical manner. For the most part they have remained critics, and thus even today they are unable to convince themselves of a clear, definite, positive decision on either domestic or foreign policy. This is due in part to insecurity and indecision, but in part also to the fear that they might provide their opponents with an easy target for their own critiques. So they wish to make a thousand improvements but cannot decide on even a single step because even this step, again, is not completely satisfactory and has its questionable aspects—in short, it has its dark side, which they recognize and which frightens them. Now, healing the body politic of a profound and serious sickness does not involve finding a prescription that is completely nontoxic; rather, it is not uncommon to counteract one poison with another. In order to eliminate circumstances that are recognized as deadly, one must have the courage to push through and implement decisions that also harbor inherent dangers. As a critic, I am entitled to sort through all foreign policy options and to attack each one in detail, based on the questionable aspects or possibilities it contains. As a political leader who wishes to make history, however, I must decide on a certain path even if sober consideration says a thousand times that this path also holds dangers and may not lead to a completely satisfactory outcome. I cannot renounce a success simply because it is not complete. If the position in which I currently find myself will soon bring certain death, I cannot refrain from taking a step simply because it may not be a complete one. I also cannot reject a political action simply because it will benefit another people as well as my own. No, I cannot do that—even if the benefit to the other will be greater than to us—if failure to act means certain disaster for my people.

Today, many people from the purely critical approach have presented me with the stiffest opposition. They recognize this and this and this as good, but they nevertheless cannot join in because this and this and this is questionable. They know that Germany and our people will perish, but they cannot join in the rescue operation because they discover this or that is at least a cosmetic defect in it. In short, they see the decline and are unable to muster the determination to fight it, because in this act of resistance itself some questionable possibility will be sniffed out again.

This sad mentality [arises] owes its existence to yet another evil. Today there are more than a few—especially so-called educated people—who, when they decide to support or even promote a certain action, first carefully weigh up what the probability of success is, in order to then gauge their own exertion according to these percentages. That means, for example, that because a certain foreign or domestic policy decision is not completely satisfactory and success is not completely assured, they also cannot support this decision completely with the commitment of all their strength. These unfortunate ones do not understand that the reverse is true: a decision that I deem necessary, but whose success does not seem completely assured or whose success will provide only partial satisfaction, must be pushed through with greater energy; that which is lacking in the probability of success must be made up for in the energy of the execution. So only one question must be asked: whether a situation demands a certain decision or not. If such a decision is assessed and recognized as unquestionably necessary, then it must be implemented with the most brutal ruthlessness and greatest application of strength, even if every time the final result itself will be unsatisfactory or in need of improvement or perhaps even have a very low probability of success.

If a person appears to have cancer and must undoubtedly die, then it would be absurd to decline an operation because it had only a low probability of success or because even if it did succeed the sick one would still not be 100 percent well. It would be even more absurd if the physician himself were to operate with only reduced or half energy as a result of these limited prospects. But these people expect these greatest of absurdities all the time in domestic and foreign policy matters. If the success of a political operation is not completely certain or its result may not be completely satisfactory, they not only refuse to implement it but they also expect, if it is going to take place anyway, that it will succeed with the application of only partial strength, without complete commitment—always in the silent hope of being able to hold open a back door for retreat. This is the soldier who, [as a result of the] in view of the uncertainty of success, resists with only half his strength when attacked by a tank in an open field. His back door is flight and his end certain death.

No, today the German people has been ambushed from within and without by a pack of looting enemies. The continuation of this situation is our death. Every opportunity to change our circumstances must be seized, even if the result itself also has a thousand weaknesses or questionable aspects. [He who is a slave to the devil has little choice in his allies] And every such opportunity must then be fought through with the utmost energy.

The [victory] success of the battle of Leuthen[97] was uncertain, but the engagement was necessary. Frederick the Great did not triumph because he confronted the enemy with only half his strength, but rather because he compensated for the uncertainty of success with the abundance of his ingenuity, the boldness and decisiveness of his orders, and the daring with which his regiments fought.

I fear, however, that I will never be understood by my bourgeois critics, at least not until success proves the correctness of our actions. The man of the people has a better [instinct] advisor here. In place of the reflective wisdom of our intellectuals, he relies on the certainty of his [feelings] instincts and the beliefs of his heart.

But when I address foreign policy in this work, I do so not as a critic but as the leader of the National Socialist movement, which I know will make history. When I am nevertheless forced to observe the past and present critically, I do so only to justify and explain our own positive path. Just as the National Socialist movement does not present only criticism in the domestic policy arena, but rather possesses its own ideologically grounded program; in the same way, it must not only recognize what others have done incorrectly in terms of foreign policy but must derive its own actions from this recognition.

I know without a doubt that even our best success will not bring 100 percent happiness; with human shortcomings and the general circumstances they condition, ultimate completion lies always only in programmatic theory. Furthermore, I also know that no success can be attained without sacrifice, just as no victory can be achieved without casualties. But the recognition of the incompleteness of a success will never be able to prevent me from preferring such an incomplete success to certain complete demise. I will then commit myself [*to*] attempting to offset that which is lacking in the probability or degree of success with greater determination, and to transmitting this spirit to the movement I lead. Today we are fighting against an enemy front that we must break through and will break through. We measure our own sacrifices, ponder the size of the possible success, and will stride toward attack, regardless whether it will come to a halt ten or a thousand kilometers behind our current lines. Because wherever our success ends, that will always be the starting point of a new battle.

[CHAPTER V]

[The Policies of the NSDAP]

I am a German nationalist. That means I am openly committed to my *Volkstum* [ethnic community]. All of my thoughts and actions belong to it. I am a socialist. I see before me no class or rank, but rather a community of people who are connected by blood, united by language, and subject to the same collective fate. I love the people and hate the current majorities only because I do not see them representing either the greatness or the happiness of my people.

The National Socialist movement, which I lead today, sees as its goal the internal and external liberation of our people. Internally, the movement wishes to provide our people with those ways of life that seem adapted to the people's essence and which, in turn, benefit the people as an expression of this essence. It wishes to preserve the essence of this people and, through the systematic support of its best individuals and best virtues, raise it to a higher level. It advocates the external freedom of the people, because only under such conditions can this life be organized in a way that is most beneficial to the people. It fights for the daily bread of this people, because it [in hunger] advocates this people's right to life. It fights for the necessary space, because it represents this people's right to exist.

The National Socialist movement understands the concept of domestic policy as the promotion, strengthening, and consolidation of the life of our people through the introduction of laws and ways of life that correspond to the essence of our people and are able to bring to bear its fundamental strengths.

Foreign policy is understood as the securing of this development through the preservation of freedom and the procurement of the necessities of life.

The National Socialist movement differentiates itself from the previous bourgeois parties more or less as follows: The foreign policy of the bourgeois world is in truth always only focused on borders, whereas the National Socialist movement, in contrast, will pursue a policy focused on space. The German bourgeoisie will, with its boldest plans, perhaps attain unification of the German nation, but in reality it usually ends in bungling border adjustments.

The National Socialist movement, in contrast, will always allow its foreign policy to be determined by the need to secure the necessary space for our people. It knows no Germanization, as the national bourgeoisie does, but only the expansion of our own people. The movement will never see subjugated, so-called Germanized Czechs or Poles as a strengthening of the nation or of the people; rather this represents a racial weakening of our people. The national conception will not be determined by previous patriotic notions of state, but rather by ethnic and racial perceptions. Thus, the starting point of the movement's ideas is completely different from that of the bourgeois world. Some of what therefore appears to the national bourgeoisie as past and present political success we see as either failure or the cause of a later disaster. And much of what we view as self-evident appears to the German bourgeoisie as incomprehensible or even atrocious.

Nevertheless, at least some German youth from bourgeois circles will be able to understand me. And neither I nor the National Socialist movement expect to find support from the circles of the currently active national political bourgeoisie, but we know very well that at least some of the youth will find their way into our ranks.

[For it][98]

[*Chapter VI*]

[*From the Unification of the Reich to a Policy of Space*]

A people's foreign policy is determined partly by factors that lie within the people and partly by factors [determined] presented by the environment. Internal factors are generally the reasons for the necessity of a particular foreign policy as well as the extent of the strength present to carry it out. Peoples with impossible territory will always—at least as long as they are well led—make the effort to expand their territory and therefore their Lebensraum. This process, originally based only on a shortage of food, appeared so beneficial in its fortunate resolution that it gradually took on the glory of success itself. In other words, territorial expansion, which was at first only a purely expedient measure, became, over the course of human development, a heroic act which then took place even if the original preconditions or causes were absent. From the attempt to adjust Lebensraum to an increased population later came unfounded wars of conquest, whose lack of motive contained the seed of future setback. The answer to that is pacifism. Pacifism has been present in the world since the time that there have been wars whose purpose is not the conquest of territory for the sustenance of a people. Since then, pacifism has always accompanied war. It will disappear again as soon as war ceases to be an instrument of greedy or power-hungry individuals or peoples, and as soon as it again becomes the final weapon with which a people fights for its daily bread.

However, the expansion of a people's Lebensraum to obtain bread will, in the future, also always require the commitment of a people's full strength. If it is the task of domestic policy to prepare for this commitment, then it is the task of foreign policy to lead it in such a way that the greatest possible success appears assured. But this is determined not only by the strength of the people wishing to act, but also by the force of the opposition. The imbalance in the strength of the peoples struggling against each other for land always leads to the attempt, by way of unions, either to conquer or to resist the superior conqueror.

This is the beginning of alliance policies.

After the successful war of 1870-71, the German people had attained an infinitely respected position in Europe. A large number of German states that were previously only loosely allied with each other—and historically were not infrequently hostile to each other—were united into one Reich, thanks to the successes of Bismarck's[99] statecraft and the achievements of the Prussian-German army leadership. A province of the old Holy German Empire, lost 170 years earlier (which had been definitively annexed by France in a brief theft), came back to the motherland.[100] Numerically, the greatest portion of the German nation, at least in Europe, was thus united in a single state entity. It was problematic that this state included...[101] million Poles and...[102] from Alsace and Lorraine who had become French. This conformed neither to the idea of a nation state nor to that of an ethnic state. The bourgeois view of the nation state would at least have to ensure the unity of the state language—down to the last school and the last street sign. It would also have to instill

German thoughts in these people, through [the] education and life, and turn them into bearers of these ideas.

This was weakly attempted, possibly never seriously desired, and in reality the opposite was achieved.[103]

The ethnic state, in contrast, could under absolutely no circumstances annex Poles with the intention of turning them into Germans one day. It would instead have to decide either to isolate these alien racial elements in order to prevent the repeated contamination of one's own people's blood, or it would have to immediately remove them entirely, transferring the land and territory that thus became free to members of one's own ethnic community.

The fact that the bourgeois national state was not capable of such an action is self-evident. Neither had the idea ever been thought of, nor would such a thing never[104] have been done. But even if the will to do it had been present, the strength would not have sufficed to carry it out—due not so much to repercussions in the rest of the world as to the complete lack of understanding for such an action could be found in the ranks of our own so-called national bourgeoisie. The bourgeois world once thought it could overthrow the feudal world, but in reality the same mistakes were perpetuated by the bourgeois nouveau riche, [professors] lawyers, and journalists. The bourgeoisie never had an original idea—just excessive vanity and money.

But with that alone one cannot overthrow a world, nor build up another. That is why, in world history, the period of bourgeois rule will be just as short as it is shockingly pathetic.

Thus, upon the establishment of the Reich, poison was also absorbed into the body of the new state, and its destructive effects could not fail to appear, especially when into the bargain civil equality[105] gave the Jews the opportunity to use it as its most reliable shock troops.

But aside from that, although the Reich included the largest part of the German nation, it was still only part, even if the new state had no great foreign policy goals of an ethnic nature, it would have made sense for it—as a so-called civil national state—to at least pursue as its smallest foreign policy goal the further unification and integration of the German nation. Something that the Italian bourgeois national state never forgot.[106]

Thus the German people obtained a nation state that in reality did not include the entire nation.

The new borders of the Reich were, from a national political perspective, incomplete. They ran straight through the German-speaking area, through parts that previously had belonged to the German Confederation, if only in the loosest manner.

But these new borders were even more unsatisfactory when viewed from the military perspective. Exposed, open terrain everywhere—areas which, especially in the west, were also of decisive importance for German industry far beyond the border regions. These borders were all the more unfavorable from a military-political standpoint, considering that [on the edge] Germany was bordered by several major powers whose foreign policy goals were as aggressive as their military resources were abundant. Russia in the east, France in the west. Two military states, one of which was eyeing East and West Prussia while the other had for centuries tirelessly pursued the foreign policy goal of establishing a border on the Rhine. Then there was England, the greatest naval power on earth. While the German land borders in the east and west were broad and exposed, the possible operational basis for naval warfare was, in contrast, confined. Nothing facilitated the fight against German submarine warfare more than the spatial constriction of the base from which it could be launched. The *nasse Dreieck* [watery triangle][107] was easier to blockade and monitor than a coastline extending, say, six hundred or eight hundred kilometers. All things considered, from a military perspective there was nothing satisfactory about the new borders of the Reich. No natural barriers or natural protection anywhere. Instead, highly developed military powers everywhere, with anti-German ulterior motives behind their foreign policy. Bismarck's premonition that his heirs would have to defend again with the sword the new Reich he had established[108] was well founded. Bismarck articulated what came to pass forty-five years later.

But as unsatisfactory as the new Reich borders were from a national and military-political standpoint, they were even more inadequate from the standpoint of the possibility of feeding the German people.

Germany was actually always an overpopulated area. This was due to the nature of the wedging in of the German people in central Europe on the one hand, and to the cultural and actual significance of the people and its pure human fertility on the other. From its historic entry into world history, the German people already found itself short of space. Yes, its very first political appearance was forced by this shortage. And since the beginning of the migration, our people have never been able to eliminate this need except by military conquest or by a reduction in our own population. This reduction was soon provided by hunger, by emigration, and sometimes by endless disastrous wars, and is being arranged recently by a voluntary decrease in the birth rate.

The wars of [18]64, [18]66, and [18]70-71[109] had their meaning in the national political integration of a portion of the German people and the consequent final end of the German political fragmentation. The flag of the new Reich—black, white, and red—therefore did not have the slightest ideological meaning, but only a German national meaning in the sense of overcoming previous political strife.[110] The black, white, and red flag thus became the symbol of a German federal state that had overcome this fragmentation. The fact that the state nonetheless and despite its youth enjoyed practically idolatrous veneration was due to the nature of the christening, which singled out the birth of the Reich itself far above similar events. Three victorious wars—of which the last became a positive miracle of German statecraft, German military leadership, and German heroism—were the actions from which the new Reich came into existence. And when it was finally announced to our fellow men in the emperor's proclamation, by the empire's greatest herald,[111] [droning] the din of the batteries of the encirclement front around Paris droned in the music of the fanfares.[112]

An empire had never before been proclaimed in such a way.

But the black, white, and red flag appeared to the German people as the symbol of this unique event, just as the black, red, and yellow flag is and will remain the symbol of the November revolution.[113]

Although the individual German states became more and more integrated with each other under this flag, and although the new Reich secured for them political prestige and external recognition, the founding of the Reich did not change anything about our people's primary hardship, the need for additional territory. The greatest military-political acts of our people had been unable to give the German people borders within which it could sustain itself. On the contrary: To the degree that the new Reich increased the esteem in which the German nation was held, it became harder for an individual to turn his back on such a state and emigrate; at the same time, a certain national pride and a love of life—which for us today is almost incomprehensible—saw a wealth of children as a joy rather than a burden.

After 1870-71, the population increase in Germany was strikingly rapid.[114] The need for food was partially met by the diligent industriousness and the great scientific expertise with which the Germans cultivated their fields within the now secure national boundaries. But a great—if not the greatest—portion of the increase in German land productivity was devoured by an at least equivalent increase in the overall demands of the citizens of the new state. The "nation of sauerkraut eaters and potato consumers," as the French sneeringly called it, now [*sic*] gradually began to match its standard of living to that of the rest of the world. But that left only a portion of the increase in German agricultural productivity available to support the pure increase in population.

Actually, the new Reich never knew how to alleviate this shortage either. In the new Reich as well, attempts were initially made to preserve the balance between population and land within reasonable bounds through continual emigration. The most striking evidence of the correctness of our claim about the paramount significance of the relation between population and land lies in the fact that as a result of this imbalance, in Germany in the '70[s], '80[s], and '90s, the land shortage led to an emigration epidemic that by the early '90s had swelled to a rate of nearly 1¼ million people per year.[115]

However, the problem of feeding the German people that remained was also not solved by the establishment of the new Reich.[116] A further increase in the population of the German nation could not take place at all without such a solution. Regardless of how such a solution might turn out, it had in any case to be found. The most important issue in German foreign policy after 1870-71 therefore had to be the question of solving the sustenance problem.

[CHAPTER VII]

[The Misguided Economic and Alliance Policies of the Second Reich]

O f all the countless dictums of Bismarck, hardly any were quoted more readily by the bourgeois political world than the statement that [art] politics is the art of the possible.[117] The smaller the political minds who had to administer the legacy of the great man, the greater the attraction the words held. With this sentence, one can excuse—even vindicate—the most pathetic political bumbler. One simply invokes the great one and attempts to prove that nothing other than what one is doing would be possible at the moment, but that politics is the art of the possible and that one is therefore acting in the Bismarckian spirit and sense. In that way, even a Herr Stresemann[118] can get something Olympic [*laurel*] around his head— which, if not exactly Bismarckian, is at least also bald [*sic*].

Bismarck had a precisely delimited and clearly defined political goal in mind. It is an impertinence to claim that he achieved his life's work through an accumulation of particular political possibilities and not through mastery of the particular situations in view of the political goal he had in mind. This political goal of Bismarck's was to solve the German question through blood and iron.[119] To eliminate the Habsburg-Hohenzollern dualism. To form a new German Reich under Prussian-Hohenzollern leadership. To provide this Reich maximum security against external threats. To organize its internal administration according to the Prussian model.

In pursuit of this goal, Bismarck used every opportunity to work with diplomatic means, as long as they promised success; he threw the sword into the balance when only force could bring about a decision. Bismarck was a master of politics whose operational territory ranged from the parquet of the drawing room to the blood-soaked ground of the battlefield.

This was the master of the politics of the possible.

His successors have neither a political goal nor even a single political thought. On the contrary—they struggle clumsily from today to tomorrow and from tomorrow to the day after, and then invoke with conceited impudence that man for whom they themselves and their spiritual forebears caused the greatest worries and bitterest conflicts,[120] in order to present their politically meaningless, pointless, and ruinous babble as the art of the possible.

When Bismarck established the new Reich—with three wars,[121] but all thanks to his brilliant political activity—this was the highest possible achievement that could be attained initially. But it was also the inevitable and necessary precondition for every subsequent political representation of the vital interests of our people. Because without the creation of the new Reich, the German people would never have had the power structure necessary to carry out the future struggle with destiny. Just as clear was the fact that although the new Reich had initially been unified on the battlefield, internally the members still had to become familiar with each other. Years of assimilation would be required before this merger—initially into a confederation—of German states could become a true federal state. This was the time when the Iron Chancellor set aside the Kürassier boots[122] and, with infinite cleverness, patience, wise understanding, and wonderful feeling, replaced the force of the Prussian hegemony with the power of trust. This achievement—turning a coalition of states drawn together on the battlefield into a Reich bound by heart-warming love—is one of the greatest [*sic*] ever attained by the art of politics.[123]

The fact that Bismarck initially limited himself to this was just as much due to the wisdom of his insight as it was fortunate for the German nation. These years of peaceful internal development were necessary to avoid an obsession with conquest—conquest whose results would have been even more uncertain in that the inner strength to carry it out would still have lacked that homogeneity necessary for the melting in [*sic*] of additional territories.

Bismarck had achieved his life's goal. He had solved the German question, eliminated the Habsburg-Hohenzollern dualism, raised Prussia to be the leading German power, then unified the nation, consolidated the new Reich internally as much as possible at the time, and developed the military defense in such a way that this entire process of refounding the internal Reich, which would take decades, could not be significantly disrupted by anyone.

Although Bismarck could, as elderly chancellor of the old Reich, look back on a completed life's work, this work does not signify the completion of the life of the German nation. Through Bismarck's establishment of the new Reich, the German nation, after hundreds of years of decline, had again found an organic form that not only united the German people but also gave these united people an expression of strength that was just as real as it was ideal in nature. If the flesh and blood of this people was the substance whose preservation on this earth had to be attempted, then the new Reich emerged as the instrument of power through which the nation could henceforth again realize its right to life in the context of the rest of the world.

It was the task of the post-Bismarck era to determine the further steps that must be taken in the interests of sustaining the substance of the German people.

More specific political acts would depend on these decisions, which were to be fundamental in character and which would therefore signify a new purpose. In other words, in the same way that Bismarck as an individual adopted a purpose for his political dealings—which only then allowed him, as each case arose, to pursue every opportunity to reach this goal—the post-Bismarck era should have established a definite goal (both necessary and possible) whose achievement would authoritatively promote the interests of the German people and in whose achievement all options, from the arts of diplomacy to the art of war, could be used.

This setting of a goal, however, did not take place.

It is not necessary or even possible to itemize all of the reasons that were the cause of this failure. The primary reason is the lack of a genuinely brilliant, preeminent political personality. But hardly less significant are the causes that can be found to some extent in the nature of the establishment of the new Reich itself. Germany had become a democratic state, and even if the leadership of the Reich was responsible for imperial decisions, these decisions could only with difficulty defy the general public opinion that found its particular expression in the parliamentary institution—an institution whose makers, however, were the political parties and the press, who themselves took their ultimate instructions from invisible manipulators. Thus, the interests of the nation began to play an increasingly secondary role to the interests of certain particular groups. This situation was exacerbated because there was very little clarity among the broad public about the true interests of the nation, whereas the interests of specific political parties or news organizations were, in contrast, much more concrete. Because Germany was now a nation state. Except that the concept of a national ethos was, in the end, viewed strictly in terms of state, patriotism, and dynasty. It had practically nothing to do with ethnic awareness. Thus, there was a general lack of clarity about the future and about the future objectives of foreign policy activity. From the national point of view, the next task of the state after the completion of its internal state development would have been to resume and carry out the unification of the nation. To the then purely formal nation state, no goal should have been more important from a foreign policy perspective than the incorporation of those German areas in Europe which, due in part to their previous history, must be a natural component not only of the German nation but of a German Reich. Such an obvious goal was not adopted, however, because aside from other obstacles, the so-called national conception was far too unclear and had not been thought out or worked through well enough to provide adequate motivation for such a step. Using every possible means to [implement] envision and implement the integration of the ethnic Germans of the old Reich's Ostmark[124] as the next goal would have gone against notions of patriotism and legitimacy as well as hard-to-define sympathies.

But the venerable house of Habsburg would thereby have lost its throne. The whole beer-table patriotism would also have been most seriously damaged, but this would nevertheless—from the standpoint of a so-called nation state—have been the only reasonable next task that the new Reich could have assigned itself. Not only because it would have brought about a significant numerical strengthening of the Germans living in the Reich area (which naturally would have expressed itself militarily as well), but it would have been the only way to save that which is lamented today as lost. If Germany itself [*had*] taken part in the breaking up of the impossible Habsburg state, [then] and if this division had been set for national political reasons as our own political goal, then the entire development of Europe would have taken a different direction. Germany would not have made enemies of a whole number of states that have nothing against Germany per se, and in the south the border of the Reich would not be at the Brenner [Pass]. At least the predominantly German part of South Tyrol would belong to Germany today.

But what prevented this was not only the lack of national consciousness at the time, but just as much the particular interests of particular groups. The Center Party circles wanted, at all costs, a policy of preserving the so-called "Catholic" Habsburg states,[125] which people falsely spoke of as "blood brothers" while knowing very well that precisely these blood brothers in the Habsburg monarchy were slowly but surely being pushed against the wall and deprived of their family membership. But for the Center Party, even in Germany German points of view were not authoritative. Every Pole and every Alsatian traitor and Francophile was dearer to those gentlemen than the German who did not wish to affiliate himself with such a criminal organization.[126] Under the pretext of representing Catholic interests, this party already helped during peacetime to damage and wreck in all possible ways the principal stronghold of a truly Christian worldview—Germany. And this dishonest party never balked at going arm in arm in deepest friendship with avowed atheists and desecrators of religion when it believed the German nation state and thus the German people could thereby be harmed.[127]

So the Center—the pious Christian Catholic Center—always had the Jewish-atheist Marxists as beloved allies at its side during the establishment of the absurd German foreign policy.

Just as the Center fought tooth and nail against an anti-Habsburg policy, the Social Democrats (who were the representatives of Marxist ideology at the time) opposed it as well, although for other reasons.[128] But the ultimate aim of both parties was the same: maximum damage to Germany. The weaker the state, the more absolute the dominance of these parties becomes—and therefore the more profitable for their leaders.

If for national political reasons the old Reich again wanted to take up the integration of the German people in Europe, then, in conjunction with the inevitable associated breakup of the Habsburg conglomerate of states, Germany would have to create its own grouping of European powers. It was obvious that such a dissolution of the Habsburg state could not be considered without entering into relations with other states that had to pursue similar interests. To reach this goal, and in pursuit of all opportunities, a European coalition would have arisen that would have determined the destiny of Europe for at least the next few decades.

But then the Triple Alliance[129] would first have to have been officially dissolved as well. I say "officially" because in reality the dissolution had already taken place long ago.

The alliance with Austria made sense for Germany as long as it could hope, through this alliance, to obtain an increase in strength for the hour of danger. The alliance became pointless from the moment that the additional military strength gained failed to outweigh the military burden the alliance placed on Germany. In effect, this was the case from the very first day of the Triple Alliance, because in part due to this alliance or as a consequence of this alliance Russia became an enemy of Germany. Bismarck also weighed this carefully and therefore decided to conclude the so-called Reinsurance Treaty with Russia.[130] The point of the reinsurance treaty was, in brief, that if the alliance with Austria were to drive Germany into a conflict with Russia, Germany would abandon Austria. Thus, Bismarck recognized already in his time the problematic nature of the Triple Alliance, and, according to his art of the possible, he provided what was needed in all situations.

This Reinsurance Treaty helped lead to the banishment of the greatest German statesman of the modern era.[131]

But after the occupation of Bosnia by Austria-Hungary,[132] an action which powerfully stirred up the pan-Slavic movement, the situation Bismarck feared in the early '90s had actually already come to pass. The alliance with Austria had brought enmity with Russia.[133]

This enmity with Russia was [*the*] reason why Marxism, although it did not exactly support the German foreign policy, then at least in reality made any other policy impossible.[134]

The relationship between Austria and Italy was, in principle, always the same. Italy joined the Triple Alliance out of wariness of France, not out of love for Austria. Bismarck, however, also correctly recognized the "intrinsic cordiality" of Austro-Italian relations when he pronounced that between Austria and Italy there were only two possible conditions: either alliance or war. In Italy there was—aside from a few Francophile fanatics—true fondness only for Germany. And that was also explainable. The immeasurable political illiteracy and ignorance of the German people, in particular its so-called bourgeois national intelligentsia, are revealed in the notion that it would be possible to carry the legally constructed Triple Alliance over into friendly affection. That was never even the case between Germany and Austria, because even here the Triple Alliance (or, rather, the alliance with Germany) was humanly anchored in the hearts of only relatively few of the Germans in Austria. The Habsburgs would never have entered the Triple Alliance if there had been any other way to preserve the cadaver of their state. In July of 1870, when the German people rose up in indignation at the outrageous provocation of France and hastened to the old battlefields [*sic*] in the defense of the German Rhine, in Vienna they hoped the hour of revenge for Sadowa[135] had come. One conference followed another, one royal counselor relieved the next, messengers flew back and forth, and the first conscription orders were distributed, but the first reports from the theater of war were also already arriving. And when Weissenburg was followed by a Wörth, and after Wörth a Gravelotte, a Metz, a Mars la Tour, and finally a Sedan,[136] only then, under the impact of the new German idea—now suddenly crying out as if just released—did the Habsburgs begin to discover their German heart as well. If Germany had only lost the first battles, then the Habsburgs (and with them Austria) would have done what they later reproached Italy for. And, moreover, what they not only planned for the second time in the Great War but also committed, as the basest treason against the state that had pulled the sword for them.[137] Germany took upon itself the greatest casualties for this state, and was betrayed by this state not just in a thousand individual cases, but also by its leader[138] himself who said numerous things and truths that our bourgeois national patriots would rather keep quiet about in order to be able to scream against Italy today.

When the house of Habsburg later crept into the Triple Alliance, it was only because without the Triple Alliance this house would long ago have been swept away to where it finds itself now. If I survey the sins of this house against the history of the German people, then one thing strikes me as painful: that this time God's mill was being driven by powers lying outside the German people.

And the Habsburgs also had every other reason to desire the alliance, particularly with Germany, because this alliance in reality abandoned the German people in Austria. The denationalization policy in Austria, the Czechization and Slavification of ethnic Germans, would never have been possible if the Reich itself had not provided moral cover for it. Because what right did the German Austrian have to protest, for national reasons, against a state policy that was backed by the essence of the German national consciousness and which embodied it for the German Austrians in the Reich? And conversely, how could Germany exercise any pressure at all to prevent the gradual de-Germanization in Austria, at a time when the Habsburgs themselves were allies of the Reich? One must know the weakness of the political leadership of the Reich in order to know that nothing would have been more impossible than even the attempt to have a genuinely influential effect on the ally whose internal conditions were concerned. The clever Habsburgs knew that very well, as Austrian diplomacy far surpassed German diplomacy in terms of cunning and cleverness. Precisely these Germans, in contrast, as if struck by blindness, appeared to have no inkling of their allies' internal activities and conditions. It took the war to open most people's eyes.[139]

But for this very reason the Habsburgs' eagerness to ally with Germany was even more disastrous, as it ensured the ultimate undermining of the conditions for the alliance. Because the Habsburgs were now in a position to eliminate the German people in Austria in complete peace and without concern over German interference, the value of this whole alliance for Germany itself became increasingly questionable. What could an alliance that was never intended seriously by the dynasty mean to Germany? The house of Habsburg would never have thought to consider the alliance applicable when German interests were at stake as well, and under its effects the only real friends of this alliance would gradually be de-Germanized. Because in the rest of Austria, the alliance was at best seen as neutral, and in most cases it was privately hated.

Even the press in the capital city of Vienna, in the last twenty years before the war, had a much more pro-French than pro-German orientation. The press in the Slavic provinces, however, was decidedly anti-German. But to the degree that the Slavic community was as far as possible culturally supported by the Habsburgs and now had its own cultural centers in its capital cities, centers of particular political desire emerged as well. It is history's retribution on the house of Habsburg: it did not see that this national hatred which was first mobilized against the German people would one day consume the Austrian state itself. But for Germany the alliance with Austria became particularly absurd in that moment when, thanks to the actions of the traitorous German-Austrian Marxists, so-called universal suffrage definitively broke the dominance of the ethnic Germans in the Austrian state.[140] Because ethnic Germans actually only numbered one-third of the population of Cisleithania—the Austrian half of the Austro-Hungarian state. As soon as universal suffrage became the basis of Austrian political representation, the situation of the ethnic Germans became hopeless. It became even more so when the clerical parties wanted a conscious representation of national points of view no more than the Marxists, who deliberately betrayed it. In the old Austria this same Social Democracy, which today hypocritically speaks of the Germans in South Tyrol, betrayed and sold the ethnic Germans in the most shameless manner at every opportunity.[141] The Social Democrats themselves always stood at the side of our people's enemies. The most shameless Czech arrogance always found its representative among the so-called German Social Democrats. Every act of oppression against the Germans always found their approval, and when the Germans were pushed back, German Social

Democracy saw in this every time assistance for itself. What could Germany expect under such circumstances from a state whose political leadership, to the extent that it expressed itself in parliament, was four-fifths consciously and deliberately anti-German?

In reality, the advantages of the alliance with Austria lay all on Austria's side, while Germany had to bear all the disadvantages. And they were not few.

Due to the character of the Austrian state, a considerable number of surrounding states viewed the breakup of Austria as the goal of their national policy. What the post-Bismarck era in Germany had never achieved, even the smallest Balkan states possessed: a specific foreign policy goal which they attempted to attain by all possible means. All of these nation states—some newly created—on Austria's border saw as their supreme future task the "liberation" of those who belonged to their ethnic communities but who lived under the Austrian and Habsburg scepter. It was understood that this liberation could take place only through military conflicts. It was also understood that this would lead to the breakup of Austria. Austria's own strength of resistance did not represent a major impediment because it relied primarily on those who were to be freed. In the case of a coalition war in which Russia, Romania, and Serbia would oppose Austria, the northern and southern Slavic elements would immediately drop out of the Austrian defense, so that at most Germany and Hungary would remain as protagonists in the primary battle. But as we know from experience, the withdrawal of certain forces for ethnic reasons leads to a disruption and therefore paralysis of the front in general. Austria itself would in reality have had very little defensive strength to resist such a general war of aggression. This was very well known in Russia as well as in Serbia and Romania. The only thing that sustained Austria was the strong ally upon which it was able to lean. But what was more natural was the formation of the perception, in the minds of the anti-Austrian leading statesmen as well as public opinion that the road to Vienna must therefore lead through Berlin.

The more states imagined themselves as Austria's heirs, but were unable to attain this because of Austria's military alliance with Germany, the more these states had to view Germany itself as an enemy.

By the turn of the century, the significance of the enemies Austria created for Germany outweighed many times over the possible military assistance that Austria itself might ever be able to provide Germany.

That turned the inner logic of this alliance policy into exactly the opposite.

The matter was made even more difficult by the third alliance partner, Italy. As already mentioned, the relationship between Italy and Austria was never an affair of the heart. It was not even based on reason; rather, it was only the result and consequence of a compelling force. The Italian people, above all, and the Italian intelligentsia were always able to conjure up affection for Germany. At the turn of the century there was already every good reason for an alliance between Italy and Germany alone. The idea that Italy is by nature a faithless ally is so stupid and dumb that it can only be held by the armchair politicians of our nonpolitical so-called national bourgeoisie. The most striking counterevidence is provided by the history of our own people, namely when Italy was previously allied with Germany—against Austria, in fact.[142] Of course, Germany at that time was Prussia, led by the genius of Bismarck, and not the mishandled Reich botched by later political incompetents.

Certainly Italy suffered battlefield defeats on land and at sea,[143] but it fulfilled its alliance obligations honorably. Austria, in contrast, in the Great War (into which Germany was pushed by Austria), did not. When Italy was offered a separate peace that would have given it everything it could have achieved later, Italy rebuffed the offer proudly and indignantly,[144] despite the military defeats it had suffered. The Austrian state leadership, however, not only cooed [*sic*] for such a separate peace but was ready to abandon all of Germany.[145] That this did not take place was due not to the strength of character of the Austrian state but much more to the nature of the enemy's demands, which in practice meant the breakup of the state. But the fact that the Italy of 1866 suffered military defeats could not really be interpreted as a sign of its faithlessness as an ally. Certainly one would rather have had victories than defeats, but the Italy of that time could not be compared to Germany then or later, because Italy lacked the superior military crystallization power that Germany had in Prussia. A German Confederation without the fundamental strength of the Prussian army would have been just as inferior as Italy in the face of an attack by a long-standing military power—not yet torn by national rivalries—such as Austria. The important thing was that Italy, by binding a large and significant portion of the Austrian army, enabled an outcome in Bohemia that made the future German Reich possible. Because anyone who examines the critical situation on the day of the battle of Königgrätz will not be able to claim that Germany's fate would not have been affected if Austria had been on the battlefield with 140,000 men more than it was able to bring because they were tied down by Italy.

Italy, of course, did not conclude this alliance agreement in order to enable the national unification of the German people, but rather that of the Italian people. The ability to see in that a cause for reproach or vilification really shows the proverbial political naiveté of a person who just joins patriotic clubs. The idea of maintaining an alliance in which, from the beginning, only one member has the prospect of success or advantage is childish stupidity.[146] In the same way, the Italians would have had the right to accuse Prussia and Bismarck of the same thing: that they concluded the alliance in pursuit of their own interests rather than simply out of love for Italy. Unfortunately, I would almost like to say, it is embarrassing that this stupidity was committed only north of the Alps and not to the south as well.

Such a stupidity can only become understandable if one views the Triple Alliance or, better, the alliance between Germany and Austria—namely, the very rare case in which one state, Austria, gains everything from an alliance and the other, Germany, absolutely nothing. An alliance in which one deploys its interests and the other its "gleaming arms."[147] The one [expedient rationality] cold expediency and the other *Nibelungentreue*.[148] It has existed only once in the history of the world, at least to such an extent and in such a way, and Germany received the most terrible bill for this type of political leadership and alliance policy.

So if the alliance with Italy, at least in terms of relations between Austria and Italy, was of questionable value from the beginning, then it was not because Italy was a fundamentally flawed partner, but rather because this alliance with Austria promised Italy absolutely nothing of value in return.

Italy was a nation state. Its future inevitably had to lie on the edges of the Mediterranean Sea. Every adjacent power is thus more or less an obstacle to the development of this nation state. If one adds to that the fact that Austria itself had more than 800,000 Italians[149] within its borders, and [vice versa] these same Habsburgs—who on the one hand brought Slavification to the Germans and on the other hand knew very well how to play the Slavs and Germans against the Italians—had every interest in gradually denationalizing these 800,000 Italians, then the future task of Italian foreign policy was hardly in doubt. Regardless of how pro-German it was, it had to be anti-Austrian. And this policy also found lively support—even glowing enthusiasm—among` the Italian people itself. What Italy had suffered at the hands of the Habsburgs over the course of the centuries (and Austria was their political weapon in this) was, seen from the Italian standpoint, outrageous.[150] For centuries, Austria was the obstacle preventing the unification of the Italian people. The Habsburgs continually supported the corrupt Italian dynasties, and around the turn of the century in Vienna hardly a party convention of the clerical and Christian Social movement ended without the call to give Rome back to the pope. No secret was made of the fact that this was viewed as the goal of Austrian policy, but the Austrians had the brazenness to expect that in Italy itself intense enthusiasm would be shown for the alliance with Austria. Austrian policy over the course of the centuries had in no way treated Italy with kid gloves. The role France played for centuries in Germany, Austria played for centuries in Italy. The north Italian lowlands were repeatedly used as the operational field upon which the Austrian state applied its friendship policies against Italy. Croatian regiments and Hungarian foot soldiers were the cultural ambassadors and bearers of the Austrian civilization, and it is only a pity that all of this came to rest on the German name to some degree as well. Today when one hears from Italian mouths frequent arrogant disparagement or even scornful denigration of German culture, then the German people can thank that state which was externally disguised as German but which revealed to the Italians the character of its inner nature through a mob of coarse and brutish soldiers who were viewed as a true divine scourge by those who experienced them within the Austrian state itself. The military renown of the Austrian army was in part built on successes that awakened for all times the everlasting hatred of the Italians.

It was a misfortune for Germany never to have understood this. A misfortune to have supported it instead—if not directly then indirectly. Because in this way Germany lost the state that, as things stood, could have been our most faithful ally, just as it was previously a very reliable ally for Prussia.

The inner view of Italy toward relations with Austria was particularly influenced by the attitude of the general Austrian public toward the Tripolitan War.[151] Considering the circumstances, it was understandable that those in Vienna looked with jealous eyes at Italian attempts to gain ground in Albania. Austria believed its own interests there were under threat. What was not understandable was the widespread and clearly artificially inflamed agitation against Italy, when Italy prepared to conquer Tripolitania. Yet the Italian step was a natural one. No one could take it amiss if the Italian government attempted to raise the Italian flag in areas that, based on their location, had to be the appropriate Italian colonial area. The Italian actions should have been welcomed by Germany and Austria, not only because the young Italian colonizers were following ancient Roman tracks, but also for another reason. The more Italy became engaged in North Africa, the more the natural opposition between Italy and France would develop. In consideration of the increase in French military strength that might otherwise also take place on European battlefields, a superior German state leadership would at least have attempted to use every means possible to create difficulties for the threatening expansion of French hegemony across North Africa and the French occupation of the black continent in general. The French government and especially its military leadership made it absolutely clear that for them the African colonies had another significance besides [plantations] demonstrations of French civilization. These colonies were already being viewed as the source of troops for the next European conflict. It was also clear that this conflict could only involve Germany. What would have been more natural than for Germany to promote every interference by another power, especially when this other power was an ally? Moreover, the French were sterile[152] and had no need to expand their Lebensraum, whereas the Italian people, like the Germans, had to find some way out. No one should say that it would have involved robbing Turkey. All colonies then are robbed areas; the European just cannot live without them. But we did not and could not have any interest in precipitating an estrangement with Italy out of false feelings of sympathy for Turkey. If ever in a foreign policy action, in this one Austria and Germany could stand behind Italy completely. But the way the Austrian press reacted to the Italian action, that in its ultimate goal was nothing other than the annexation of Bosnia and Herzegovina by Austria itself, was simply scandalous. Then hatred suddenly flared up; this showed the true inner disposition of the Austro-Italian relationship even more clearly, as there was no actual reason for it. I myself was in Vienna at that time,[153] and I was inwardly shocked by the stupid and unconscionable way in which our ally was stabbed in the back. Under such circumstances, demanding of this ally a loyalty that would in reality have been suicide for Italy is at least as incomprehensible as it is naive.

Furthermore, the natural military-geographic situation of Italy will always force this state to pursue a policy that does not bring it into conflict with a superior naval power that the Italian fleet and its allies would not, as far as can be judged, be in a position to defend against. Italy will never be able to adopt an anti-English attitude as long as England possesses undisputed naval supremacy and as long as this dominance can be strengthened by a French Mediterranean fleet, without Italy plus and [*sic*] its allies being in a position to offer promising resistance. One can never demand of a state's leadership that it abandon its own to certain destruction, out of foolish sympathy for another state whose reciprocal love was clearly shown by the Tripoli war. But anyone who subjects the coastal situation of the Italian state to even the most cursory inspection must immediately be convinced that it would not only be hopeless but absurd for Italy to fight England under the present circumstances. But Italy found itself in exactly the same situation in which Germany had found itself: Just as Bismarck once saw the risk of an Austrian-provoked war with Russia as so enormous that, in the event of such a situation, he committed himself by the famous Reinsurance Treaty, to disregard the otherwise binding alliance conditions, in the same way Italy's alliance with Austria became unsustainable the moment it made England into an enemy. Anyone who does not comprehend or wish to understand this is incapable of thinking politically and is therefore at best capable of making policy in Germany. However, Germany is now seeing the results of the policies made by this sort of person, and Germany has to bear the consequences.

These are all points that had to reduce the value of the alliance with Austria to a minimum. It was certain that Germany, because of its alliance with Austria, would in addition to Russia, Romania, and Serbia presumably also make an enemy of Italy. Because, as already mentioned, there is no alliance that can be built upon ideal sympathy or ideal loyalty or ideal gratitude. Alliances are so much the stronger the more the individual parties are able to hope to thereby gain personal advantages. Trying to base an alliance on any other foundation is fanciful. I would never expect Italy to enter into an alliance relationship with Germany out of sympathy for Germany, out of love for Germany, and with the intention of being useful to Germany. Nor would I ever be able to enter into a contractual relationship out of love for another state, out of sympathy for it, or out of a desire to help it. Today when I advocate an alliance relationship between Italy and Germany, I do so only because I believe that it can provide both states with useful advantages. Both states will make profitable dealings.

But the benefits of the Triple Alliance lay exclusively on the Austrian side. Due to determining factors in the policies of the individual states, only Austria could ever be the beneficiary of this alliance. The essence of the Triple Alliance lacked every aggressive tendency. It was a defensive alliance, which, according to the provisions of the agreement, was at most only intended to secure the maintenance of the status quo. Because of the impossibility of sustaining their people, Germany and Italy were forced to adopt an offensive policy. Austria alone had to be pleased to at least maintain (which was really impossible by then) the corpse of the state. Because Austria's own defensive forces would never have been adequate for this task, the offensive forces of Germany and Italy were, through the Triple Alliance, strained in the service of maintaining the Austrian state. Germany remained in the harness and therefore collapsed. Italy jumped out and saved itself. The only person who could consider that reason for reproach would be someone who does not view politics as the duty to preserve the existence of a people, using all means and pursuing all opportunities.

Even if the old Germany, as a formal nation state, had set itself the foreign policy goal of only unifying the German nation, Germany would immediately have had to let go of the Triple Alliance or change its relationship with Austria. An immense number of enmities, which were in no way offset by Austria's commitment of forces, could thereby have been avoided.

But prewar Germany could no longer allow its foreign policy to be determined by purely formal national viewpoints if these did not lead to ethnically necessary goals.

Already in prewar times, the future of the German people was a question of solving the food supply problem. The German people could no longer find its daily bread in the available territory. The greatest diligence and efficiency, and all the scientific methods of land management, could at best alleviate this need somewhat but not definitively eliminate it any more. Even in exceptionally good harvest years it was no longer possible to completely cover the nation's food requirements. In the case of average or poor harvests, reliance on imports reached a very sizable percentage. In certain industries, serious difficulties were also encountered in the supply of raw materials, which could only be obtained from abroad.[154]

There could have been various ways to eliminate this hardship. From the standpoint of the nation state at that time, emigration and a reduction in the birth rate had to be categorically rejected—due less to the recognition of the biological consequences than the fear of numerical decimation. Thus, there were really only two possibilities if Germany was to secure the preservation of the nation for the long term without having to reduce the population itself. The nation could either attempt to alleviate the land shortage, in other words, conquering new territory, or transform the Reich into a huge export firm. That is to say, production of certain goods would be increased beyond the level of internal requirements in order to be able to export these goods in exchange for foodstuffs and raw materials.

The recognition of the necessity of expanding the German Lebensraum did exist at that time, if only partially. People believed the best way to deal with this was to usher Germany into the ranks of the great colonial powers. In reality, however, there was already a breakdown in the inner logic of this idea, due especially to the mode of execution. The point of a healthy territorial policy lies in the expansion of a people's Lebensraum by allocating to the excess population new areas for colonization; however, if this process is not to take on the character of emigration, the colony must maintain close political and national relations with the mother country. This no longer applied to the colonies that were still available at the end of the nineteenth century. The physical distance but also especially the climatic conditions prevented colonization like that previously carried out by the English in their American colonies, the Dutch in South Africa, and the English again in Australia. Added to that was the whole character of the internal arrangement of the German colonial policy. The settlement problem was left completely in the background, to be replaced by corporate interests that matched only to a limited degree the collective interests of the German people. Thus, from the beginning, the value of the German colonies lay more in the possibility of obtaining certain markets, which—as suppliers of various colonial products and also some raw materials—could make the German economy self-sufficient.

In time, this would no doubt have succeeded to a certain degree; however, this approach would not have solved Germany's overpopulation problem in the least—unless the decision was made to guarantee the German people's food supply through a fundamental increase in the nation's export industry. Then, of course, the German colonies could one day assist various industries to achieve greater competitiveness in international markets by supplying less-expensive raw materials. In this way, however, German colonial policy became fundamentally not a territorial policy but an accessory to Germany industrial policy. And in actuality, the direct numerical relief provided by colonial settlements was completely insignificant in terms of the overpopulation of Germany.

In addition, if one wished to shift to a true territorial policy, then the colonial policy pursued before the war was even more nonsensical, as it was unable to lead to a tangible reduction in the German overpopulation,[155] yet at the same time the execution of this policy, as far as can be judged, would one day require the same blood sacrifice that would have been required only in the worst case under a truly advantageous territorial policy. Because this type of German colonial policy could at best bring only a strengthening of German industry, it would inevitably one day become a contributing cause of brutal conflict with England. A German global economic policy could never have avoided Armageddon with England. That power which—from the same self-preservation standpoints as Germany—had already felt compelled to tread this path much earlier would then have had to protect its export industry, international trade, colonies, and merchant fleets with the sword. So as long as England could count on destroying the German competition through purely economic means, the peaceful economic battle for a place in the sun[156] could take place—because then we would never come out of the shade. But if Germany succeeded in pushing England back on this peaceful economic course, then it was obvious that this phantom peaceful economic world conquest would be replaced by the resistance of bayonets.

Without doubt, allowing the German people additional population growth by increasing industrial production and sales on the international market was at least a political idea. It was not an ethnic idea, but it fit the perceptions of the then dominant bourgeois-nationalist world. This path could certainly have been followed, but it gave German foreign policy a very tightly defined responsibility: German international trade policy could only end in war with England. German foreign policy would then have the task of arming itself, through far-sighted alliance measures, for conflict with a state that based on hundreds of years' experience would itself leave no stone unturned to effect a general mobilization of supportive states. If Germany wanted to defend its economic and industrial policies against England, then it first had to seek rear cover from Russia. Russia was the only state that could [*come*] into consideration as a valuable alliance partner at that time, as it was the only one without significant conflicts with Germany—at least for the moment. However, the purchase price of this Russian alliance, as things then stood, could only be the abandonment of the alliance with Austria. In that case the Dual Alliance with Austria was madness—yes, insanity. Only if Germany had complete rear cover from Russia could the nation shift to a naval policy that aimed deliberately at the day of reckoning. Only then could one commit the enormous resources necessary to upgrade a fleet that lagged five years behind[157]—not in every way, but in terms of construction, especially in speed and therefore [*sic*] displacement.

But the entanglement in the Austrian alliance was so great that a solution could not be found. Consequently, Russia, which began to realign itself after the Russo-Japanese War,[158] ultimately had to be pushed away. For that reason, however, the entire German economic and colonial policy became an extremely dangerous game. The fact was that Germany dreaded the final conflict with England and, accordingly, allowed its behavior to be determined for years by the principle of not provoking the enemy. This affected every German decision that would have been necessary to safeguard the German economic and colonial policy—until, on August 4, 1914, the English declaration of war concluded this period of disastrous German delusion.

Had Germany at that time been governed less by bourgeois-nationalist than by ethnic viewpoints, only the other path to resolving the German need would have come under consideration: an expansive territorial policy within Europe itself.

The German colonial policy that would inevitably bring us into conflict with England, and in which France could always be seen standing on the side of the enemy, was especially irrational for Germany because our European base was weaker than that of any other colonial power of international political significance. Because ultimately, of course, the destiny of the colonies would be decided in Europe. Therefore, German foreign policy was primarily focused on strengthening and securing Germany's military position in Europe. In this, we could expect only very little significant help from our colonies. In contrast, every expansion of our [in Europe] European territorial base would automatically have led to a strengthening of our situation. It is not all the same whether a people possesses a cohesive settlement area of 560,000 or, say, 1 million square kilometers. Aside from the difficulty of supplying food in the case of a war (which should remain as independent as possible from the impact of the enemy), the size of the territory itself already provides some military protection, in that the operations that oblige us to fight on our own soil are significantly easier to bear.

The size of a state territory already provides some protection against frivolous attacks.

Above all, however, only through a territorial policy in Europe could the population resettled there, be preserved for our people including their military utilization. An additional 500,000 square kilometers of land in Europe[159] can provide millions of German farmers with new homesteads, and can add to the strength of the German people millions of soldiers available for the decisive moment.

The only area in Europe that could be considered for such a territorial policy was Russia. The sparsely populated western areas bordering Germany[160] (which had already once welcomed German colonizers as bearers of culture) also came into consideration for the new European territorial policy of the German nation. But then the goal of German foreign policy would necessarily have to have been to free up the back facing England and instead to isolate Russia as much as possible. Then, with ruthless consistency, we would have to give up our economic and international trade policies and, if necessary, renounce our fleet entirely in order to again concentrate the collective strength of the nation, as once before, on the land army. But then, more than ever, we would have had to give up the alliance with Austria, as nothing stood more in the way of isolating Russia than the defense—guaranteed by Germany—of a state whose breakup was desired by a large number of European powers, but who would only have been able to achieve this in alliance with Russia. Because these states saw in Germany the strongest safeguard of Austria's preservation, they had to oppose even more the isolation of Russia, as the czarist empire appeared more than ever to be the only possible power capable of breaking Austria.

Clearly, all of these states certainly could not wish for a strengthening of Austria's only support at the expense of the strongest opponent of the Habsburg state.

In this case France would also always have taken the side of Germany's enemies, so the possibility of an anti-German coalition would always have been present if we did not decide to finally liquidate the alliance with Austria (at least by the turn of the century), abandon the Austrian state to its fate, and rescue the German portions of it for the Reich.

It happened differently. Germany wanted world peace. It thus avoided a territorial policy that could only have been fought out aggressively, and ultimately turned to a never-ending economic and trade policy. Germany expected to conquer the world by peaceful economic means and did not rely on the support of one power or another but clung ever more convulsively—the more general political isolation set in as a result—to the dying Habsburg state. Significant numbers within Germany welcomed this, in part out of true political incompetence, out of incorrectly understood notions of patriotism and legitimacy, and in [part] also out of the quietly nurtured hope of thereby being able one day to bring about the collapse of the hated Hohenzollern empire.

On August 2, 1914, with the bloody explosion of the Great War, the alliance policy of the prewar period sustained its actual defeat, in reality already complete. In order to help Austria, Germany was pressed into a war which then should have revolved more around its own existence. Its enemies were those who objected to its world trade as well as to its overall size in general, along with those hopeful of Austria's collapse. Its friends were the impossible state formation of Austria-Hungary on the one hand and the eternally ailing and weak Turkey on the other. Italy, however, took that step[161] which Germany should have taken and would have taken if instead of frail philosophers[162] and boastful jingoists the brilliance of a Bismarck had managed Germany's fate. The fact that offensive action was later finally taken against a former ally is in accordance with the prophetic foresight of Bismarck that between Italy and Austria only two conditions were possible: alliance or war.

[Chapter VIII]

[The Necessity of Military Power—The Borders of 1914 Not a Goal]

On November 11, 1918, in the forest of Compiègne, the armistice agreement was signed.[163] For this, fate had destined a man who hadbeen one of the chief culprits in the disintegration of our people. Matthias Erzberger,[164] representative of the Center Party—and, according to various claims, the illegitimate son of a maid and a Jewish employer[165]—was the German negotiator who then also signed his name to a document which, unless one assumes a deliberate intent to destroy Germany, appears incomprehensible in light of the four and a half years of heroism demonstrated by our people.

Matthias Erzberger was no bourgeois annexationist himself—one of those men who tried, particularly at the beginning of the war, to remedy in their own way the lack of an official war aim. Because even though in August 1914 the entire German people instinctively sensed that this was a battle for its very existence, as soon as the flames of initial enthusiasm died down there was no clarity

at all about either the threatening extinction nor the necessary continued existence. The dimensions of the notion of a defeat and its
consequences were gradually countered by propaganda that had
been given free rein within Germany, and the true war aims of the
Entente were cleverly and dishonestly distorted or totally denied.
Thanks to this propaganda, in the second and especially the third
years of the war the German people's fear of defeat was mitigated
to such a degree that they no longer believed in the scope of the
enemy's destructive intent. This was all the more terrible because
conversely nothing could be done to make the people recognize
the minimum that must be achieved in the interests of its future
preservation and as compensation for its outrageous sacrifices.[166]
The discussion of a possible war aim thus also took place only in
more or less irresponsible circles and also took on the expression
of the mindset and general political perceptions of their respective
representatives. The cunning Marxists, knowing full well the debili-
tating effects of the absence of a specific war aim, now refused to
tolerate one at all, and spoke only of the restoration of peace without annexations and reparations; however, at least some of the bourgeois politicians tried to respond to the casualties and the outrage
of the aggression with specific counterclaims.[167] All of these bourgeois proposals were strictly border corrections and had nothing at
all to do with notions of territorial policy. At most, these people
intended to satisfy the expectations of individual unemployed German princes through the creation of buffer states, and so even the
establishment of the Polish state appeared to the bourgeois world,
with a few exceptions, as a wise decision from a national policy perspective.[168] Several emphasized economic viewpoints according to
which the border should be configured (for example, the necessity
of winning the ore basin of Longwy and Briey), while others focused on strategic ideas (for example, the need to take control of
the Belgian fortifications on the Maas).

It should be obvious that this was no aim for a war of one state
against twenty-six,[169] in which this state would have to take upon

itself the most enormous casualties ever seen in history, while at home a whole people was literally handed over to starvation. It was an impossible rationale upon which to base the necessity of persevering in the war, and this helped to bring about its unfortunate conclusion.

When the homeland therefore collapsed, knowledge of war aims was all the more lacking, as their previous feeble representatives had in the meantime distanced themselves from a few of their previous demands. And that was actually understandable, because it would be truly unjustifiable and outrageous to want to wage a war of this unheard of magnitude in order to have the border run through Liege instead of through Herbesthal,[170] or in order to install a little German prince as potentate over some Russian province instead of a czarist commissar or governor. Because of the nature of the German war aims—to the extent that they were under consideration at all—they were later all disavowed. Because in truth, for the sake of these trifles one really could not leave a people even one hour longer in a war whose battlefields had gradually become a hell.

The only war aim that would have been worthy of these enormous casualties would have been to promise the German troops that so many hundreds of thousands of square kilometers of land would be allotted to the frontline soldiers as property or made available for colonization by Germans.[171] In that way, the war would also immediately have lost the character of an imperial undertaking and would instead have become a matter of concern to the German people. Because ultimately, the German soldiers did not really shed their blood so that the Poles could obtain a state or so that a German prince could be installed on a plush throne.

In 1918 we thus stood at the conclusion of a completely pointless and aimless waste of the most valuable German blood.[172]

Once again, our people offered up infinite heroism, courage in the face of sacrifice—yes, courage in the face of death—and willingness to accept responsibility, and [*sic*] nevertheless had to leave the battlefield [*sic*] defeated and weakened. Victorious in a thousand battles and engagements, yet still conquered by the losers in the end. The writing on the wall for the German domestic and foreign policy of the prewar period and the four and a half years of bloody conflict itself.

Now after the collapse the fearful question arises: whether our German people learned something from this catastrophe, whether those who thus far have deliberately betrayed our people will continue to determine its fate, [and] whether those [or] who thus far have failed so miserably will also dominate the future with their rhetoric, or whether at last our people will be educated to think differently about domestic and foreign policy and will change its actions accordingly.

Because unless a miracle is performed on our people, its path will be one of ultimate ruin.

What is the current situation of Germany, and what are the prospects for its future, and what type of future will it be?

The collapse that the German people suffered in 1918 was not due, as I will establish again here, to the demise of its military organization or the loss of its weapons, but rather to the internal decay that was revealed back then and is increasingly evident today. This internal decay lies just as much in the area of the deterioration of the people's racial value as in the loss of all those virtues that determine the greatness of a people, guarantee its continued existence, and promote its future.

The German people is gradually being threatened with the loss of its genetic quality, assertion of identity, and self-preservation drive. Instead, internationalism is triumphing and destroying the value of our people, democracy is spreading by smothering the individual identity, and a nasty pacifist sewage is ultimately poisoning the mindset of bold self-preservation. We see the effects of these human vices appearing everywhere in the life of our people. Not only in the area of political concerns—no, also in the economic area, and last but not least a downward sliding [*sic*] is noticeable in our cultural life. If this descent is not halted, our people will no longer be able to be counted among those nations with a promising future.

Eliminating these general aspects of decay is the great domestic policy task of the future. This is the mission of the National Socialist movement. From this work, a new body politic must come into being, which must also overcome the most serious disadvantage of the present, the division between the classes, for which the bourgeoisie and the Marxists are equally culpable.[173]

The goal of this domestic policy reformation work, however, must ultimately be the regaining of our people's strength to carry out its struggle for survival, and thus the strength to represent its vital interests to the outside world.

This will also give our foreign policy the task it must fulfill. Because while domestic policy must provide foreign policy with the instrument of the people's strength, foreign policy must also, through its adopted practices and measures, promote and support the development of this instrument.[174]

If the initial foreign policy task of the old bourgeois national state had been the further unification of the members of the German nation in Europe—in order to swing over to a higher, ethnically aware territorial policy—then the foreign policy task of the postwar period must initially be one of promoting the internal instrument of power. Because the foreign policy aims of the prewar period had at their disposal a state that was perhaps not terribly appealing ethnically, but one that at least had a wonderful army organization. Although the Germany of that time had long since lost the military emphasis of, say, the old Prussia, and thus was surpassed by other states, particularly in terms of the size of the army organization,[175] the inner quality of the old army was incomparably superior to all similar organizations. This best instrument of the art of war was available at that time to a bold foreign policy state leadership. Because of this instrument, as well as the generally high regard that it enjoyed,[176] the freedom of our people was not only a [matter] result of our actually tested strength, but rather that general credit that we [enjoyed] possessed due to this unique army instrument and also partly due to the rest of the exemplary clean state apparatus.

The German people today no longer possesses this most important instrument for the defense of a people's interests—or at least only on a completely inadequate scale and far removed from the foundation that determined its earlier strength.

The German people have been given a mercenary army.[177] This mercenary army in Germany is in danger of deteriorating into a police force armed with particularly sophisticated weapons.[178] The German mercenary army compares unfavorably with that of the English. The English mercenary army has always been the bearer of the notions of military defense and attack, as well as of the English military tradition. England, with its mercenary army and peculiar militia system, possessed an army organization that was adequate, even appropriate, considering its island location, for defending English vital interests.[179] [The type of this] The idea expressed in this structuring of the English defensive force was to spare the English people nationwide casualties—an idea which by no means arose from cowardice. On the contrary. England fought with mercenaries as long as the mercenaries sufficed for the defense of English interests. It called for volunteers as soon as the conflict required a greater commitment. It introduced universal conscription as soon as the need of the fatherland required it.[180] Because regardless of the appearance of the particular organization of the English defensive force, it was always deployed for ruthless fighting on behalf of England. And the formal army organization in England was always only an instrument to fight for English interests, mobilized by a will that did not shrink back from calling upon the blood of the entire nation when necessary.[181] And where England's interests were decisively at stake, it in any case knew how to protect a dominance which, from a purely technical standpoint, extends to the requirement of the "two-power standard."[182] When one compares the infinitely [careful] responsible concern represented by this with the carelessness with which Germany—national bourgeois

Germany—neglected its armaments buildup in the prewar period,[183] one must feel deep sadness even today. Anyone who knew, like England, that his future—yes, his continued existence—depended on the strength of his fleet, then bourgeois national Germany should have known that the continued existence and future of the German Reich depended on the strength of our land forces [*sic*]. Germany should have countered the two-power standard at sea with the two-power standard on land. And just as England, with iron resolve, saw a provocation of war in every violation of this standard, in the same way Germany, in Europe, should have prevented—by means of a military resolution, which we could have brought about and for which there was more than favorable opportunity—every attempt by France and Russia to outstrip its army. In this situation as well, the bourgeoisie misused Bismarck's words in the most absurd way. The statement by Bismarck that he did not intend to fight any preventive wars[184] was joyfully seized by all the feeble, weak, and also irresponsible armchair politicians as cover for the disastrous results that must arise from their policy of just letting everything happen. But in doing so, they completely forgot that allthree wars that Bismarck fought were wars that—at least in the judgment of these anti-preventive-war peace philosophers—could have been avoided. Imagine, for example, what affronts by Napoleon III in 1870 would have to have been inflicted on the German republic of today before it would have decided to ask Herr Benedetti[185] to moderate his tone a bit. Neither Napoleon nor the entire French people could ever have succeeded in provoking today's Germany to a Sedan. Or do people believe that the war of 1866 could not have been prevented if Bismarck had not desired the decision? Now one could argue that these were wars to achieve clearly set goals, and not ones based only on fear of attack by the enemy. But in reality that is splitting hairs. Because Bismarck was convinced that war with Austria was unavoidable, he prepared for it and carried i out in a way that was favorable for Prussia.[186] The French army reform introduced by Marshal Niel[187] clearly revealed the intention of French policy and French chauvinism to use the powerful weapon to attack Germany. Actually, it would without doubt have been possible for Bismarck to have brought the conflict to some sort of peaceful settlement in 1870.[188] But it was more expedient to fight this war at a time when the French army organization had not yet reached full effectiveness. In addition, all of these interpretations of Bismarck's sayings suffer from the fact hat they confuse Bismarck the diplomat with a republican parliamentarian. The way Bismarck himself judged such statements is best shown by his reply, before the outbreak of the Prussian-Austrian war, to a questioner who wanted to know if Bismarck really ntended to attack Austria. Bismarck, with an impenetrable mien, responded, "No, I do not intend to attack Austria, but I would alo not intend to tell you that if I did happen to wish to attack it."[189]

In addition, the most difficult war that Prussia ever had to fight was a preventive wa. When Frederick the Great finally found outthe intention of his old adversary from a petty-minded person, he did not—based on a fundamental rejection of preventive war—wait until the others attacked, yet [*sic*] [strode] shifted immediately to attack himself.[190]

Every violation of the two-power standard while[191] should, for Germany, have been occasion for a preventive war. Because [would have] what would have been easier to justify before history: a preventive war that—in 1904, when Russia seemed tied down in East Asia[192]—would have thrown France down, or the Great War that resulted from the failure to do this, costing many times the blood and thrusting our people into the deepest defeat?

England never had such qualms. Its two-power standard at sea seemed the prerequisite to maintaining English independence. As long as it had the strength, it allowed no changes to this situation. After the Great War this two-power standard was abandoned, but only under the force of circumstances that were stronger than any opposing English aims. With the American union, a new power factor has emerged on a scale that threatens to nullify all the previous state power relationships and hierarchies.

But in any case, the English fleet has until now always been the most striking proof of the idea that regardless of the structure of the land army, the will to sustain England was the decisive determining factor [*sic*]. For that reason, however, the English mercenary army never took on the negative attributes of other mercenary troops. It was a combat and conflict crowd that had wonderful individual training with outstanding equipment and a sportingly felt notion of service. What gave this small army organization particular meaning was the direct contact with the visible expressions of life of the British world empire. This mercenary army had fought for England's greatness in almost every part of the world, and had thereby also come to know England's greatness. The men who soon represented England's interests at times in South Africa, at times in Egypt, and at times in India as bearers of England's armed forces thus also received indelible impressions of the enormous magnitude of the British empire.

This opportunity is completely lacking for today's German mercenary troops. Yes, the more one feels obligated to make concessions of this spirit in the small army itself, under the influence of pacifist democratic—in reality treasonous—parliamentary majorities, the army becomes less and less an instrument of war and becomes instead a police force for maintaining peace and order, i.e., peaceful submission.[193] One cannot form an army with great intrinsic worth if the purpose of its existence is not preparation for war. There are no armies to maintain the peace—only to wage victorious warfare. The more people in Germany try to raise the Reichswehr out of the tradition of the old army, the more it will be without tradition itself. Because the value of a unit's traditions do not lie in successfully overcoming a few internal strike revolts or in preventing the looting of food supplies; rather, it lies in the glory achieved through successful battles. To the extent that it ceases to represent the national idea, however, the Reichswehr distances itself further each year from the tradition of this glory.[194] The more it kills the consciously national (i.e., nationalistic) spirit within its own ranks and excludes the representatives of this spirit[195] in order to give positions to democrats and completely ordinary careerists, the more alien it will become to the people. Because those clever gentlemen should not imagine that they can find a connection with the people by making concessions to the pacifist democratic segment of our population. This segment of the population inwardly hates every military organization in principle, as long as it is a military and not a security company for international-pacifistic stock-market interests. The only segment to which an army in the militarily valuable sense can have a close inner connection is that nationally aware core of our people that not only thinks in soldierly terms out of tradition but also is the only group ready—out of national love—to put on the gray uniform in the defense of honor and freedom. But it is necessary that an army organization maintain the close connection to those who can replenish it in the hour of need, and not to those who will betray it at every opportunity. That is why the current leaders of our so-called Reichswehr can act as democratic as they wish, but they will still never be able to achieve a close connection with the German people, because the German people that is inclined in that direction is not to be found in the camp of the democrats. The former head of the German Reichswehr, General von Seeckt,[196] not only did not resist the removal of experienced, consciously nationally minded officers and leaders, but even [himself] advocated it himself; thus, they finally created that instrument themselves which then let him go relatively lightheartedly.

Since the resignation of General von Seeckt,[197] however, the democratic pacifist influence has been working tirelessly to turn the German Reichswehr into what the regents of today's state see as the most beautiful ideal: a republican democratic parliamentary guard.

With such an instrument, however, one obviously cannot conduct foreign policy.

Therefore, the next task of German domestic policy would be to give the German people again a functional military organization of its national strength But because the structure of today's

Reichswehr will never be adequate for this purpose—and, instead, is determined by foreign policy factors—it is the task of German foreign policy to bring about all the opportunities that could allow a German people's army to be organized again. Because it must be the unshakable goal of all the political leadership in Germany to one day replace the mercenary army with a true German people's army again.

Because as badly as the general qualities of the Reichswehr must develop in the future, the current purely technical-military qualities are outstanding. This is without doubt the achievement of General von Seeckt and the Reichswehr officer corps in general. Therefore, the German Reichswehr really could serve as the framework for the future German people's army. As the task of the Reichswehr itself must be: to train the mass of [future] officers and sergeants for the future people's army, with the instructional emphasis on the national responsibility for war.

No true nationally minded German can argue with the fact that this goal must be kept consistently in view. Nor with the fact that it will only be possible to attain this goal if the nation's foreign policy leadership secures the overall necessary preconditions.[198]

Thus, the first task of German foreign policy is the creation of conditions that will enable the reestablishment of a German army. Because only then will the vital needs of our people be able to find their practical representation.

Fundamentally, however, one must further note that the political actions that are to ensure the reestablishment of a German army must take place in the context of necessary future developments for Germany.

It does not need to be emphasized that a change in the present army organization, quite apart from the current internal political situation, cannot take place for foreign policy reasons either as long as only German interests and German viewpoints argue for such a change.

The nature of the Great War and the intention of Germany's primary enemy was to settle this biggest combat operation on earth in such a way as to ensure that as many states as possible had an interest in the perpetuation of the settlement. This was achieved through a system of land distribution, so that even states with otherwise very divergent wishes and goals were held together in cohesive enmity out of the fear of suffering losses from a revitalized Germany. Because when it is still possible ten years after the end of the Great War,[199] against all previous historical experience, to maintain a type of coalition of victorious states, then the reason lies only in the fact—truly glorious for Germany—of the memory of that conflict in which our fatherland stood up to a total of twenty-six states.

This will remain as long as the fear of suffering losses at the hand of a powerful resurgent German Reich is greater than the difficulties these states experience among themselves. And it is also obvious that there is for a long time no desire to allow the German people armaments that could be seen as a threat by these "victor states." However, out of the recognition that (1) German vital interests cannot be truly represented in the future by an inadequate German Reichswehr, but only by a German people's army, (2) the formation of a German people's army will be impossible as long as the current foreign policy strangulation of Germany continues, but (3) a change in the foreign policy resistance to the organization of a people's army will only appear possible when such a new formation is not generally seen as a threat, leads to the following reality for the currently possible German foreign policy:

The Germany of today must under no circumstances see its foreign policy task in a formal border policy. As soon as restoration of the 1914 borders is established as the foreign policy objective, Germany will confront a cohesive phalanx of its former enemies.[200] But then every possibility of replacing the form of our army (determined by the peace treaty) with another that better furthers our interests is [*impossible*]. But thus the foreign policy rallying cry, "restoration of the borders," becomes nothing more than empty words, because without the necessary strength it can never be realized.

It is typical that the so-called German bourgeoisie—here again with the patriotic organizations in the lead, in fact—has brought [*itself*] to accept this stupidest of all foreign policy objectives. They know that Germany is powerless. They also know that quite apart from our internal decay, means of exercising military power would be necessary to restore our borders; they also know that because of the peace treaty we do not possess these means and that due to our opponents' cohesive front we cannot obtain them either; [They also know that the borders of 1914] however, they still use a foreign policy rallying cry that—precisely because of its most basic essence—takes from us forever the possibility of obtaining those means of power that would be necessary to carry it out.

So something like this is called bourgeois statecraft, and the fruits we see before us show the incomparable spirit that governs it.

Seven years, from 1806 to 1813, were enough for Prussia to resurrect itself back then.[201] [And in ten years] In the same amount of time, bourgeois statecraft, in collaboration with Marxism, led Germany to Locarno.[202] Which is a great success in the eyes of the bourgeois Bismarck of today, Herr Stresemann, because it represents what is possible for this Herr Stresemann to achieve. And politics is an art of the possible. If Bismarck had ever suspected that he would be damned by fate to endorse with this dictum the statesmanlike qualities of Herr Stresemann, he would either not have made this statement or, in a very brief comment, he would have barred Herr Stresemann from the right to appeal to it.[203]

The rallying cry of restoring the German borders as a foreign policy objective of the future is doubly dumb and dangerous because in reality it does not encompass any goal that is at all beneficial or desirable.

The German borders of 1914 were borders that represented something just as unfinished as peoples' borders always are. The division of territory on the earth is always the momentary result of a struggle and an evolution that is in no way finished, but that naturally continues to progress.[204] It is dumb to simply take the border from any given year in the history of a people and establish it as a political goal. Instead of establishing the border of 1914, one could just as well take the one from 1648 or 1312, and so on, and so on. Especially because the 1914 border was not at all satisfactory from a national, military, or territorial policy perspective. It was just the momentary situation at that point in our people's struggle for survival, which has been rolling on [*sic*] for millennia and which would not have had its ending in 1914 even if the Great War had not come.

If the German people actually did achieve the restoration of the 1914 borders, the sacrifices of the Great War would nevertheless have been for nothing. But the future of our people would not gain anything either through such a restoration. This purely formal border policy of our national bourgeoisie is just as unsatisfactory in its potential end result as it is intolerably dangerous. It also may not apply to itself the [demand] dictum about the art of the possible, because that is simply a theoretical phrase that seems suitable for destroying every practical possibility.

In fact, such a foreign policy objective cannot stand up to a genuinely critical scrutiny either. Thus, people attempt to base it on motives that are not so much logical reasons as reasons of "national honor."

National honor requires that we restore the borders of 1914. This is the tenor of the statements made during the beer evenings that the representatives of national honor put on everywhere.

First, national honor has nothing to do with an obligation to conduct a dumb and impossible foreign policy. Because the result of a bad foreign policy can be the loss of a people's freedom, the consequence of which is then enslavement, which certainly cannot be interpreted as a condition of national honor. Of course one can preserve a certain degree of national dignity and honor even under oppression, but then this is not a question of clamor or national rhetoric and so on; rather, in contrast, it is the expression—found in a people's integrity—with which it bears its fate.

People should not speak of national honor, particularly in today's Germany, and people should not attempt to give the impression that national honor can [again] be preserved through any sort of outwardly directed rhetorical barking. No, that cannot be done—because it no longer exists at all. And it has by no means disappeared because we lost the war or because the French occupied Alsace-Lorraine,[205] the Poles stole Upper Silesia,[206] or the Italians took South Tyrol.[207] No, our national honor is gone because the German people, in the most difficult time of its struggle for survival, demonstrated a lack of conviction, shameless servility, and cringing, groveling tail-wagging that can only be called shameless. Because we gave in pathetically without being forced to do so, because the leadership of this people, against historical truth and its own knowledge, assumed the war guilt[208]—yes, burdened our entire people with it—because there was no oppression by the enemy that would not have found within our nation thousands of creatures willing to be compliant helpers. Because instead people shamelessly reviled the time of the greatest deeds of our people, spit on the most glorious flag of all time, yes, tore off the glorious cockades from dirty homebound soldiers before whom the world had trembled, threw feces at the flag, tore off medals and decorations, and debased in a thousand ways the memory of Germany's greatest era. No enemy had reviled the German army like the representatives of the November knavery defiled it. No enemy had disputed the greatness of the German army leadership like the villainous representatives of the new state idea slandered them. And what was really more dishonorable for our people, the occupation of German areas by enemies, or the cowardice with which our bourgeoisie handed over the German Reich to an organization of panderers, pickpockets, deserters, profiteers, and newspaper scribblers? As long as they bow to the authority of dishonor, those gentlemen should not now babble on about German honor. One has no right to want to conduct foreign policy in the name of national honor when the domestic policy is the most antinationalist shamelessness ever inflicted on a major people.

Anyone who today wants to act in the name of German honor must first announce the most relentless fight against the intolerable defilers of German honor. But those are not our former opponents; rather, they are the representatives of the November crime. That collection [of] Marxist, democratic-pacifist, and Centrist traitors that pushed our people into its current state of powerlessness.

Upbraiding one-time enemies in the name of national honor while acknowledging as gentlemen the dishonorable allies of these enemies in our own midst—that fits with the national dignity of this current so-called national bourgeoisie.

I admit most frankly that I could reconcile myself with every one of those old enemies, but that my hate for the traitors in our own ranks is unforgiving and will remain.

What the enemies did to us is serious and humiliating for us, but the sins committed by the men of the November crime—that is the most dishonorable, dastardly crime of all time. By attempting to bring about circumstances that will someday force these creatures to accountability, I am helping to restore German honor.

However, I must reject the idea that in the establishment of German foreign policy, other factors could override the responsibility to secure freedom and future life for our people.

But the whole pointlessness of the patriotic-bourgeois national border policy arises from the following consideration:

The German nation, if one bases it on commitment to the German mother tongue, numbers…[209] million persons.

Of that number, …million reside in the motherland.

In the[210]

Chapter IX

[Neither Border Policies Nor Economic Policies Nor Pan-Europe]

C onsequently, of all the Germans in the world, only [...]²¹¹ mil lion, that is…percent of the total number of our people, re-side within the current Reich area. Of the Germans not united with the motherland, the [...]²¹² must, as a result of the circumstances, be considered fellow countrymen doomed to be gradually lost, that is to say, a total of approximately…²¹³ million Germans find themselves in a situation that in all probability will one day mean their de-Germanization. But under no circumstances will they be able to participate any longer in the motherland's struggle with destiny in any significant way, nor in the cultural development of their people. Whatever the Germans in North America achieve specifically, it will not be credited to the German people, but is forfeited to the body of culture of the American union. Here the Germans really are only the cultural fertilizer for other peoples everywhere. Yes, in reality the greatness of these peoples, to a high degree, is not infrequently [*attributable*] to achievements contributed by Germans. As soon as one sees the extent of this confirmed loss of people, the limited significance of the border policy sponsored by the bourgeois world becomes immediately apparent.

Even if German foreign policy were to reestablish the borders of 1914, the percentage of Germans living within the Reich—that is, members of our nation—would still only rise from …[214] to…percent. And in doing so, the possibility of significantly increasing this percentage could hardly be considered again.

If the German people in foreign countries nevertheless want to remain loyal to the nation, then this can initially involve only a linguistic and cultural loyalty, which will grow into a deliberately demonstrated sense of community the more the motherland of the German nation honors the German name through the dignity of its representation of our people.

The more that Germany itself, as a world empire, transmits the impression of the greatness of the German people, the more the Germans who have ultimately been lost to the state will be stimulated to boast at least mentally about their affiliation with this people. However, the more pathetically the motherland itself safeguards the interests of the German nation and accordingly also makes a bad impression externally,[215] the weaker the inner inducement to belong to such a people.

But because the German people does not consist of Jews, the [*Germans?*] in Anglo-Saxon countries in particular will, unfortunately, nevertheless become progressively more anglicized. They will presumably also become spiritually and intellectually lost to our people in the same way that their practical work achievements are already lost to our people.

But with regard to the fate of those Germans who were forcibly cut off from the German body politic through the Great War and the peace treaties, it must be said that their fate and their future is a question of politically regaining the power of the motherland.

Lost territories are not regained through protest campaigns but by a victorious sword. And so anyone who today wants to liberate some area in the name of national honor must also be ready to take responsibility for this liberation with iron and blood; otherwise, a babbler like that can hold his tongue. For this reason, then, the duty also arises to weigh up, first, whether one has the strength to carry through such a fight, and second, whether the casualties can and will lead to the desired success, and third, whether the achieved success will be commensurate with the casualties.

I protest most solemnly against the idea that there could be a duty to national honor that forces one to allow two million men to bleed to death on the battlefield in order to gain, at best, a quarter million men, women, and children altogether.[216] That is not national honor appearing here, but unscrupulousness or insanity. But it is not national honor for a people to be ruled by insane people.

Certainly an important people will also protect its last citizen with the commitment of the whole community. But it is a mistake to attribute this to a feeling, to honor, rather than, first of all, the understanding of intelligence and human experience. As soon as a people would allow an injustice to be inflicted on individual citizens, it would gradually weaken its own position more and more, because such toleration would serve just as much to provide inner strength to an enemy disposed to attack as it would to erode the citizens' trust in the power of their own state. We know all too well from history the results of continual compliance in little things, to not be able to judge the necessary consequences in big things. Thus, a careful state leadership will all the more readily safeguard the interests of its citizens even in the smallest things, since the risk of its own involvement decreases to the degree that that of the opponent increases. When an injustice is committed today against an individual English citizen in some state, and England takes on the protection of its citizen, the danger of becoming entangled in a war because of this individual Englishman is no greater for England than it is for the other state that committed the wrong. Thus, the decisive action of a respected polity in defense of even one individual person is in no way an unbearable risk, because the other state will have just as little interest in letting a war break out because of the trifle that one individual person may have suffered. From this awareness and the thousand-year application of this principle, namely, that a powerful state protects every one of its individual citizens and defends them with all its strength, a general notion of the concept of honor has been formed.

Furthermore, facilitated by the nature of the European hegemony, a certain practice has emerged over time of demonstrating this concept of honor with [less] more or less cheap examples, in order to confer on the individual European states increased esteem, or at least continuity. As soon as a Frenchman or Englishman in certain weak and militarily less powerful countries was wronged—or, often, only alleged or pretended to have been wronged—[one] began to take on the defense of these subjects with force of arms. That is to say, a few warships staged a military demonstration, which in the worst case was target practice with live ammunition, or some expeditionary corps was landed in order to chasten the power that was to be punished. Not infrequently, the wish (to obtain the provocation for an intervention) was the father of the thought.

It would probably never occur to the English even to exchange a diplomatic communication with North America over a trifle that they took bloody revenge on Liberia for.

So although in a strong state one will take on—for reasons of pure expediency—the protection of individual citizens by all possible means, one cannot expect a completely defenseless, powerless Reich, to adopt—for reasons of national honor—foreign policy measures that must necessarily lead to the destruction of the last prospects for the future. Because if the German people bases its current border policy, advocated in so-called nationalist circles, on the necessity of representing German honor, then the result will not be the restoration of German honor but the perpetuation of German dishonor. It is in fact not at all dishonorable to have lost territory, but it is dishonorable to pursue a policy that must inevitably lead to the complete enslavement of one's own people. And all of this just to give free rein to evil rhetoric and to be able to avoid action. Because it is all just rhetoric. If one really wanted to aim for a policy of national honor, then one would at least have to entrust this policy to people who could be esteemed in line with general conceptions of honor. But as long as the German Reich's domestic and foreign policy is managed by powers who declare in the Reichstag with cynical grins that for them there is no fatherland called Germany, the next task of these national bourgeois and patriotic rhetoric heroes is to create, through their domestic policy, the most basic legitimacy for the idea of national honor in Germany. But why do they not do this? Why do they instead, at the expense of this so-called national honor, join coalitions with declared traitors? Because otherwise a difficult struggle would be required—a struggle in whose conclusion they have little confidence, and, yes, which could possibly even lead to the destruction of their existence. This own private existence is more sacred to them than the defense of the national honor inside the country. The future existence of the entire nation, however, they willingly jeopardize for a few phrases.

The national border policy becomes more absurd than ever when one looks away from the hardships and also the tasks of the present to the necessities of an organizing principle for our people in the future.

The border policy of our bourgeois patriotic circle is thus particularly absurd because it requires the greatest casualties but offers the least prospect of future success for our people.

The German people is today even less in a position than in the years of peace[217] to feed itself from its own land and territory. All attempts to bring about an increase in German food production, whether through increases in actual crop yields or through the cultivation of the last wastelands, are not able to feed our people from the resources of our own land and territory. And even the population living in Germany today would no longer be satisfied from the output of our land. Each further increase in output did not support an increase in our population, however, but was completely used up by the increasing general requirements of individuals.[218] Here a standard of living was created as an example, primarily through the knowledge of circumstances and life in the American union.[219] Just as the living requirements in the countryside increase with the gradual awareness and influence of city life, in the same way the living requirements of entire peoples also increase under the influence of life in better-off and richer nations. Not infrequently, a people will view as inadequate a standard of living that thirty years earlier would have seemed the maximum, simply because in the meantime knowledge was gained of another people's standard of living. Just as humans in general, even at the lowest levels, today take facilities for granted that eighty years ago were still unheard of luxury for the highest strata. But the more that distance is bridged by technology and especially travel and the peoples move closer together, and the more intensive their reciprocal relations thus become, the more living conditions will also rub off on each other and attempt to mutually conform to each other. It is not true that through an appeal to perceptions or ideals, a people of a certain cultural competence and also actual cultural significance can be held long term below an otherwise universal standard of living. The broad masses, in particular, will rarely be understanding of that. They feel the hardship and rail against those they believe to be responsible, something that at least in democratic states is dangerous, since they thus represent a reservoir for all subversive attempts [*sic*], or they attempt to bring about an improvement through their own measures, corresponding to the extent of their own knowledge and originating from their own insight. The war against the child begins. People want to live life the way others do and cannot do so. What is more natural than blaming the abundance of children for this, and not only taking no more pleasure in them but attempting to reduce their number—as a burdensome evil—as much as possible?

Therefore it is wrong to believe that the German people can, in the future, obtain the possibility of a further population increase by increasing the productivity of the land. What happens is, in the best case, a satisfaction of the increased standard of living require-ments. But because the increase in these living requirements is de-pendent upon the living standards of other peoples who, however, have a much more favorable ratio of population to land area, these peoples will also in the future always lead the way in the standard of their lives. Consequently, this drive will never disappear, and one day either a distance will develop between the standards of living of these peoples and those poorly provided with land and territory, or the latter will be forced, or at least believe themselves to be forced, to reduce their numbers even further.

The prospects for the German people are bleak. Neither the current Lebensraum nor that achieved through a restoration of the borders of 1914 permits us to lead a life comparable to that of the American people. If we wanted this, either our people's territory would have to be very significantly expanded or the German economy would again have to follow paths that are already familiar to us from the prewar period. In both cases, power is then neces-sary—first in the sense of the restoration of the inner strength of our people, but then in a military version of this strength as well.

Today's national Germany, which sees the fulfillment of the national duty in its limited border policy, cannot deceive itself into thinking that that will solve the nation's food-supply problem in any way. Because even the greatest success of this policy of restoring the 1914 borders would only bring back the economic conditions of 1914. In other words, the problem of feeding our people—com-pletely unresolved then as now—would inevitably drive us back onto the path of the global economy and international exports. In real-ity, the German bourgeoisie, along with the so-called national or-ganizations, thinks only in terms of economic policy. Production, export, and import—those are the catchwords they bandy about and from which the future salvation of the nation is promised. They hope, through an increase in production, to raise the export capa-bilities and thus be able to meet the import needs. They completely forget, however, that this whole problem for Germany, as already emphasized, is not at all a problem of increasing production but a question of sales opportunities. The export difficulties will not be remedied at all through a decrease in German production costs, as our bourgeois geniuses suppose. Because to the degree that this is only possible to a certain extent, due to our limited internal market, increasing the competitiveness of German export goods—through a decrease in production costs, perhaps brought about by a dismantling of our social legislation and the duties and burdens resulting from it—will only bring us to where we landed on August 4, 1914.[220] It really reflects the incredible bourgeois-national naiveté to think that England would or even could tolerate the threat of German competition. And these are the same people who know very well—and also emphasize constantly—that Germany did not want war in 1914 but was literally pushed into it.[221] And that it was England that, out of pure competitive envy, gathered the other enmities in Europe and let them loose against Germany. Today, however, these inveterate economic visionaries imagine that after England jeopardized the very existence of its world empire in a monstrous four-and-a-half-year world war, and remained the victor, it would now view German competition in a different light than back then. As if this whole question were just a sporting matter for England. No. For decades before the war, England attempted to break the threatening German economic competition, the growing German maritime trade, and so on, with economic countermeasures. When England finally had to accept that this would not succeed—and, on the contrary, Germany demonstrated through the buildup of its naval fleet that it was truly determined to carry out its economic war to the point of peacefully conquering the world—England called upon force as a last resort. And now, after England remained the victor, people believe the game can be played over again from the beginning, even though Germany on top of everything is not at all in a position today to throw any sort of significant power factor into the balance, thanks to its domestic and foreign policy.

The attempt to restore and maintain the sustenance of our people by increasing our production and by making it less expensive will ultimately fail because a lack of military power will prevent us from taking this fight to its final conclusion. It will end with a collapse of the German food supply and thus of all of these hopes. Quite apart from the fact that in addition to all the European states that are struggling for the world market as export nations, the American union is now also the stiffest competitor in many areas. The size and wealth of its internal market permits production levels and thus production facilities that decrease the cost of the product to such a degree that, despite the enormous wages, underselling no longer seems at all possible. The development of the automotive industry can serve as a cautionary example here. It is not only that we Germans, for example, despite our ludicrous wages, are not in a position to export successfully against the American competition even to a small degree; [*at the same time?*] we must watch how American vehicles are proliferating even in our own country.[222] This is only possible because the size of the internal American market and its wealth of buying power and also, again, raw materials guarantee the American automobile industry internal sales figures that alone permit production methods that would simply be impossible in Europe due to the lack of internal sales opportunities.[223] The result of that is the enormous export capacity of the American automobile industry. At issue is the general motorization of the world—a matter of immeasurable future significance. Because the replacement of human and animal power with the engine is just at the beginning of its development; the end cannot yet be assessed at all today. For the American union, in any case, today's automobile industry leads all other industries.

Thus, our[224] continent will increasingly appear as an aggressive economic factor in other areas as well, thereby helping to intensify the market competition. Taking all factors into consideration, particularly in view of the inadequacy of our own raw materials and the resulting worrying dependence on other countries, the future of Germany must appear very bleak and sad.

But even if Germany were to master all the economic difficulties, then it would still only be where it was on August [4], 1914. The final determination of the outcome of the contest for the world market will be made by force and not by economics activity itself.

It has been our curse, however, that already in peacetime a large share of the national bourgeoisie was steeped in the opinion that economic policy would enable us to renounce force. And even today the chief advocates of this idea are to be found in those more or less pacifistic circles that, as opponents and enemies of all heroic national virtues, wish to see the economy as a state-maintaining—yes, even state-forming—force. But to the extent that a people subscribes to the belief that it can preserve its life through economic activity alone, it is precisely its economy that is handed over to ruin. Because ultimately the economy is a strictly secondary concern in the life of a people, tied to the primary existence of a powerful state. The sword must stand before the plow, and an army before the economy.

If people believe they can renounce this in Germany, then the sustenance of our people must fail as a result.

But as soon as a people first satisfies its life with the idea of being able to find its daily sustenance through economic activity alone, it will be less likely in the event of a failure of this attempt to think of a solution involving force; rather, on the contrary, it will be all the more likely to seek to pursue the easiest path—one that will eliminate the economic failure without having to risk blood. In reality, Germany is already in this situation today. Emigration and a reduced birth rate are the medicines [*sic*] extolled by the representatives of the pacifist economic policy and the Marxist view of the state as the medicines [*sic*] of our body politic.

The consequence of following these suggestions, however, would have a disastrous impact, particularly for Germany. From a racial standpoint, Germany is composed of such unequal base elements that continual emigration will inevitably extract the more robust, bold, and resolute individuals from our community. Today it is these people above all who will be the carriers of the Nordic blood, like the Vikings of old. This gradual removal of the Nordic element within our people leads to a lowering of our overall racial quality and thus to a weakening of our technical, cultural, and also political productive forces. The consequences of this weakening will be particularly grave for the future because now a state is appearing as an active participant in world history which for centuries, as a true European colony, obtained through emigration Europe's best Nordic forces, which has now, facilitated by the commonality of the original blood, formed these forces into a new national community of the highest racial quality. It is not by chance that the American union is the state in which by far the greatest number of bold, sometimes unbelievably so, inventions are currently taking place. Compared to old Europe, which has lost an infinite amount of its best blood through war and emigration, the American nation appears as a young, racially select people.[225] Just as the achievements of a thousand degenerate Levanters in Europe—say, on Crete— cannot equate with the achievements of a thousand racially much superior Germans or Englishmen, the achievements of a thousand racially questionable Europeans cannot equate with the capabilities of a thousand racially first-rate Americans. Only a deliberately ethnic racial policy could save the European nations from losing the power of the initiative to America as a result of the lower quality of the European peoples in comparison to the Americans. But when instead the German people allows—in addition to a Jewish-instigated systematic bastardization with lower-quality human material, and a resulting decline in the racial level itself—the best bloodlines to be removed through the ongoing emigration of hundreds of thousands of individual specimens, it will gradually deteriorate into a low-quality and therefore incapable and worthless people. The danger is particularly great ever since—with complete indifference on our part—the American union itself, motivated by the theories of its own racial researchers, established specific criteria for immigration.[226] By making an immigrant's ability to set foot on American soil dependent on specific racial requirements on the one hand as well as a certain level of physical health of the individual himself, the bleeding of Europe of its best people has become regulated in a manner that is almost bound by law. Something that our whole so-called national bourgeois world and all of our economic policymakers either do not see at all or at least do not want to hear because it is awkward for them and because it is much cheaper to slide away from these things with a bit of general nationalist rhetoric.

To this naturally necessary lowering of the general quality of our people through the emigration forced by our economic policies is then added, as a second detriment, the reduction in the birth rate. I have already described the consequences of the battle against the child. They include a reduction in the number of individual entities brought to life, so that a further selection can no longer take place. People then try instead to preserve, under all circumstances, the life of everything that has ever been born. But because capability, energy, and so on are not necessarily tied to being firstborn, but instead only become visible in individuals during the course of the struggle for survival, one thus eliminates the possibility of a sieving and selection according to such traits. The peoples become poor in talents and energies. Again, this is particularly dire in the case of nations in which the lack of homogeneity among the racial base elements reaches right into the families. Because now, according to Mendel's laws of differentiation,[227] a division of the children emerges in every family, with some reflecting the one racial side and some the other. But if these racial qualities are of different value to a people, then even the value of the children of one family will thus already be differentiated based on racial factors. It is in the best interest of a people that—because the firstborn is in no way required to reflect the more racially valuable side of the two parents— later life at least select, through the struggle for survival, the racially more valuable out of the total number of children, is preserved for the nation, and in turn gives the nation possession of the achievements of these racially superior individual beings. But if a person himself prevents the siring of a large number of children and limit themselves to first- and at most second-born, then if these do not have the racially more valuable characteristics, he will strive all the more to make the nation preserve these racially inferior elements nonetheless. He artificially impedes the selection process, hinders it, and thus helps impoverish a people of strong characters. He destroys the highest values of a people.

The German people, which itself does not have the average quality of, for example, the English, will rely especially heavily on the quality of individual persons. The extraordinary extremes that we can observe everywhere in the life of our people are only the after effects of our genetic fragmentation into higher- and lower-quality individual racial elements. The Englishman will, overall, have a better middle average. He may never reach the dangerous depths of our people, but neither will he reach the illustrious heights. His life will thus move along a more intermediate line and reflect a greater consistency. The German life, in contrast, is constantly fluctuating and turbulent in everything, and it obtains its significance only through the extraordinary highest achievements through which we again offset the questionable aspects of our society. But as soon as an artificial system removes the persons responsible for these highest achievements, the achievements themselves cease to exist. Our people then moves in the direction of a lasting depletion of personal qualities and thus to a decline in its overall cultural and intellectual significance.

When this situation has continued for a few hundred years, at least our German people will be so weakened in its overall importance that it will no longer be able to make any sort of claim to be identified as a world-class people: in any case, it will no longer be in a position to keep pace with the achievements of the considerably younger and healthier American people. We will then, due to a great number of reasons, experience that which more than a few old civilized peoples have demonstrated in their historical development. Because of its vices and thoughtlessness, the carrier of Nordic blood—as the most racially valuable element of the culture bearers and state founders—was gradually eliminated, leaving behind a human jumble of such slight inner significance that the power of taking the initiative was wrested from their hands and given to younger and sounder peoples.

The entire southeast of Europe, but especially the even older cultures of Asia Minor and Persia, as well as the Mesopotamian lowlands, offer object lessons for the progression of this process.

Just as history was gradually shaped here by the racially superior peoples of the Occident, the danger arises that the significance of racially inferior Europe will gradually lead to a new determination of the fate of the world by the people of the North American continent.

In any case, a few already recognize that this danger is threatening all of Europe. But the fewest want to know what this means for Germany. If in the future our people continues living with the same political thoughtlessness as in the past, it will ultimately have to renounce the claim to international significance. It will become more and more stunted racially, until it finally deteriorates into degenerate, brutish gluttons who will not even remember the past greatness. In the context of the future international state hierarchy, it will be at most what Switzerland and Holland were in the previous Europe.

That will be the end of the life of a people whose history has been world history for two thousand years.

This fate will not be changed anymore by dumb, national-bourgeois rhetoric whose practical absurdity and worthlessness should already have been demonstrated by the results of the developments thus far. Only a new reformation movement, which counters racial thoughtlessness with deliberate recognition and draws all conclusions from this recognition, can still tear our people back from this abyss.

It will be the duty of the National Socialist movement to transfer the either already existing or [through][228] future findings and scientific insights of racial theory—as well as the world history it elucidates—into practical, applied policy.

Because the economic fate of Germany today vis-à-vis America is to some degree also the fate of other European nations, there is again, particularly among our people, a movement of devout adherents that wishes to counter the union of the American states with a European one, in order to prevent the world hegemony of the North American continent.

The pan-European movement truly seems to these people, at least at first glance, to have some impressive points in its favor.[229] Yes, if one could judge world history based on economic points of view, this might even be the case. For those who see history in mechanical terms and mechanical politicians, two are always more than one. But in the life of the people, quality decides, not quantity. That the American union is able to rise to such a threatening height is not based on the fact that...[230] million people form a state there, but on the fact that...million square kilometers of the most fertile and richest soil are inhabited by...million people of the highest racial quality. [Whereas already the fact that it] That these people form a state despite the physical size of their living area has greater significance for the rest of the world insofar as a unified organization exists, thanks to which the racially determined individual quality of these people can find a cohesive, inclusive commitment to fight the struggle for survival.

If this were not true, and the importance of the American union were therefore to lie only in the population alone or also in the size of the territory or in the relationship between this territory and the size of the population, then Russia would be at least just as dangerous for Europe. Today's Russia encompasses...[231] million people on...million square kilometers. These people are also united in a polity whose value, viewed traditionally, should be even higher than that of the American union, except that it would nevertheless not occur to anyone to therefore fear a Russian world hegemony. The size of the Russian population is not accompanied by such an intrinsic worth that this size could become a danger for the freedom of the world. At least not in the sense of an economic or power-political domination of the rest of the world, but at most in the sense of an inundation with sickness-causing bacteria, which are currently found in Russia.

But if the significance of the menacing American hegemonic position appears to be determined primarily by the quality of the American people and then only secondarily by the size of the Lebensraum given to this people and the resulting favorable relation between population and land area, then this hegemony will not be eliminated by a purely formal numerical merger of European peoples, if their intrinsic worth is not higher than that of the American union. Otherwise, today's Russia in particular would appear to be the greatest danger to this American union, and even more China, which is populated by more than 400 million people.[232]

Thus, the pan-European movement rests from the beginning on the fundamental basic mistake that quality of population can be made up for with quantity of population. This is a purely mechanical view of history that completely avoids exploring all the forces that shape life; instead, it sees numerical majorities not only as the creative sources of human culture but also as the history-forming factors. This view fits as well with the pointlessness of our western democracy as with the cowardly pacifism of our *Überwirtschaftskreise* [leading economic circles] [*sic*]. It is obvious that this is the ideal of all inferior or half-breed bastards. Likewise, that the Jew particularly welcomes such a concept; in its consistent observance it leads to racial chaos and confusion, to a bastardization and niggerization [*sic*] of civilized humanity, and finally to such a deterioration in its racial value that the Hebrew who keeps himself free from it can gradually rise to be masters of the world. At least he imagines that he can one day [ascend] become the brain of this humanity that has been made worthless.

But aside from this fundamental basic mistake of the pan-European movement, the thought of creating a union of European peoples out of the force of a common insight into an impending emergency is a fanciful, historically impossible puerility. By that I do not wish to say that such a union under Jewish protectorate and

Jewish instigation would be impossible per se from the outset, but only that the result could not match the hopes for which the whole magic was set in action. Because one should not believe that such a European coalition would be able to mobilize any sort of force that could make an appearance externally. We know from past experience that lasting unions can only take place when the peoples in question are of equal racial quality and related, and second, when their union takes place in the shape of the slow process of a struggle for hegemony. That was how Rome once conquered the Latin states, one after the other, until finally its power sufficed to become the crystallization point of a world empire. But this is also [through] the history of the emergence of the English world empire. Furthermore, Prussia ended the fragmentation of the German states in the same manner, and it is only in this way that a Europe could one day arise that could safeguard its people's interests in a cohesive political form. But this could only be the result of a centuries-long struggle, as an infinite amount of old lore and tradition would have to be overcome and an equalization would have to take place between peoples that are already exceedingly divergent racially. The difficulty of giving such an entity a unified state language could also only be solved in a centuries-long process.

But then all of this would not be the [fulfillment] realization of the current pan-European idea, but the result of the struggle for survival of the most powerful nation in Europe, and what remained would be no more a pan-Europe than the unification of the Latin states was once a Latin Federation. The power that carried out this unification process back then, in centuries-long battles, also gave the whole entity its enduring name. And the power that would create a pan-Europe in such a natural way today would thereby at the same time also rob it of the pan-Europe designation.

But even in this case the desired success would fail to materialize. Because as soon as any European great power—and it could of course only be a power with a high-quality, racially significant people—were to bring Europe to unification in this manner today, the final achievement of this unification would signify the racial decline of its founders, thus eliminating the ultimate value of the whole entity after all. It would never be possible to create an entity in this way that would be able [*to*] stand up to the American union.[233]

In the future, the only state that will be able to stand up to North America will be the state that has understood how—through the character of its internal life as well as through the substance of its external policy—to raise the racial value of its people and bring it into the most practical national form for this purpose. But by making such a solution seem possible, a great number of nations will be able to participate in it, which can and will lead to greater strengthening already as a result of the mutual competition.

It is, again, the duty of the National Socialist movement to strengthen and prepare our own fatherland to the greatest degree possible for this task.[234]

However, the attempt to realize the pan-European idea through a purely formal union of European peoples, without being brought about by force in centuries-long battles by a European supreme power, will lead to an entity whose entire strength and energy will be absorbed by internal rivalries and conflicts—as happened once with the strength of the German tribes in the German Confederation. Not until the internal German question was ultimately solved by Prussian superiority could the nation exert its united strength outward. But it is thoughtless to believe that the conflict between Europe and America would always be of a peaceful economic nature, when economic factors finally develop into life-determining factors. It was due to the nature of the origin of the North American state that it could initially show little interest in foreign policy problems. Not only as a result of the lack of a long national tradition, but simply as a result of the fact that there were extraordinarily large areas within the American continent itself that were available to satisfy the natural human appetite for expansion. For this reason, the policy of the American union, from the moment of disengagement from the European mother states up to most recent times, was primarily only a domestic policy. Yes, even the battles for independence were basically nothing more than the shaking off of foreign policy ties in favor of a life conceived exclusively in domestic policy terms. But as the American people progressively fulfill the internal colonization task, the natural activist drive, which is inherent particularly in young peoples will turn outward. The surprise, however, which the world could then perhaps still experience, would least of all be countered with serious resistance by a pacifist, democratic, pan-European muddled state. This pan-Europe, according to the view of the biggest bastard in the world, Coudenhove,[235] would play the same role opposite the American union or a nationally awakened China as the old Austrian state played opposite Germany or Russia.

But the idea really does not need to be refuted that because in the American union people from various ethnic origins have been amalgamated, the same must be possible in Europe as well. The American union did indeed merge together those from various ethnic affiliations to create a young people. Closer examination, however, reveals that the overwhelming majority of these different ethnic members belong to racially equal or at least related base elements. Because the emigration process in Europe was a selection process of the most capable, but because in all European peoples this competence lay primarily in the Nordic admixture, the American union actually extracted from peoples who were very diverse in principle the [racially] Nordic elements dispersed among them. If one adds to this that these were people who did not carry any particular national political disposition and therefore did not appear burdened by any tradition, plus the magnitude of the impression of the new world, which all people more or less succumb to, then it becomes understandable how it could be possible that in barely two hundred years a new national people could arise out of individuals from all European nations. It must be considered, however, that in the last century this process of amalgamation already became more difficult to the extent that Europeans went to North

American under the compulsion of hardship and, as members of European nation states, not only felt themselves still connected to their people but valued in particular their national tradition higher than citizenship in their new homeland. The American union was also unable to merge foreign people with a pronounced national feeling or racial instinct. The American union's power of assimilation failed with the Chinese as well as with the Japanese elements. People sense this quite clearly and know it, and thus would prefer to exclude these foreign elements from immigration.[236] With that alone, the American immigration policy itself confirms that the previous amalgamation did indeed presuppose people of certain equal racial foundations, and that it immediately fails as soon as people of a fundamentally different type are involved. The fact that the American union feels itself to be a Nordic-Germanic state and not at all an international mishmash of peoples can moreover seem the way in which the immigration quotas for the European peoples are allotted.[237] Scandinavians—that means Swedes, Norwegians, also Danes—then Englishmen and finally Germans are allocated the largest contingents. Romanians and Slavs very limited; Japanese and Chinese one would rather exclude altogether. It is a utopia to want to oppose this consequently racially [dominant] predominantly Nordic state with a European coalition or a pan-Europe consisting of Mongols, Slavs, Germans, Romanians, and so on, in which anything but Germans would dominate, as a factor capable of resistance. Indeed, a very dangerous utopia when one considers that many countless Germans see a rosy future again without having to make the most serious sacrifices for it. The fact that this utopia originates in Austria[238] of all places does not lack a certain comic element. This state and its fate are the clearest example of the enormous strength inherent in such artificially glued together but intrinsically unnatural entities. It is the rootless spirit of the old Reich capital, Vienna—that hybrid city of Orient and Occident—that speaks to us in this way.

[CHAPTER X]

[No Neutrality]

In summary, it can again be said that our bourgeois national policy, whose foreign policy goal is to restore the 1914 borders, is absurd and even disastrous. It brings us inevitably into conflict with all the states that took part in the Great War. It thereby guarantees the further survival of the coalition of victors that is slowly strangling us. It thereby ensures for France a positive public opinion in the rest of the world for its perpetual proceedings against Germany. Its results, even if it were successful, would mean nothing for the future of Germany, but would nevertheless force us to fight with blood and steel. Furthermore, it impedes, in particular, any stability at all in German foreign policy.

One of the characteristic features of our prewar policy was that it had to give outside observers the picture of erratic and often unfathomable decisions. If one excludes the Triple Alliance itself, whose maintenance could not be a foreign policy aim but only a means to such an end, one can discover no consistent idea in the guidance of the fate of our people in the prewar period. This is naturally incomprehensible.[239] At the moment in which the foreign policy goal was no longer defined as fighting for the interests of the German people but instead maintaining world peace, the ground fell out from under our feet. I can certainly outline and establish the interests of a people and, regardless of how the individual possibilities of representing it turn out, still keep the big goal consistently in view. Gradually the rest of humanity will also obtain a general knowledge of a people's particular, definite, guiding foreign policy thoughts. This then provides the possibility of managing the relationships among each other on a more stable basis, whether in the sense of an intentional opposition to the recognized action of such a power, or a fair notice of it, or also in the sense of an understanding, as one's own interests may be achieved by collaborating.

This foreign policy stability can be identified in quite a number of European states. Russia shows, in long periods of its development, certain foreign policy goals that then govern all of its actions. France has pursued consistent foreign policy aims over the course of centuries, regardless of who embodies the political power in Paris at the time. Of England one can say not only that it is the state with a traditional diplomacy, but above all that it is the state whose foreign policy idea has become a tradition. In the case of Germany, such an idea could only be detected periodically in the Prussian state. In the short era of Bismarckian statecraft, we see Prussia fulfill its German mission, but with that, every comprehensive foreign policy goal ends as well. The new German Reich, particularly since Bismarck's departure, has not possessed such a goal, as the rallying cry of preserving peace—that is, the maintenance of an existing situation—possesses no stable content or character. Just as every passive slogan is in reality condemned to become the plaything of the offensive desire. Only he who wishes to act himself is also able to determine his actions according to his own will. That is why the Triple Entente,[240] which wanted to act, also retained all the advantages that lie in the self-determination of action, whereas the Triple Alliance was disadvantaged to that same degree through its contemplative bias toward the preservation of world peace. Thus the war was also determined, in timing and initiation, by the nations with definite foreign policy goals, while the Triple Alliance powers, in contrast, were surprised in an hour that was anything but favorable. If one had had even the most limited bellicose intentions in Germany, then it would have been possible, through a number of measures that could have been perfunctorily implemented easily, to give [in] the beginning of the war already a completely different look. But Germany had no definite foreign policy goal in view, had no aggressive steps in mind to realize this goal, and was therefore surprised by the events.

From Austria-Hungary one could hope for [*sic*] no other foreign policy goal than to wriggle through the dangers of European policy in such a way that the rotten state entity did not bump up against anything, and thus be able to conceal the true inner character of this monstrous cadaver of a state.

The German nationalist bourgeoisie—of whom I can always only speak here because international Marxism itself knows only the goal of destroying Germany—has even today learned nothing from the past. Today they still do not feel the necessity of establishing for the nation a foreign policy goal that can be seen as satisfactory for the future of Germany and that can thus give a certain stability to our foreign policy aspirations on a more or less long-term basis. Because not until such a potential foreign policy goal appears defined in principle can one discuss in detail the possibilities that can lead to success. So only then does politics enter into the phase of the art of the possible. But as long as this whole political life is not governed by any guiding idea, the individual actions will not have the character of utilizing all possibilities to achieve a certain result; instead, they are then always only individual stations along the path of aimless and purposeless struggling from one day to the next. Then, above all, that perseverance which is always required in fighting toward major goals will be lost. In other words: One will try this today and that tomorrow, and the day after tomorrow one will envisage this foreign policy possibility and suddenly pursue a completely opposite aim, provided this obvious chaos as chaos corresponds in the end to the wishes of that power that rules Germany today and in reality does not wish our people ever to rise again. Only international Jewry can have an active interest in a German foreign policy that—through its perpetual unreasonable-appearing leaps—precludes any clear plan and has, at best, as its only justification: "No, we do not know what should be done either, of course, but we are doing something because something must be done." Yes, one can hear not infrequently that these people are themselves so little convinced by the inherent significance of their foreign policy actions that, as highest-level motivation, they can put forward only the question of whether someone else would have known something better. This, then, is the foundation upon which the statecraft of a Gustav Stresemann then rests.

However, it is necessary precisely today, more than ever, that the German people establish a foreign policy goal that meets its actual internal needs and also grants its foreign policy action unconditional stability for the foreseeable future. Because only if our people's interests are fundamentally defined and then persistently fought for in such a way can it hope to induce one state or another whose interests are not opposed to ours (now finally established)—and, yes, are even corresponding—to enter into a closer alliance with Germany. Because the idea of trying to resolve our people's distress through the League of Nations[241] is just as unjustified as the idea of allowing the German question to be decided by the federal parliament in Frankfurt was.[242]

The satisfied nations dominate in the League of Nations. Yes, it is their instrument. They have, for the most part, no interest in allowing any change to take place in the division of territory on the earth, aside from [*sic*] it would be to their advantage again. And when they speak of the rights of the small nations, they really only have the interests of the largest ones in view.

If Germany wishes to attain true freedom again, and to be able to give the German people its daily bread under its blessing, then the measures to achieve this will have to be carried out outside the League of Nations parliament in Geneva. Then, however, due to a lack of strength on our own part, it will be necessary to find allies who can believe that they will be able to serve their own interests by associating with Germany. Such a situation will never arise, however, if Germany's true foreign policy aim has not become completely clear to these peoples. And, above all, Germany itself will never obtain the power and inner strength for the persistence that is necessary to clear away the oppositions of world history. Then one will never learn to be patient with the small things, and when necessary also to forego them, in order ultimately to be able to reach the big goal that is indispensable to life. Because even among allies the relationship will never be completely frictionless. Disruptions in mutual relations can repeatedly arise and take on a threatening aspect if the scope of the once-established foreign policy goal does not contain the strength to overcome minor inconveniences and disputes. Here the French state leadership in the decade before the war can serve as a characteristic example. The way they—in contrast to our jingoists, who were perpetually bawling and not infrequently barking at the moon—passed over everything minor and were even silent in the face of very bitter events, in order not to lose the opportunity to organize the war of revenge against Germany.

But the putting up [*sic*] of a clear foreign policy goal appears particularly important because otherwise it will always be possible for the representatives of other interests within the nation to confuse public opinion and turn minor, sometimes even provoked, incidents into the occasion for a revision of the foreign policy position. In this way, out of minor quarrels that arise either from the state of things themselves or that are also artificially fabricated, France will keep trying to cause resentments, even alienation, among the peoples that, according to the whole nature of their true vital interests, should be dependent on each other and should collaborate for common action against France. But such attempts will only succeed when, as a result of the lack of an unshakable foreign policy goal, our own political actions have no real stability and thus, above all, lack also the persistence necessary to prepare those measures that are useful for the fulfillment of our own political objectives.

The German people, which has neither a foreign policy tradition nor a foreign policy goal, will in principle always be easily prone to endorse utopian ideals and thus to neglect its real vital interests. What all [has] our people not doted on in the last one hundred years? First it was the Greeks that we wanted to rescue from Turkey,[243] then again Turks to whom we gave our affection, against Russians[244] and Italians,[245] and then our people again found a fascination in doting on Polish freedom fighters,[246] and then in sympathizing with Boers,[247] and so on, and so on. But what did all these dumb effusions—effusions of a soul as politically incompetent as it was garrulous—cost our people?

Thus the relationship with Austria, as was emphasized with particular pride, was not one of hardheaded reason, but a true inner bond of affection. If only the head had spoken instead of the heart at that time, and reason had decided, then Germany would be saved today. But precisely because we are a people that allows its political actions to be determined too little on the basis of a truly sensible, intellectual understanding, and because we cannot at all look back on any great political tradition, we must at least for the future give our people an unshakable foreign policy goal that seems capable of making the details of the political measures of the state leadership comprehensible also to the broad masses. Only in this way will it be possible one day for millions, in anticipating faith to stand behind a state leadership that implements decisions that individually may be somewhat painful. This is a prerequisite to creating a mutual understanding between people and state leadership, and indeed also a prerequisite to anchoring a certain tradition in the state leadership itself. It will not do for every German government to have its own foreign policy goal. Only the means can be argued about—those can be disputed—but the goal itself must be established, once and for all, as unalterable. Then politics can become the great art of the possible; that is to say, the brilliant abilities of individual state leaders allow them, as the case arises, to seize the opportunities that will bring the people and the Reich closer to its foreign policy goal.

This foreign policy objective does not exist at all in Germany today. This also explains the boundless, erratic, and uncertain safeguarding of the interests of our people, and also the whole chaos of our public opinion, as well as all the unbelievable wild leaps of our foreign policy which always end disastrously without the people even being discriminating enough to truly hold accountable those who are responsible. No, one does not know what should be done.

Yes, there are indeed not a few people today who actually believe that we should not do anything. They adopt the position that Germany must be prudent and reserved today, that it must not engage itself anywhere, and that we must watch the development of events carefully, but not take part in them ourselves, in order then one day to take on the role of that laughing third party who pockets the success while two others quarrel.

Yes, yes, our current bourgeois statesmen are so clever and wise. A political judgment that is unclouded by any knowledge of history. There are more than a few proverbs that have become a real curse for our people. For example, "The more intelligent one backs down," or "The clothes make the man," or "With hat in hand one comes through the whole land," or also "When two quarrel, the third is pleased."

In the life of the people at least, this last proverb is of limited relevance [and this for the following reasons], namely only when two within a nation are quarreling futilely; then a third who is outside the nation can prevail. But in the life of the peoples together, the ultimate success will always be to [*sic*] states that fight deliberately, because conflict is the only way to increase their power. There is no historical event in the world that cannot be judged from two viewpoints. The advocates of neutrality on one side are always faced by the interventionists on the other. And the neutral parties will always lose, while the interventionists can more likely claim the success for themselves, provided[248] the party to which they are attached doesn't lose.

In the life of the peoples, that means the following: In this world, if two powerful peoples are fighting, the surrounding more or less small or large states can take part in this struggle or stay away from it. In one case, the possibility of gain is not excluded, provided the participation takes place on the side that obtains the victory. But regardless of who wins, the neutral parties will never have any other fate than enmity with the remaining victorious state. None of the large states of the world has ever reached ascendancy through neutrality as a principle of political action, but only through conflict. If there are preeminently powerful states on the earth, smaller peoples are left with no other choice than either to renounce their future entirely or to fight together under the protection of favorable coalitions, thus multiplying their own power. Because the role of the "laughing third" always presumes that this third already has power. But those who are always neutral will never attain power. Because although the strength of a people also lies in its inner value, it does find its ultimate expression in the organizational form of a people's armed forces—created by the will of this inner value—on the battlefield. But this form will never emerge if it is not exposed to practical testing from time to time. Only under the sledgehammer of world history will the eternal values of a people become the steel and iron with which history is then made. But those who avoid battles will never attain the strength to fight battles. And those who never fight battles will never be the beneficiaries of those who engage each other in swordplay. Because the beneficiaries in world history to date have never been peoples with cowardly views of neutrality, but rather young peoples with the better sword. Neither in antiquity, nor in the Middle Ages, nor in the present time has there been even [still] one example of powerful states emerging in any other way than through constant conflict. The peoples who have been the beneficiaries of history, however, have always been powerful states. Certainly a third can also be the beneficiary when two fight, in the life of the peoples, but then this third one is already from the beginning a power that deliberately allows two others to fight in order to then ultimately defeat them without great casualties of its own. But in this case neutrality completely loses the character of a passive lack of participation in events and instead takes on that of a deliberate political operation. Of course, no intelligent state leadership will begin a fight without weighing up the extent of its own possible commitment and comparing it with that of the opponent. But when it realizes the impossibility of fighting against a certain power, then it will be all the more compelled to fight alongside this power. Because then, through this shared struggle, the strength of the previously weaker power can grow to the point where it will be able to fight for its own vital interests, when necessary against this stronger power as well. That is not to say that no power will therefore enter into an alliance with a state that could perhaps become a threat itself one day. Alliances do not represent political ends, but only means to those ends. One must use them today, even if one knows a thousand times that later developments could lead to the opposite. There is no alliance that is permanent. Fortunate are those peoples who, as a result of the complete divergence of their interests, are able to enter into an alliance relationship for a certain time without being forced into conflict with one another after its termination. But particularly a weaker state that wishes to attain power and greatness must always take an active part in the general political events of world history.

When Prussia entered into its Silesian war,[249] this was also a relatively minor occurrence next to the immense conflict between England and France that had just then reached its climax.[250] Perhaps one could accuse Frederick the Great of having pulled English chestnuts out of the fire. But would that Prussia with which a Bismarck was able to create a new German Reich ever have emerged if at that time the Hohenzollern throne had been occupied by a prince who maintained his Prussia in docile neutrality in recognition of the coming greater events of world history? The three Silesian wars brought Prussia more than Silesia. These battlefields were where those regiments originated that subsequently carried the German flags from Weissenburg and Wörth to Sedan,[251] in order finally to greet the new emperor of the new Reich in the Hall of Mirrors in the palace of Versailles. Prussia was certainly a small state then, insignificant in population size and territory; however, because this small state jumped into the middle of the great actions of world history, it obtained the legitimation for the establishment of the future German Reich.

And the neutralists did win in this Prussian state once as well. That was during the era of Napoleon I. At that time, people initially believed that Prussia could maintain its neutrality; they were later punished for that with the most terrible defeat.[252] And in 1812 the two views still stood in harsh opposition. The one for neutrality and the other—led by Reichsfreiherr von Stein [*sic*][253]—for intervention. The fact that the neutralists won in 1812 cost Prussia and Germany an infinite amount of blood and brought infinite suffering. And the fact that the interventionists finally gained acceptance in 1813 saved Prussia.

The Great War gave the clearest response to the opinion that political successes could be gained by maintaining a careful neutrality as a third power. What did the neutral states in the Great War achieve? Were they, perhaps, the "laughing third"? Or do people believe that in a similar occurrence German would play a different role? One certainly doesn't think that only the size of the Great War was to blame. No, in the future, all wars, to the extent that they involve the major nations, will be total wars of the most gigantic proportions. But as a neutral state in any future European conflict, Germany would have no greater significance than Holland or Switzerland or Denmark or the like in the Great War. Do people really believe, then, that after the events we would possess the strength—out of nothing—to play the role opposite a remaining victor that we did not dare to play in alliance with one of the two conflicting powers?

The Great War did, in any case, prove one thing unmistakably: Those who remain neutral in the great conflicts of world history may perhaps initially be able to carry out a little trade; in terms of power politics, however, they will for that reason ultimately be excluded from participating in the determination of the fate of the world.

If the American union had remained neutral in the Great War, regardless of whether England or Germany had emerged victorious the American union would today be viewed as a second-rate power. The fact that it entered the battle[254] raised it in terms of naval power to the strength of England, but marked it in terms of world politics as a power of decisive significance. The assessment of the American union has become completely different since its entry into the Great War. It is the nature of human forgetfulness [to forget] to no longer remember already after a short time already [*sic*] how a situation was generally judged a few years before. Just as today we sense in the speeches of many foreign statesmen a complete disregard for the former greatness of Germany, we cannot, in contrast, estimate the extent to which the valuation of the American union has increased in our own judgment since its entry into the Great War.

This is also the most compelling statesmanlike reason for Italy's entry into the war against its former allies. If Italy had not taken this step, then today, regardless of how the dice had fallen, it would share the role of Spain. The fact that it took this highly criticized step and participated in the Great War brought an enhancement and strengthening in its position, which has now found its ultimate crowning expression in fascism. Without entry into the war, this would also have been a completely unthinkable occurrence.

Germans can think about that with or without bitterness. The important thing is to learn from history, but particularly when its lessons speak to us in such an insistent manner.

So it is false and foolish to believe that through a careful, re-served neutrality in the face of developing conflicts in Europe and elsewhere, successes can one day be gained as a "laughing third." One does not obtain freedom through begging or cheating, or through labor and industriousness either, but exclusively through fighting—fighting one's own battles. It is easily possible that the will, in this case, will count for more than the deed. Peoples have not infrequently achieved successes in the context of intelligent alliance policies that do not stand in relation to the successes of their weapons. But with a people that commits itself boldly, fate does not always measure according to the scope of the deeds, but very often according to the extent of the will. The history of the Italian unification in the nineteenth century is notable for this. But the Great War also shows how a great number of states were able to achieve extraordinary political successes less through their military [successes] achievements than through the audacious boldness with which they took sides, and through the tenacity with which they persevered.

If Germany wishes to end its period of subjugation by all, it must by all means attempt actively to push its way into a power combination, in order actively to participate in the future power-political formation of European life.

The objection that such participation contains a serious risk is correct. But do people really believe, then, that freedom can be attained without incurring any risk? Or do they think that there was any deed in the history of the world that was not connected with a risk? Was, say, the decision of Frederick the Great to undertake the first Silesian war not linked with any risk? Or was the unification of Germany by Bismarck without danger? No, and a thousand times no! Beginning with the birth of the human until his death, everything is doubtful. The only thing that seems certain is death itself. But that is exactly why the final commitment is not the most difficult, because it will one day be demanded in one way or another.

Of course, it is a matter of political intelligence to choose the stakes in such a way that the greatest possible benefit results. But not to bet at all out of fear of perhaps getting the wrong horse means renouncing the future of a people. The accusation that such action then has the character of a high-stakes game of chance can most easily be refuted with a simple reference to historical experience thus far. A high-stakes game of chance is defined as one in which the possibilities of greatest gain [*sic*] are from the beginning determined solely by luck. This will never be the case in politics. Because although the final decision lies in the obscurity of the future, the belief in the possibility or impossibility of a success is built upon humanly recognizable factors. It is the task of the political leadership of the people to weigh up these factors. But the result of this review must then also lead to a decision. This decision thus arises from one's understanding and is supported by the belief, based on this understanding, in possible success. Thus, I cannot label a decisive political deed as a high-stakes game of chance simply because its outcome is not 100 percent certain, any more than I can do so in the case of an operation performed by a physician when the outcome likewise need not necessarily be successful. Since the beginning of time, it has always been part of the essence of great men to carry out with the utmost energy even questionable deeds with uncertain results, if the necessity was clear and after careful examination of all the circumstances these supported only this one certain action.

In the struggle between the peoples, the willingness to take responsibility and make important decisions will increase to the degree that those who are acting can, when observing their people, come to the conclusion that even a failure will not destroy the vital strength of the nation. Because a people that is internally very healthy will in the long run never be able to be extinguished through battlefield defeats. So if a people possesses this internal healthiness, under the precondition of adequate racial significance, the courage for difficult operations will be able to be greater, because even the failure of these would not, by far, mean the downfall of such a people. And here Clausewitz[255] was correct when he established in his *Bekenntnisse* that in the case of a healthy people, such a defeat can always lead to a later renewal, but that cowardly submission—surrender to fate without a struggle—can, in contrast, lead to ultimate destruction.[256] Neutrality, however, which people today praise as the only possible action for our people, is in reality nothing more than weak surrender to a fate determined by foreign powers. And therein alone lies the distinguishing feature and possibility of our decline. If, however, our people had made even failed attempts at freedom, then the demonstration of this disposition would already represent a factor that would benefit the vital strength of our people. Because no one can say that it is state-political wisdom that holds us back from such steps. No, it is pathetic cowardice and lack of principle that in this case, as so often in history, people attempt to confuse with wisdom. Of course, a people can in some cases be forced, under the compulsion of foreign powers, to suffer foreign oppression for years. But although a people is not then able to do anything serious outwardly against the superior powers, its inner life will press toward freedom and leave nothing untried that could be capable of changing the current situation one day by mobilizing the collective strength of such a people. They will then bear the yoke of the foreign conqueror but will watch with clenched fists and gnashing teeth for the hour that offers the first opportunity to do away with the tyrant. Something like this can be possible under the weight of the circumstances. But what presents itself as state-political wisdom today is actually a spirit of voluntary subjugation, of unprincipled renunciation of any resistance—yes, of the shameless persecution of those who dare to think of such resistance and whose work could clearly serve the renewal of their people. It is the spirit of inner self-disarmament and the destruction of all the moral factors that could one day serve a renewal of this people and state, and this spirit really cannot act as state-political wisdom, because it is actually state-destroying dishonesty.

And this spirit must indeed hate every attempt of our people to actively participate in the coming European development, because even the attempt at such cooperation alone involves the necessity of the fight against this spirit.

But if a state leadership seems attacked by the corruption of this spirit, then it is the task of the opposition—safeguarding and advocating and thus representing the true vital forces of a people—to write on its banners [the education] the fight for national renewal and thus national honor. It must not let itself be intimidated, then, by the claim that foreign policy is the duty of the responsible state leadership, because there has been no such responsible leadership for a long time; rather, it must take the position that beyond [from formal governments also timeless] the formal rights of the particular government there are timeless obligations that compel every member of a national community to do what is recognized as necessary for the continued existence of the community.[257] Even if this stands a thousand times in opposition to the intentions of bad and incompetent governments.

For this reason, the so-called national opposition in Germany today should have the highest obligation, in view of the baseness of the general leadership of our people, to establish a clear foreign policy goal and to prepare and educate our people for the implementation of these ideas. It must make a priority of declaring all-out war against the currently widespread hope that anything about our fate can be changed through active cooperation with the League of Nations. Furthermore it must make absolutely sure that our people gradually recognize that we cannot expect improvement in the German situation to come from institutions whose representatives [are] those interested in our current misfortune. Moreover, it must deepen the belief that if German freedom is not regained, all social hopes are utopian promises without any real value. Moreover, it must bring our people to the realization that to attain this freedom, only the mobilization of our own strength, in one way or another, comes into question. And that therefore our entire domestic and foreign policy must be such that under its effects the inner strength of our people grows and increases. And, finally, it must clarify to the people that this employment of strength must occur in pursuit of a truly worthwhile goal, and that for this purpose we cannot confront fate alone, but we must have allies.

[CHAPTER XI]

[Germany's Political Situation: No Alliance with Russia]

I n addition to the inner strength of our people—its strength of character and estimation—the size of its possible military deployment as well as the relationship between this power resource and those of the surrounding states is of decisive significance for the question of the future formation of German foreign policy.

I do not need to hold forth further in this work about the inner moral weakness of our people today. Our general weaknesses, which are based partly on genetics and lie partly in the nature of our current state organization or must be attributed to the effects of our bad leadership, are, unfortunately, all too well known to the rest of the world—perhaps less so to the German public. A large number of our oppressor's measures are based on the recognition of these weaknesses [*sic*]. But with full acknowledgement of the actual circumstances it must never be forgotten that this same people of today achieved historically incomparable attainments barely ten years ago.[258] The German people, which makes such a dejected impression at the moment, has nevertheless proven its immense worth more than once in the history of the world. The Great War itself is the most glorious testimony to our people's sense of heroism and courage in the face of sacrifice, to its death-defying discipline, and to its brilliant capability in thousands and thousands of areas in the organization of its life. Its purely military leadership also achieved immortal victories. Only the political leadership failed. It was already the precursor of today's even worse leadership.

Thus, although the inner qualities of our people today may be a thousand times unsatisfactory, they will at one stroke provide a different picture as soon as a different fist one day takes the reins of events to lead our people back out of its current decline.

We see from our history just how wonderful our people's capacity for transformation is. Prussia in 1806 and Prussia in 1813. What a difference. In 1806 the state of the saddest capitulation in every nook and corner, and the shocking pitifulness of the bourgeois attitude, and in 1813 the state of the most fervent hatred against foreign domination and the most patriotic sense of sacrifice for one's own people and the most heroically courageous will to fight for freedom. What, in truth, changed at that time? The people? No, its inner essence remained the same as before; only its leadership changed hands. The weakness of the Prussian state leadership in the post-Frederician period and the ossified and outmoded leadership of the army were now followed by a new spirit. Baron von Stein [*sic*] and Gneisenau,[259] Scharnhorst,[260] Clausewitz, and Blücher[261] were the representatives of the new Prussia. And the world forgot again in a few months that this Prussia had experienced a Jenaseven years earlier.

And was it any different before the founding of the new Reich? Barely a decade was necessary to allow—from the German decline, the German discord, and the general political dishonor—the emergence of a new Reich, which in the eyes of many seemed the strongest embodiment of German power and magnificence. A single preeminent mind, in the fight against the mediocrity of the majorities, gave the German genius its freedom to develop again. Imagine Bismarck out of our history, and only pathetic mediocrity would fill the period that was the most glorious for our people in centuries.

Just as it was possible for the German people, through the mediocrity of its leadership, to be thrown down again in few years from its unheard of greatness into its current chaos, in the same way it can also be pulled up again by an iron fist. Its inner quality will then appear so obvious to the whole world that even the fact of its existence must compel the regard and estimation of this fact.

But if this quality is initially dormant, then it is even more important to create clarity about the real value of Germany's currently existing power.

I have already attempted to sketch a brief picture of the current German military power instrument, the Reichswehr. Here I would like to outline the general military situation of Germany in relation to the surrounding world.

Germany is currently encircled by three power factors or power groups. England, Russia, and France are currently Germany's militarily most threatening neighbors. And the power of France appears to be strengthened by a system of European alliances that reaches from Paris to Warsaw[262] and from Prague to Belgrade.[263]

Germany lies wedged between these states, with completely open borders. What is particularly threatening is the fact that the western border of the Reich runs through Germany's greatest industrial area. [And further, that the coastline defenseless the entire overseas trade on a few.] But this western border, as a result of its length and the lack of any real natural obstacles, also offers very few opportunities for defense by a state whose military power resources seem exceedingly limited. [The attempt, the Rhine as a military defensive line.] The Rhine cannot be viewed as a militarily effective defensive line either. It is not only that the peace treaties have taken from Germany the possibility of making the necessary technical preparations for this;[264] the river itself offers even less of an obstacle to the crossing of modern, well-equipped armies, as the limited

German defensive resources would be spread out along too long of a front. In addition, this river runs through Germany's greatest industrial area, and therefore a battle for it would from the beginning mean the destruction of the industrial locations and factories that are in terms of technology most necessary for national defense. If, however, as a result of a German-French conflict, Czechoslovakia also came into consideration as an additional enemy for Germany, then a second large industrial area that could contribute industrially to the war effort would be exposed to the greatest war danger: Saxony. Here as well, of course, the border runs unprotected down to Bavaria, so wide and open that successful defense could hardly be considered. If Poland were also to take part in such a conflict, then the entire eastern border, with the exception of a few inadequate fortifications, would likewise be defenseless and open to attack.

So whereas on one hand the German borders are military vulnerable and open in long stretches and surrounded by enemies, our North Sea coastline in particular is short and restricted. The naval power resources to protect it are ridiculous and completely worthless. The warship matériel that we call our own today is, starting with our so-called battleships, at best scrap metal for enemy target practice. The few newly constructed modern light cruisers do not have decisive value—or even any apparent value at all.[265] The fleet allowed us is inadequate even for the Baltic Sea. All things considered, the only value of our fleet is at most that of a floating firing school.[266]

For this reason, in the case of a conflict with any naval power, not only is German trade immediately halted, but the danger of landings is also present.

The entire adversity of our military situation arises from the following consideration:

The Reich capital, Berlin, is barely 175 kilometers from the Polish border. It is barely 190 kilometers from the closest Czech border; the linear distance to Wismar and to the Stettiner Haff is the same. That means, therefore, that with modern aircraft Berlin can be reached from these borders in less than an hour. If one draws a line sixty kilometers to the east of the Rhine, then almost the entire western German industrial area lies within it [*sic*]. From Frankfurt to Dortmund, there is hardly a major German industrial location that does not lie within this zone. As long as France has occupied a portion of the left bank of the Rhine,[267] it is in a position to advance with aircraft into the heart of our western German industrial area in less than thirty minutes. Munich lies as far from the Czech border as Berlin from the Polish and Czech borders. Czech military aircraft would need approximately sixty minutes to reach Munich, forty minutes to reach Nuremberg, and thirty minutes to reach Regensburg— yes, even Augsburg is only 200 kilometers from the Czech border and could easily be reached with today's aircraft in just under an hour. And Augsburg's distance from the French border is about the same as its distance from the Czech border. From Augsburg to Strasbourg the distance by air is 230 kilometers, but to the nearest French border it is only 210 kilometers. Thus, Augsburg also lies in a zone that can be reached by enemy aircraft within the course of an hour. Yes, if we analyze the German borders from this point of view, then it emerges that within an hour's flight time the following can be reached: The entire industrial area in western Germany, including Osnabrück, Bielefeld, Kassel, Würzburg, Stuttgart, Ulm, Augsburg. In the east: Munich, Augsburg, Würzburg, Magdeburg, Berlin, Stettin. In other words, with the current state of the German borders, there is only a very small area of a few square kilometers that could not be visited by enemy aircraft already within the first hour.

France comes into question as the most dangerous enemy, because thanks to its alliances only it is in a position to be able to threaten almost all of Germany with airplanes within an hour of the outbreak of a conflict.

Germany's military counteraction against the application of this weapon is, all things considered, currently nil.

This single observation alone shows the bleak situation in which the German resistance against France would immediately find itself if left to its own devices. He who has himself frequently been exposed to the impact of enemy air attacks in the field knows best how to assess in particular the resulting effects on morale.

But even Hamburg and Bremen, and all of our coastal cities, would no longer escape this fate today, as the great navies possess the ability to bring floating airfields close to the coasts with aircraft carriers.[268]

But it is not only against air attacks that Germany today lacks technically effective weapons in adequate number. In other respects as well, the purely technical equipment of our small Reichswehr is hopelessly inferior to that of our enemies.[269] The lack of heavy artillery could be endured more easily than the lack of any real defensive possibility against tanks. If Germany were pushed into a war against France and its allies today, without being in a position to make even the most necessary preparations for defense beforehand, the decision would come in a few days, based purely on the technical superiority of our opponent. The measures that would be necessary to defend against such an enemy attack could no longer be taken in the conflict itself.

The idea that we could resist for a certain time through improvisational means is also wrong, because a certain amount of time is already needed for these improvisations, but in the case of a conflict this time is no longer available. Because the events will happen and thus create realities faster than the time that would be left to us to organize countermeasures against these events.

Therefore, we can also view the foreign policy options from whatever perspective we wish, and one case is fundamentally excluded for Germany: Supported only by our own military power resources, we will never be able to proceed against the forces currently mobilized in Europe. Any combination that brings Germany—without giving it the possibility of thorough preparation beforehand—into conflict with France, England, Poland, Czechoslovakia, and so on, is thus eliminated.

This fundamental recognition is important because in Germany today there are still well-intentioned national men who believe in all seriousness that we must enter into an association [*sic*] with Russia.[270]

Considered even from a purely military perspective, such an idea is unfeasible or disastrous for Germany.

Just as prior to 1914, today we can also always assume it to be absolutely certain that in every conflict in which Germany will become entangled—regardless of the reasons and regardless of the causes—France will always be our enemy. Whatever European combinations may appear in the future, France will always cooperate with the anti-German ones. This is due to the traditionally deep-seated purpose of French foreign policy.[271] It is incorrect to believe that the conclusion of the war changed that in some way. On the contrary. The Great War did not bring France the complete fulfillment of the war aim it had in mind.[272] Because this goal was not the regaining of Alsace-Lorraine at all; on the contrary, Alsace-Lorraine itself represented only one small step in the direction of the French foreign policy goal. The aggressive anti-German tendencies of French policy are in no way softened by possession of Alsace-Lorraine; this is evidenced most decisively by the fact that the anti-German tendency of French foreign policy was nevertheless present also when France already possessed Alsace-Lorraine. The year 1870 showed France's fundamental intentions more clearly than 1914. At that time there was no reason to camouflage the offensive character of French foreign policy. In 1914, however, people thought it seemed better—perhaps because of wisdom gained through experience, or perhaps influenced by England—to hold up universal human ideals on the one hand and on the other to limit their goal to Alsace-Lorraine. These tactical considerations, however, do not at all indicate a renunciation of the former goals of French foreign policy, but only a concealment of them. The central idea of French foreign policy is still the conquering of the Rhine border; the tearing up of Germany into individual states, as loosely attached to one another as possible, is viewed as the best defense of this border. The fact that the European security France achieves in this way is intended to serve greater international political goals does not end[273] anything about the fact that these French continental political intentions are a question of life and death for Germany.

Actually, France has never taken part in a coalition that would also have advanced German interests in any way. In the last three hundred years, up to 1870, Germany has been attacked by France twenty-nine times. A fact that induced Bismarck, on the evening of the battle of Sedan, to confront the French general Wimpffen most fiercely when he attempted to obtain an easing of the capitulation conditions.[274] It was Bismarck at that time who, in response to the statement that France would not forget a concession by Germany and would forever preserve a grateful memory, immediately became angry and held out to the negotiator the hard, naked facts of history. He emphasized that France had attacked Germany so many times in the last three hundred years—regardless of what system of government it was ruled by—that he would forever be convinced that regardless of how the capitulation was formulated, France would immediately attack Germany again as soon as it felt strong enough to do so, either by its own power or through the power of allies.

Bismarck thus assessed the French mentality more accurately than our current political German leaders. He could do this because having a political goal in mind himself, could also possess an inner comprehension of the political objectives of others. For Bismarck, the aim of French foreign policy was clearly established. It is incomprehensible to our current so-called statesmen, however, because they also lack any clear political ideas themselves.

Moreover, if France, on the occasion of its entry into the Great War, had had only the intent of regaining Alsace-Lorraine as its definitive goal, the energy of the French war effort would not have been nearly as great as it was. But then the political leadership in particular would not have struggled through with a determination that in some situations during the Great War seems worthy of the greatest admiration. But due to the nature of this greatest coalition war of all time, complete fulfillment of all wishes was all the less feasible, as the inner interests of the participating nations themselves were in great opposition to each other. [The French desire] The French goal of complete obliteration of Germany in Europe still stood in opposition to the English desire to prevent a French position of absolute hegemony just as much as a German one.

An important factor in the curtailing of French war aims was the fact that the German collapse took place in ways that initially did not allow the public to become completely aware of the entire extent of the catastrophe. In France they learned to know the German infantryman in a way that would allow them to view only with doubt a possibility that perhaps would have compelled France to move by itself to the realization of its ultimate political goal. But later—under the impression of the now generally visible internal collapse of Germany—if such action had been decided upon, the war psychosis of the rest of the world was already so reduced that an individual action in pursuit of such great final aims could no longer have been carried out by France without protest from its former allies.

That is not to say, however, that France has renounced its goal. On the contrary—it will persistently attempt, as it has thus far, to achieve in the future what the present prevented. France will also always in the future as soon as it feels capable, either through its own strength or the strength of allies—strive to break Germany up and attempt to occupy the Rhine bank in order in this way to be able to deploy French strength in other locations unthreatened from the rear. That France is not at all confused in its aims by changes in the German form of government is all the more understandable because the French people itself also adheres consistently to its foreign policy ideas regardless of its particular constitution. A people that always pursues a certain foreign policy goal itself, regardless of whether it is ruled by republic or monarchy, bourgeois democracy or Jacobin terror, will not understand that another people might perhaps also undertake a change in its foreign policy goals through a change in its form of government. Therefore, nothing will change in France's attitude toward Germany, regardless of whether an empire or a republic represents the German nation, or even if [a] socialist terror were to rule the state.

Naturally, France does not face the internal German activities with indifference, but its attitude will be determined only by the likelihood of a greater success—a facilitation of its foreign policy actions—through a certain form of German government. France will wish for Germany the constitution that would allow France to expect the least resistance in the destruction of Germany. When, therefore, the German republic attempts to cite French friendship as a special sign of its worth, then this is in reality the most crushing evidence of its incapacity. Because it is only welcomed in Paris since it is then viewed by France as lacking value for Germany. But that is not at all to say that France will face this German republic differently than it faced similar weakened conditions of our national existence in the past. On the Seine, they always loved German weakness more than German strength, because that seemed to ensure easier success for France's foreign policy activities.

This French tendency also will not be altered at all by the fact that the French people does not have a shortage of space. Because in France, for centuries, policy has been determined least by pure economic concerns but rather by motives of sentiment. France is a classic example of how the sense of a sound policy of territorial conquest can also easily turn into the reverse, as soon as ethnic principles are no longer decisive and so-called state-national principles appear instead. French nationalist chauvinism has removed itself so far from ethnic viewpoints that in order to satisfy a pure urge for power the French allow their own blood to be niggerized [*sic*] just to be able to maintain the numerical character of a "Grandnation" [*sic*]. France will thus also be a perpetual international troublemaker until a decisive and thorough instruction of this people is undertaken one day. For the rest, no one has characterized the character of French vanity better than Schopenhauer with his dictum: "Africa has its monkeys and Europe its French."[275]

French foreign policy has always obtained its inner drive from this mixture of vanity and megalomania. Who in Germany can hope and expect that, although France is increasingly estranged from rational, clear thought as a result of its general niggerization [*sic*], it will nevertheless one day undertake a change in its attitude and its intentions against Germany?

No, regardless of how the next developments in Europe proceed, France will always attempt—by exploiting the respective German weaknesses and all the diplomatic and military options available to it—to inflict damage on us and disunite our people in order to be able ultimately to bring it to a complete disintegration.

Thus, any European coalition that does not mean tying down France is automatically prohibited for Germany.

The belief in a German-Russian understanding is fanciful as long as a government that is preoccupied with the sole effort to transmit the Bolshevist poison to Germany rules in Russia.[276] Thus, when communist elements agitate for a German-Russian alliance,[277] this is then natural. They justly hope that in doing so, they can bring Bolshevism to Germany itself. But it is incomprehensible when nationalist Germans believe that they can arrive at an understanding with a state whose highest interest includes the destruction of precisely this nationalist Germany. It goes without saying that if such an alliance were to materialize today, its result would be the complete dominance of Judaism in Germany, just as in Russia. The idea that we could enter a conflict against the capitalistic western European world with this Russia is likewise incomprehensible. Because, first, today's Russia is anything but an anticapitalist state. It is indeed a country that has destroyed its own national economy, but only in order to safeguard the possibility of absolute dominance by international finance capital.[278] If this were not the case, how then, second, would precisely to[279] capitalistic world in Germany come to take a position for such an alliance? It is precisely the Jewish press organs of the most noted stock market interests that advocate a German-Russian alliance in Germany. Do people really believe that the *Berliner Tagblatt*[280] or the *Frankfurter Zeitung*[281] and all of their illustrated sheets[282] speak more or less openly for Bolshevist Russia because this is an anticapitalist state? It is always a curse when in political things the wish becomes the father of the thought.

Indeed, it would be conceivable that in Russia itself an inner change could occur within the Bolshevik world, such that the Jewish element could perhaps be displaced by a more or less Russian nationalist element. Then it would also not be impossible for today's actually Jewish-capitalist Bolshevik Russia to be driven to [a] nationalist-anticapitalist tendencies. In that case, which perhaps seems to be evident in some respects, it would then indeed be conceivable that western European capitalism would adopt a serious anti-Russian attitude. But even then an alliance between Germany and this Russia would be utter insanity. Because the idea that such an alliance could somehow be kept secret is just as unfounded as the hope of arming for the conflict through silent military preparations.

There would really be only two possibilities in this situation: Either this alliance would or would not be viewed as a danger by the western European world then coming forward against Russia. If yes, then I do not know who seriously believes that we would have time to obtain armaments that would be capable, at least, of preventing a collapse for the first twenty-four hours. Or do people seriously believe that France would then wait until we had upgraded our air defense and antitank defense? Or do people believe that this could happen secretly in a land in which betrayal is no longer considered shameless but a courageous deed worthy of admiration?[283] No, if Germany really wished to conclude an alliance with Russia against western Europe today, then tomorrow Germany would again be a battlefield of history. And then it would be a very unusual fantasy to imagine that Russia somehow—I don't know in what way— could come to Germany's assistance. The only result of such an action would be that Russia could thus perhaps for a certain time still get by [*sic*] the catastrophe by initially driving into Germany. But [*sic*] a more popular reason for such a war against Germany could not exist particularly in the western states. Imagine Germany allied with a truly anticapitalist Russia, and then envision how the democratic international Jewish press would mobilize all the instincts of the other nations against Germany. How especially in France complete harmony would immediately be restored between French nationalist chauvinism and the Jewish financial press. Because one cannot confuse such an instance with the battles of the White Russian generals against Bolshevism back then. In [*19*]19 and [*19*]20 nationalist White Russia[284] fought against the Jewish-financial (in reality, in the truest sense, international-capitalistic) Red revolution. Today, however, anticapitalist Bolshevism—which has become nationalist—would be at war with international Jewry. Those who know the significance of the propaganda of he press, and its unlimited opportunity to agitate and make the people stupid, can imagine what orgies of hatred and passion the western European nations would be whipped up to against Germany. Because then Germany would no longer be allied with the Russia of a great, remarkable, ethical, and bold idea, but with the desecrators of human culture.

There could, particularly for the French government, be no better opportunity to master its own internal difficulties than to take up a fight against Germany that in such a case would be completely without risk. The French nationalist chauvinists could be all the more content if then, under the protection of a new international coalition, they could move significantly closer to the fulfillment of their ultimate war aim. Because regardless of the nature of the alliance between Germany and Russia, militarily Germany would have to endure the most terrible blows alone. Aside from the fact that Russia does not share a direct border with Germany and would therefore have to first overrun the Polish state, even in the case of a defeat of Poland by Russia—which is already unlikely[285]—such Russian assistance would essentially [*sic*] at best be able to reach the German area when there is no longer a Germany. But the idea of a landing of Russian divisions somewhere in Germany can be totally excluded as long as England and France completely dominate at sea, including the Baltic. In addition, the landing of Russian troops in Germany would fail anyway due to countless technical defects.

So if a German-Russian alliance were one day to have to stand the test of reality—and there are no alliances without thoughts of war—then Germany would be exposed to the concentric attacks of all of western Europe without being able to mount any serious resistance of its own.

But now the question remains of what purpose a German-Russian alliance should have anyway. Only that of protecting Russia from obliteration and in return sacrificing Germany? Because regardless of how this alliance would end, Germany could not reach an ultimate foreign policy objective. In terms of the fundamental vital question—yes, the critical need of our people—nothing will be changed by this. On the contrary, Germany would then be prevented more than ever from pursuing a single, rational policy of space, in order to occupy its future with quarrels over insignificant border adjustments. Because the question of space for our people cannot be solved either in the west or in the south of Europe.

However, the hope of a German-Russian alliance—a hope that is haunting the minds of many nationalist German politicians—is very doubtful for yet another reason.

It generally seems self-evident in nationalist circles that Germany cannot very well ally itself with a Jewish-Bolshevist Russia because the result in all likelihood would be the Bolshevization of Germany itself. It is obvious that they do not want this. But they base their hope on the disappearance one day of the Jewish and therefore fundamentally international-capitalistic character of Bolshevism, to be replaced by a nationalist, anticapitalist communism. This Russia, once again filled with nationalist tendencies, would then very much come into consideration for an alliance relationship with Germany.

This is a very grave error. It is based on an extraordinary lack of knowledge of the psyche of the Slavic people's soul. One cannot be astonished by this if one considers how little knowledge even politicizing Germany had about the mental state of its former allies. Otherwise we would never have fallen so far. If these Russophile nationalist politicians attempt today to motivate their policy through references to analogous positions of Bismarck, then they ignore a whole series of important factors that argued for a pro-Russian policy back then and against today.

The Russia that Bismarck knew was not a typical Slavic state, at least in terms of political leadership. Slavic peoples themselves generally lack state-forming powers. Particularly in Russia, state formation was always managed by foreign elements. Since the time of Peter the Great, there were above all many Germans (Baltics!)[286] who formed the framework and the brain of the Russian state. Over the course of centuries, countless thousands of these Germans were Russified, but only in the same sense that our national bourgeoisie wishes to Germanize or Teutonize Poles and Czechs. Just as in this case the fresh-baked "German" is in reality only a German-speaking Pole or Czech, these artificial Russians, according to their blood and thus their capabilities, remained Germans—or better, Teutons. Russia owed its existence as a state, as well as the little cultural value present, to this Teutonic upper class.[287] Without this essentially German upper class and intelligentsia, a Greater Russia would not have emerged, nor could it have preserved itself. Now as long as Russia was a state with autocratic forms of government, this upper class (which in reality was not at all Russian) also decisively influenced the political life of this huge empire. And Bismarck, at least to a certain degree, still knew this Russia. The master of German statecraft undertook political dealings with this Russia. But already during his lifetime, the reliability [especially with which one from Russia] and stability of Russian policy, both internally and externally, had become precariously shaky and somewhat unpredictable. This was due to the gradual pushing back of the Germanic upper class. This process of the conversion of the Russian intelligentsia was partly a consequence of the great losses suffered by the Russian people as a result of countless wars, which—as already mentioned in this book—decimate primarily the racially more valuable forces. In reality, the officer corps in particular was for the most part of non-Slavic descent, but in any case not of Russian blood. In addition, there was the more limited reproduction rate of the upper levels of the intelligentsia itself, and finally the training upward of a true ethnic Russian people, artificially achieved through education. The limited state-maintaining value of the new Russian intelligentsia itself was genetically based and showed itself perhaps most clearly in the nihilism of the Russian system of higher education.[288] At the most fundamental level, however, this nihilism was nothing but the genetically based opposition of the real Russian people against the racially foreign upper class.

As the Germanic state-forming upper class in Russia was replaced by a racially pure Russian bourgeois class, the Russian notion of the state was confronted with the pan-Slavic idea. From the very hour of its birth, it was completely ethnic [Russian] Slavic and anti-German.

But the anti-German disposition of the newly developing Russian people, especially among the so-called intelligentsia, was not simply a pure reflex action against the previous autocratic, foreign upper class in Russia, based on some concept of political freedom; rather, at the deepest level it was a protest of the Slavic character against the German. These are two ethnic souls that have very little in common, and it must even first be established whether or not the little that they do share does not arise from the chaos of individual racial elements from which the Russian as well as the German people seem to be composed. So that which is common to us Germans and the Russians is no more a reflection of the German character than the Russian, and can only be attributed to the mixing of our blood, which has brought eastern, Slavic elements to Germany just as it has brought Nordic-German elements to Russia.

However, if one were to examine the nature of the two souls by taking a pure Nordic German—let us say, from Westphalia— and contrasting him with a pure Slavic Russian, an infinite chasm would open between these representatives of the two peoples. Actually, the Slavic-Russian people has always felt this as well, and thus has always had an instinctive aversion to Germans. The rigorous thoroughness as well as the cold logic and matter-of-fact thinking are inwardly unappealing to the true Russian, and to some degree also incomprehensible. Our sense of order will not only find no reciprocal affinity, but will instead always generate antipathy. What we see as a matter of course is thus a torment for the Russian, as it represents a limitation of his natural, different mental and motivational life. Therefore, Slavic Russia will also always feel itself drawn more and more toward France. And even to an increasing degree, as the Frankish-Nordic elements are pushed back also in France. The easy, superficial, more or less effeminate French life can captivate the Slavs more, as it is more closely related to them than is the harshness of our German struggle for survival. It is thus also no coincidence that politically pan-Slavic Russia gushed over France, just as the Russian intelligentsia of Slavic blood found in Paris the Mecca of its own needs for civilization.

The ascension process of the Russian nationalist bourgeoisie also [meant] accounted for the inner alienation of this new Russia from Germany, which could no longer build upon a racially related Russian upper class.

Indeed, the anti-German attitude of the representatives of the ethnic pan-Slavic idea was already so strong by the turn of the century, and its influence on Russian policy so developed, that even Germany's more than decent stance toward Russia with regard to the Russo-Japanese War[289] could not stop the further estrangement of the two states. The Great War came, which pan-Slavic agitation had very much helped to ignite. The true national Russia insofar as it was represented by the previous upper class, had hardly any say about this.

The Great War itself then brought about [the last] a further bleeding of Russia's Nordic-German elements, and the last remnants were finally eradicated by the revolution and Bolshevism. It is not as if the Slavic racial instinct alone deliberately carried out the extermination battle against the previous non-Russian upper class. No, in the meantime it had received its new leadership in Jewry. With the help of the Slavic racial instinct, the Jews—pushing toward the upper class and therefore upper leadership—exterminated the previous foreign upper class. Because if, with the Bolshevik Revolution, Jews took over leadership in all areas of Russian life, then this is a self-evident process, because in and of itself the Slavic people completely lacks any organizational capability and thus also any state-forming and state-maintaining power. If one were to pull out of the Slavic people all of the elements that are not purely Slavic, then the state would also immediately break up. Fundamentally, every state formation can indeed initially have its deepest cause in the coming together of peoples of higher and lower rank, whereby the carriers of the higher-quality blood—out of reasons of self-preservation—develop a certain spirit of community that first allows them the possibility of organizing and controlling the inferiors. Only the overcoming of common tasks [for] compels organizational forms. But the difference between state-forming and non-state-forming elements lies in the fact that it is possible for the former to create an organization to preserve their kind over other beings, whereas those who are incapable of state formation are themselves incapable of finding that organizational form that would ensure their existence above others.

Thus, current Russia—or, better, the current Slavic people of Russian nationality—obtained the Jew as masters [*sic*], who first eliminated the previous upper class and now had to prove its own state-forming power. But due to the overall tendency of Judaism, which is ultimately only destructive, this will only act as the historical "ferment of decomposition"[290] here as well. It called for help from spirits that it will no longer be able to get rid of, and the fight of the inwardly antinational pan-Slavic idea against the Bolshevik Jewish notion of the state will end with the destruction of Jewry. But what will then remain will be a Russia with limited national power and a deep-rooted anti-German attitude. Because this state will no longer possess a state-maintaining upper class that is anchored in any way, it will become a source of perpetual agitation and uncertainty. A gigantic land mass will thus be handed over to a most changeable fate, and instead of a stabilization of the relations between nations on the earth, a period of troubled changes will begin.

The first phase of these developments will be that the most varied nations of the world will attempt to establish relations with this vast state complex in order to bring about a strengthening of their own positions and intentions in this way. But such an attempt will also always be linked with the effort to exercise a spiritual and organizational influence on Russia.

Germany cannot hope to come into consideration in any way in this development. The entire mentality of current and future Russia is opposed to it. For Germany, a future alliance with Russia has no sense, neither from the standpoint of sober expediency nor from that of a human connection. On the contrary—it is fortunate for the future that this development took place in this way, because it broke a spell that would have prevented us from seeking the goal of German foreign policy in the one and only place possible: space in the East.

[CHAPTER XII]

[Principles of German Foreign Policy]

In the construction of the future German foreign policy, the following must be considered in view of Germany's hopeless military situation:

1) Germany itself cannot bring about a change in its current situation if this must be accomplished through military resources.

2) Germany cannot hope that a change in its situation will occur through the measures of the League of Nations, as long as the influential representatives of this institution are at the same time those with an interest in Germany's destruction.

3) Germany cannot hope to change its current situation through a combination of powers that brings it into conflict with the French alliance system surrounding Germany, unless Germany has prior opportunity to remedy its purely military powerlessness in order to be able to act militarily—immediately, and with likelihood of success—in the case of [an application] the inocation of alliance obligations.

4) Germany cannot hope to find such a combination of powers until its ultimate foreign policy goal appears to be established

with complete clarity and does not conflict with the interests of those states—yes, and even seems useful to them—that could come into consideration as alliance partners for Germany.

5) Germany cannot hope that these will be states outside the League of Nations; rather, it must, on the contrary, exist[291] its only hope in its success at breaking individual states away from the previous coalition of victors and creating a new interest group with new goals whose realization cannot be achieved through the League of Nations, based on its very nature.

6) Germany can only hope to attain success in this way if it definitively renounces its previous vacillating dithering policy and fundamentally decides on one direction and also takes on and bears all the consequences.

7) Germany should never hope to be able to make world history through alliances with peoples whose military worth is inferior—this being adequately identified either through the fact of their previous defeat or their general racial significance. Because the fight to regain German freedom will again raise German history to world history again.

8) Germany should not forget for one instant that regardless of how and in what way it intends to change its fate, France will be its enemy, and that any coalition of powers that turns against Germany can from the outset count on France.

[CHAPTER XIII]

[The Possible Goals]

One cannot examine Germany's foreign policy options without first achieving clarity about what Germans themselves want—how Germany itself intends to shape its future. Then one must also attempt to clarify the foreign policy aims of those European powers that, as members of the coalition of victors, have the significance of world powers.

In this book I have already addressed Germany's various foreign policy options. However, I would like to state again very briefly the possible foreign policy goals, so that [to them] [through them] they can be used as a basis for a critical examination of the relationship of these individual foreign policy goals to those of the other European states.

1) Germany can dispense with a fundamental foreign policy objective altogether. That means in reality that it can decide on everything and it does not need to commit to anything.

It will thus continue the policies of the last thirty years in the future as well, but under different conditions. Now, if the world were entirely made up of similarly politically aimless states, this would at least be endurable for Germany, though not at all justifiable. But this is not the case. So just as in everyday life a person with a clear-cut life goal, which he strives to reach under all circumstances, will always be superior to others who are aimless, it is the same in the life of nations as well. Above all, though, this is certainly not to say that a state without political objectives will be in a position to avoid the dangers that having such a one could perhaps bring. Because although [yes] he seems relieved from active operation as a result of his own political aimlessness, he can in his passivity easily become the victim of the political goals of others. Because the actions of a state are not determined by its own will alone, but also by that of others, but with the difference that in the one case the state can control its own initiative, while in the other it is forced upon it. Not wanting a war because one has a peaceful disposition certainly does not necessarily mean also being able to avoid it. And wanting to avoid a war at any cost certainly does not necessarily mean saving life from death.

Germany's position in Europe today is such that it cannot hope at all, with its own political aimlessness, to live in a situation of introspective tranquility. Such a possibility does not exist for a people that is located in the middle of the heart of Europe. Either Germany attempts to collaborate actively in the arrangement of its life, or it will be a passive object of the life arrangements of other peoples. All wisdom that previously pretended that peoples could be pulled out of historical dangers by declaring a general disinterest has thus far always been exposed as a cowardly and dumb mistake. Anyone who does not wish to be the hammer will be the anvil in history. Our German people, in its entire previous development, has had only these two options to choose between. If it wanted to make history itself, it accordingly committed itself joyfully and boldly, and then it was always the hammer. But if it believed it could renounce the obligations of the struggle for survival, then it was always the anvil upon which either others fought out their own struggle for survival, or it even served the foreigners as nourishment.

So if Germany wishes to live, it must take on the defense of this life, and here as well the best parry has always been the strike. No, Germany absolutely cannot hope to be able to do anything more for its own life arrangement if it does not create for itself a clear foreign policy objective that seems capable of bringing the German struggle for survival in prudent relation to the interests of other peoples.

But if this is not done, then the general aimlessness will lead to aimlessness in the details. This aimlessness will gradually turn us into a second Poland in Europe. To the degree that we [*allow?*] our own powers to become weaker thanks to our general political defeatism, and the only activity of our life expresses itself in domestic policy, we will, from a foreign policy perspective, be reduced to a plaything of the events of world history, events whose motivating forces arise from other peoples' struggle for survival and the pursuit of their interests.

In addition, peoples that are unable to reach a clear decision about their own future and accordingly would rather not take part in the game of world development are viewed by all the players as spoilsports and are consistently hated. Yes, then it can even happen that the aimlessness of individual political actions, based on the overall foreign policy aimlessness, is, on the contrary, viewed as a very clever, nontransparent game and is responded to accordingly. This was one of the misfortunes that befell us in the prewar period. The more nontransparent, because incomprehensible, the political decisions of the German Reich government were at the time, the more suspicious they seemed and the more particularly dangerous ideas were scented behind even the dumbest steps.

So if Germany does not bring itself to create a clear political objective today, then it thus essentially renounces all possibility of revising our current fate, without being able in the least to evade [the] further dangers in the future.

2) Germany wishes to feed the German people through peaceful economic means, as before. Accordingly, it wishes also in the

future to participate most decisively in international industry, export, and trade. For this reason it wishes to have a large merchant fleet again, coal refueling stations, and bases in the rest of the world, and desires in the end not only international markets for its goods but when possible also raw material sources of its own in the form of colonies. In the future, such a development would inevitably have to be protected, particularly by naval power.

This entire future political goal is a utopia, unless England is crushed beforehand. It again produces all the causes that in 1914 ended in the Great War. Any attempt by Germany to rebuild its past in this way must end with the deadly enmity of England, which, from the beginning, can count on France as its most reliable partner.

Viewed from the ethnic standpoint this foreign policy objective is disastrous, and from the power-political standpoint it is insane.[292]

3) Germany establishes as its foreign policy goal the restoration of the 1914 borders.

This goal is inadequate from the national standpoint, unsatisfactory from the military standpoint, impossible from the forward-looking ethnic standpoint, and insane from the standpoint of its consequences. Germany thus faces the entire previous coalition of victors as a cohesive front of adversaries in the future as well. But how the old borders could be restored, considering our current military situation, which will become worse from year to year if the current circumstances continue, is the most impenetrable secret of our nationalist-bourgeois and patriotic state politicians.

4) Germany decides [its future goal] to adopt a clear, farsighted policy of space. It thus turns away from all international industrial and international trade policy attempts and instead concentrates all of its strength on marking out a way of life for our people through the allocation of adequate Lebensraum for the next one hundred years. Because this space can lie only in the East, the obligation of a naval power takes a back seat. Germany again attempts to fight for its interests by forming a decisive power on land.

This goal corresponds equally to the highest national and ethnic requirements. It also presumes great military power resources for its implementation, but does not necessarily bring Germany into conflict with all the European great powers. France will certainly remain Germany's enemy here as well, but the nature of such a foreign policy goal does not give reason for England and especially Italy to maintain the enmity of the Great War.

[Chapter XIV]

[Germany and England]

To better understand the possibilities just mentioned, it is appropriate to examine the major foreign policy aims of the other European powers. These aims are in part identifiable through the previous actions and dealings of these states, in part they are also programmatically defined, and in part they lie in the life necessities that are so clearly identifiable that even if these states momentarily followed other paths the constraints of a harsher reality would bring them back to these goals.

That England has a clear foreign policy objective is evidenced by the fact of the existence and thus the development of this huge empire. No one can imagine that such an empire could ever be forged without having a clear will to do so. Of course, not every individual member of such a nation then goes to work every day thinking about the great foreign policy objective, but gradually the entire people will very naturally be engaged by such an objective, so that even the unconscious actions of individuals nevertheless follow the general direction of this objective and actually even assist it as well. Yes, gradually the collective political goal will be expressed in the very essence of such a people, and the pride of the English today is no different than the pride of the ancient Romans. It is mistaken to believe that world empires owed their origin to chance or that at least the events that determined their development were random historical incidents that always turned out well for a people. Ancient Rome, just like England today, owed its greatness to the correctness of Moltke's[293] dictum that in the long run luck is only with the competent.[294] This competence of a people, however, does not lie in its racial worth alone, but also in the capability and skillfulness with which this worth is employed. A world empire of the magnitude of ancient Rome or current Great Britain is always the result of marrying the highest genetic quality with the clearest political objective. As soon as one of these two factors begins to be insufficient, a weakening results initially and ultimately perhaps even a decline.

The objective of today's England is determined by the quality of the Anglo-Saxon people itself and the insular location. It was part of the Anglo-Saxon people's character to pursue space. Inevitably, this drive could only find its fulfillment outside today's Europe. Not that the English have not tried from time to time to obtain land for their expansionary appetite in Europe as well, but all of these attempts failed due to the fact that they were confronted by states with—at least at that time—no less great racial competence. The later English expansion in the so-called colonies led from the beginning to an extraordinary increase in English maritime activity. It is interesting to see how England, which first exported people, finally moved to the export of goods, in the process even reducing its own agriculture. Although a great share of the current English people now—yes, the average, generally—is below the highest German value, a centuries-long tradition has become so much a part of the flesh and blood of this people that it possesses significant political advantages over our German people. If the earth has an English world empire today, then there is also no people that would currently be more qualified for it based on its general national political attributes as well as its average political savvy.

The fundamental idea that governed English colonial policy was, on the one hand, finding outlets for the English population and maintaining their national connection to the motherland, and, on the other hand, securing markets and sources of raw materials for the English economy. It is understandable if the Englishman believes that the German cannot colonize [as], just as it is understandable if, vice versa, the German believes the same of the Englishman. The two peoples take different positions in assessing colonizing capabilities. The English was an infinitely more practical and sober one, and the German a more romantic one. When Germany pursued its first colonies, it was already a military state and thus a first-rank power in Europe. It had earned itself the label of world power through enduring achievements in all areas of human culture, but also in the area of military capability. Now, it was noteworthy that especially in the nineteenth century, a general pull toward colonization affected all peoples; the original governing idea, however, had already given way completely. Germany, for example, justified its right to colonize with its competence and its desire to disseminate German culture. This is nonsense. Because one cannot transmit culture, which is a general expression of the life of a certain people, to any other people with a completely different mindset. This would at most work with a so-called international civilization, but which has the same relationship to culture as jazz music to a Beethoven symphony. But aside from that, it would never have occurred to an Englishman at the time of the founding of the English colonies to justify his actions in any other way than with the very real and serious advantages that they would bring. When England later acted on behalf of the freedom of the seas or the oppressed nations, it never did so in order to justify its own colonial activity, but only in order to destroy difficult competitors. Thus, the English colonizing activity had to be very successful, in part for the most natural of reasons. Because the less the English thought of attempting to impose something like English culture or English civilization upon the savages, the more congenial such a government must have appeared to the savages, who were not at all culture hungry. In addition, however, there was the whip, which could also be used more easily if one never ran the risk of contradicting a cultural mission. England needed markets and sources of raw materials for its goods. And it secured these markets through power-political means. That is the point of the English colonial policy. Now, when England later nevertheless also spoke of culture, it did so strictly for the benefit of public sentiment, in order to be able to dress up its own very practical actions in moral terms. In reality, the domestic circumstances of the savages were of absolutely no interest to the English as long as they did not affect the circumstances of the English themselves. It is comprehensible and understandable that completely different notions relating to prestige politics later became linked with colonies the size of India. But no one can contest the fact that Indian interests never determined English circumstances, but rather the English determined Indian circumstances. Likewise, it also cannot be denied that the English did not establish any cultural institutions in India so that the natives could share in the English culture, but rather, at most, so that the English could gain greater benefit from their colonies. Or do people believe that England only brought railroads to India in order to give the Indians possession of European transport options, and not to use them to enable more effective exploitation of the colony as well as to guarantee easier control? Today when England again follows in the footsteps of the Pharaohs in Egypt and blocks the Nile with gigantic dams,[295] then it is certainly not doing so to make the mundane existence of the poor fellahin easier, but only to make English cotton independent from the American monopoly. But these are all points that Germany [*never?*] dared to consider openly with regard to its colonial policy. The English became educators of the natives in the interests of England, and the German was the teacher. The fact that in the end the natives perhaps might even have felt better under us than under the English would, to a normal Englishman, speak far more in favor of the English type of colonization policy than of ours.

This policy of a gradual conquest of the world, in which economic power and political power always went hand in hand, determined England's attitude toward the other states. The more England grew into its position as an international colonial power, the more it required dominance at sea, and the more dominant it became at sea, the more it in turn became a colonial power; but the more jealously it also finally began to watch over its position, so that no one would dispute its dominance at sea or the possession of its colonies.

In Germany in particular, a very erroneous idea is widespread, namely that England would immediately fight any dominant European power. This is actually not correct. England has actually not concerned itself greatly with European affairs, as long as no threatening competitor arose from among the European powers; and it always saw the threat only in terms of a development that was certain one day to impede its maritime and colonial dominance.

No European conflict exists for England in which it would not have looked after its trade and overseas interests. The wars against Spain, Holland, and later France[296] had their cause not in the threatening military power of these states per se, but only in the basis of this power as well as the effects of the same. If Spain had not been an overseas power and thus a competitor of England, then England would presumably have taken little notice of Spain. The same holds true for Holland. And even England's later gigantic war against France was not carried out against the continental France of Napoleon but against the Napoleonic France that viewed its continental policy as merely a springboard and basis for greater, not at all continental, aims. Due to its geographic location, France will be the most threatening power to England. France was perhaps the only state that could hold within itself threats to the future of England, even when pursuing a certain continental development. But it is all the more noteworthy, and instructive for us Germans, that England nevertheless decided to side with France in the Great War. Instructive because it shows that despite adhering to the great fundamental idea of English foreign policy, the English always took into account the currently available options and never simply renounced them because a threat to England could arise from them as well in some nearer or more distant future. Our "God punish England"[297] politicians always think that a good future relationship with England must always fail because England would never seriously consider supporting Germany through an alliance, only to confront it again one day as a threatening power. Of course the English will not conclude an alliance with Germany in order to promote Germany, but only to advance British interests. But England has thus far offered numerous examples of very often being able to marry the pursuit of its own interests with the pursuit of other nations' interests, and then turning to alliances despite the fact that in all probability even these must later turn into hostility. Because ultimately, political marriages always succumb sooner or later to divorce, because they do not serve the common pursuit of the two parties' interests, but only wish to employ common means to defend or advance the two states' interests which are in principle different but at the time not in conflict.

That England does not fundamentally oppose a European great power of preeminent military significance, as long as the foreign policy aims of this power are obviously of a strictly continental nature, is evidenced by its attitude toward Prussia. Or will anyone deny that under Frederick the Great the Prussian military power was without a doubt by far the strongest in Europe? One cannot believe that the only reason England did not fight this Prussia back then[298] was that despite its military hegemony it had to be counted among the smaller states because of the size of its territory in Europe. Not at all. Because when England fought its battles against the Dutch, the Dutch state territory in Europe was significantly smaller that the Prussian territory of the late Frederician period, and one could certainly not speak of a threatening hegemony or a position of superior power in the case of Holland. But when England nevertheless contended with the Dutch in decades-long battles, then the reason was exclusively due only to the threatening of English maritime and trade dominance by the Dutch, as well as to the general Dutch colonial-policy activities. And no illusions should be cherished there: If the Prussian state had not devoted itself so exclusively to strictly continental aims, then England would forever have been its fiercest enemy, regardless of the extent of Prussia's purely military power resources in Europe or the danger of Prussia becoming hegemonic in Europe. The successors of the Great Elector[299] are not infrequently bitterly reproached by our rarely-thinking nationalist patriotic politicians with the charge that they neglected the overseas possessions obtained by the Great Elector—yes, even abandoned them—and therefore also had no interest in the maintenance and expansion of a Brandenburg-Prussian fleet.[300] It was fortunate for Prussia and the future Germany that this was so.

Nothing speaks for the outstanding statesmanlike wisdom of Friedrich Wilhelm I[301] in particular [*than*] the fact that, with the greatest economy, he concentrated the extremely limited means of the small Prussian state exclusively on the support of the land army. Not only because this small state could thus obtain a superior position in one [kind of] force, but in this way he also avoided the enmity of England. A Prussia following in the steps of Holland, however, could not have fought the three Silesian wars with England as an enemy in the rear as well. Not to mention the fact that every attempt by the small Prussian state to achieve prestige as a true naval power would necessarily have failed in the end as a result of the extremely limited—and very unfavorably positioned from a military perspective—territorial basis of the motherland. Already at that time, it would have been child's play for the English to eliminate the dangerous competitor in Europe through a general coalition war. The fact that the future Prussia could arise at all from tiny Brandenburg, and a new German Reich from that future Prussia, was due only to the wise insight into the true power relations, as well as into Prussia's options at the time, which caused the Hohenzollerns—until into the Bismarckian period—to limit themselves almost exclusively to the strengthening of the land force. It was the only clear, logical policy. If German Prussia and then later Germany wanted to have a future at all, then this future could only be safeguarded through a supremacy on land that corresponded to the English supremacy at sea. It was unfortunate for Germany that people gradually moved away from this realization; the land force was inadequately expanded, and instead a naval policy was adopted which produced only half results in the end anyway.[302] Even the Germany of the post-Bismarckian period could not afford the luxury of creating and maintaining superior forces on land and at sea at the same time. But it is one of the most important principles of all time that a people must identify the weapon that is inevitably most necessary to preserve its existence, and then promote it to the utmost through the commitment of all means possible. England realized this and adhered to it. Because for England, dominance at sea was truly the be-all and end-all of its existence. Even the most illustrious military periods on the mainland, the most glorious wars, and the incomparable military outcomes could not bring the English to view the land force in the end as anything [*other than*] only secondary for England, and to concentrate the entire strength of the nation on the preservation of a superior dominance at sea. In Germany, however, people let themselves be swept along by the great colonial wave of the nineteenth century, perhaps also strengthened by romantic memories of the old Hansa[303] as well as driven by the peaceful economic policy. The exclusive focus on the land army was disregarded, and the construction of a fleet began. This policy then gained its ultimate expression in the equally perverse and calamitous statement "Our future lies on the water."[304] No, quite the contrary—for us in Europe it did and does lie on land, just as the causes of our downfall will also always be only of a purely continental nature: our position, which is disastrous in terms of space and terrible from a military-geographic perspective.

As long as Prussia limited its foreign policy desires to strictly European goals, it did not need to fear serious threats from England. The objection that a pro-France disposition nevertheless dominated in England as early as 1870-71[305] is inaccurate and proves nothing in any case. Because a pro-German attitude dominated in England then as well—yes, France's actions were even decried as an outrage from the pulpits of English churches. In addition, it is the actually officially held stance that is decisive. Because it is quite natural that in a state as significant as England, there will be ongoing fondness for France as well, especially since it is not uncommon for foreign monies to exert influence on a nation's press. France has always understood how to mobilize positive feelings for itself in a very skillful manner. In doing so, it has always played on Paris as its most excellent assisting weapon. This did not take place only in England, however, but even in Germany. In the middle of the '70-'71 war, even in the Berlin community—yes, in Berlin court circles—there was a sizeable clique that made absolutely no secret of its pro-French sympathies and in any case figured out how to delay the bombardment of Paris for quite some time.[306] In addition, it is understandable, from a human perspective, that the German military success was viewed with tempered joy in English circles. They could not in any case shift the official stance of the English state government toward any sort of intervention. The idea that this was only attributable to the Russian rear cover that Bismarck had secured does not change anything either. Because this rear cover was primarily intended against Austria. But if England had given up its neutral stance at that time, then even the Russian rear cover would not have been able to avert an extensive conflagration. Because then Austria, more than ever, would have taken part again and in one way or another the success of 1871 would have been prevented. Bismarck actually had an ongoing silent fear of the interference of other states, not only in the war but even in the peace negotiations as well. Because what happened to Russia a few years later[307] could have been arranged just as easily against Germany as well, through England's instigation of the intervention of other powers.

The change in the English attitude toward Germany can be easily traced. It parallels our development at sea, builds up to open animosity with our colonial activity, and finally, with our naval policy, ends in open hatred.[308] But the fact that the English sensed a future threat in the development of such a competent people as the Germans cannot really be held against [*sic*] a truly concerned state leadership. One can never use our German sins of omission as the standard for judging the actions of others. The carelessness with which Germany after the time of Bismarck allowed its power-political situation in Europe to be threatened by France and Russia, without seriously undertaking any countermeasures, does not in any way allow one to expect the same of other powers or to express moral indignation when they better safeguard the vital interests of their peoples.

If prewar Germany, instead of pursuing its world peace and economic policy with its disastrous repercussions, had decided to continue the previous Prussian continental policy, then it could [*sic*], first, raise its land force to the truly outstanding level that the Prussian state once reached, and second, it did not need [*sic*] to fear absolute antagonism with England. Because this much is certain: If Germany had used all the prodigious resources that it poured into the fleet[309] for the strengthening of the land army, then its interests could at least have been championed differently on the decisive European battlefields, and the nation would have been spared that fate of seeing an in parts very insufficiently equipped land army gradually bleeding to death at the hands of a crushing international coalition, while the navy, at least its major battle units, rusted away in the ports, only to end its existence with a more than disgraceful surrender.[310] One does not thereby excuse the commanders, but one must have the courage to admit that this lay in the nature of this weapon for us. Because during that same time the field army was pulled out of one battle and thrown into another, without regard for casualties or other distress. The land army was really the German weapon, grown out of a hundred-year tradition; our fleet, however, was in the end only a romantic plaything, a display piece that was created for its own sake and that again for its own sake could not be employed. The total benefit that it provided us is far outweighed by the terrible enmity that it brought upon us. [I]

[With that will be] If Germany had not undertaken this development, then we could still at the turn of the century have reached an understanding with England, which was ready to compromise at that time. However, such an understanding would only have lasted then if it were accompanied by a fundamental reorientation of our foreign policy objectives. At the turn of the century Germany could still decide to take up the earlier Prussian continental policy again and define the further development of world history together with England. The objection by our perpetual waverers and skeptics that this would have been uncertain anyway is based on nothing but personal opinion. Previous English history speaks against it, in any case. With what right does such a doubter assume that Germany could not have played the same role that Japan played? The dumb expression that the [*sic*] Germany would then pull the English chestnuts out of the fire could then just as well be applied to Frederick the Great, who ultimately also helped to facilitate, on the battlefields of Europe, England's non-European conflict with France. Also the further objection that England would have turned against Germany one day anyway is almost too dumb to mention. Because even in that case the German position would always have been better, after a successful defeat of Russia, than it was at the beginning of the Great War. On the contrary, if the Russo-Japanese War had been fought out in Europe between Germany and Russia, then Germany would have gained such an increase in purely moral power that for the next thirty years any other European power would have thought very carefully about breaking the peace and allowing itself to be badgered into a coalition against Germany. But all of these objections always arise from the mentality of prewar Germany, which even as opposition always knew everything and did nothing.

The fact is that England approached Germany back then, and further, that on the German side, due to the mentality of these perpetual hesitant waverers, no clear opinion could be reached.[311] What Germany declined at that time, Japan then procured,[312] thereby obtaining the glory of a world power in a relatively inexpensive manner.

But if those in Germany did not want to do this under any circumstances, then they should have supported the other side. 1904 or [19]05 could [*sic*] then be used for a conflict with France and would have had Russia in the rear. But these hesitators and waverers did not want that either. Out of pure caution and pure scruples and pure knowledge, they were never able to establish what they actually wanted. And the superiority of the English state leadership is based only on the fact that there they are not ruled by such know-it-alls who can then never bring themselves to take an action, but rather by very naturally thinking persons for whom politics really is an art of the possible, but who then also seize all possibilities and truly strike with them.[313]

But as soon as Germany had stepped aside from such a fundamental understanding with England which, as already mentioned, would admittedly only have made lasting sense if those in Berlin had arrived at a clear continental objective focusing on a policy of space, England began to organize the international opposition to the threat to British interests of maritime dominance.

The Great War itself, in view of the military capability of our people, unsuspected even in England, did not proceed as initially expected. Germany was indeed finally wrestled down, but only after the American union appeared on the battlefield[314] and Germany, as a result of its internal collapse, lost the rear support of the homeland.[315] But even with that the actual English war aim was not achieved. Because although the German threat to English dominance at sea was eliminated, the American one, which stands on much stronger foundations, appeared in its place. In the future, the greatest danger to England will no longer be in Europe at all, but in North America. In Europe itself, the state posing the greatest threat to England is currently France. Its military hegemony has a particularly threatening significance for England as a result of the geographic position that France occupies in relation to England. It is not only that a large number of important English population centers appear virtually defenseless against French air attacks, [*but that?*] some English cities can even be reached with long-range guns from the French coast. Yes, if modern technology succeeds in bringing about a further significant increase in the firing range of the heaviest long-range guns, then even shelling London from the French mainland would not be outside the realm of possibility.[316] But even more importantly, a French submarine war against England has a completely different base than the German one had during the Great War. France's wide coastal basis on two seas would make it very difficult to implement blockade measures such as those that succeeded easily against the constricted *nasse Dreieck*.[317]

Anyone who attempts to find natural enemies for England in today's Europe will always come upon France and Russia. France as a power with continental political aims that are in reality always only a cover for wide-ranging general global political intentions. Russia as a threatening enemy of India and a possessor of oil fields, which have the same significance today as iron and coal mines had in the past century.

If England itself remains true to its great international political aims, then its potential adversaries in Europe will be France and Russia, and in the rest of the world in the future especially the American union.

There is, however, no reason for the perpetuation of the English animosity toward Germany. Otherwise, English foreign policy would be determined by motives that are removed from all real logic, and thus perhaps only in the mind of a German professor could they have significant influence on the determination of the political relations between the peoples. No, in the future England will take its stance just as level-headedly as it has for three hundred years, based strictly on grounds of expediency. And just as England's allies have been able to become enemies and enemies allies again over the past three hundred years, this will always be the case in the future as well, provided general and particular exigencies argue in its favor. If, however, Germany arrives at a fundamental political reorientation that no longer conflicts with the maritime and trade interests of England, but instead limits itself to continental goals, then there is no longer a logical basis for English hostility, which would then just be hostility for hostility's sake. Because the European balance also interests England only as long as it prevents the emergence of an international trade and naval power that could threaten England. There is no foreign policy leadership that would have been less influenced by unrealistic doctrines than the English would. A world empire does not emerge by means of sentimental or purely theoretical policies.

Thus, levelheaded recognition of British interests will be decisive for English foreign policy in the future as well. Anyone who interferes with these interests will therefore be England's enemy in the future as well. England will not touch the existence of anyone who does not touch its interests. And England will invite onto its side any power that can be useful to it from time to time, regardless of whether it was previously an enemy and perhaps might become one again in the future.

But to reject an advantageous alliance because later it might one day perhaps end in animosity—that is something only a German bourgeois nationalist politician could achieve. To expect that of an Englishman is to isult the political instinct of this people.

If, of course, Germany does not settle upon any political objective and thus, as before, struggles forward from day to day, aimless and without any guiding ideas, or if this objective lies in the restoration of the 1914 borders and possessions and thus in the end brings us back to our international trade, colonial, and naval power policies, then English hostility will indeed be certain in the future as well. Then Germany will suffocate economically under its Dawes burdens,[318] degenerate politically under its Locarno agreements, become progressively weaker racially, and finally end its existence in Europe as a second Holland and as a second Switzerland. Our bourgeois-nationalist and patriotic armchair politicians can already achieve this; they only need to continue down the path of their current rhetorical flailing, hurling verbal protests, fighting all of Europe, and creeping spinelessly into their holes before every action. This is what is then known as the nationalist-bourgeois-patriotic policy for revitalizing Germany. Just as our bourgeoisie figured out in the course of less than sixty years how to debase and compromise the term "nationalist," in the same way, in its downfall, it is now destroying the beautiful term "patriotic" by degrading it to mere rhetoric in its associations.

But another important factor for England's attitude toward Germany appeared as well: world Jewry, which also exerts a controlling influence in England. Although the English people itself will certainly be able to overcome the war psychosis vis-à-vis Germany, it is just as certain that world Jewry will leave nothing undone to keep the old enmities alive, to prevent a pacification [*sic*] of Europe, and to enable—in the confusion of general turbulence—full expression of its disruptive Bolshevik tendencies.

One cannot speak of world politics without taking this most terrible power into account. I would therefore still like to deal with this problem separately in this book.[319]

[*CHAPTER XV*]

[*Germany and Italy*]

[A]

I f England is not compelled as a matter of principle to maintain its wartime hostility against Germany forever, then Italy even less. Italy is the second state in Europe that does not fundamentally need to be an adversary of Germany—yes, whose foreign policy goals do not need to bring it into conflict with Germany at all. On the contrary, there may be no other state with which Germany has more common interests than Italy, and vice versa.[320]

During the same time period in which Germany attempted to achieve a new national unification, the same process took place in Italy as well.[321] However, the Italians lacked a central power of gradually developing and ultimately preeminent significance, such as the developing Germany possessed in Prussia. But much as the German unification faced primarily France and Austria as true enemies, the Italian unification movement also had the most to suffer under these two powers. Essentially, it was the Habsburg state that had to and did possess a vital interest in maintaining the internal Italian fragmentation. Because a state the size of Austria-Hungary without direct access to the sea is hardly conceivable, and the only area that could come under consideration for this was, at least in the cities, inhabited by Italians, Austria had to actively oppose the emergence of a unified Italian state out of fear of the possible loss of this area in the event of the establishment of an Italian nation state. At that time, even the boldest political goal of the Italian people could focus on nothing but unification. This then had to determine the foreign policy stance as well. [The through Savoy] Thus, as the Italian unification gradually took shape, its brilliant great statesman Cavour[322] availed himself of all the possibilities that could serve this particular purpose. Italy owes the possibility of its unification to an extraordinarily wisely chosen alliance policy. The goal was always present to bring about, first and foremost, a paralysis of the chief enemy of this unification, Austria-Hungary—yes, and ultimately to induce this state to leave the northern Italian provinces. However, even after the completion of the preliminary unification of Italy, there were more than eight hundred thousand Italians in Austria-Hungary alone. The national goal of the further incorporation of people of Italian nationality initially had to be delayed, as threats of an Italian-French estrangement began to appear for the first time. Italy decided, particularly in order to gain time for its internal consolidation, to enter the Triple Alliance.

The Great War finally brought Italy—for reasons I have already mentioned—into the camp of the Entente. That carried Italian unification a massive step further forward; however, even today it is not yet completed. But the greatest event for the Italian state is the elimination of the hated Habsburg Empire. However, in its place has stepped a southern Slavic entity[323] that already represents—from general nationalist viewpoints—a danger to Italy that is not much less.

Because just as the bourgeois nationalist conception of the vital necessities of our people (always seen strictly in terms of border policy) could not be adequate for Germany in the long term, neither could the equally strictly bourgeois nationalist unification policy of the Italian state be adequate for the Italian people.

Like the German people, the Italian people lives on a land area that is too small and also not very fertile in some places. This overpopulation has forced Italy for many decades—centuries, even—to continuously export people.[324] Even though many of these emigrants were seasonal workers and returned to Italy to live off their savings there, this led to an even greater strain on the situation. This not only did not solve the population problem, but aggravated it. Just as Germany, through its exports, became dependent on the capability, possibility, and desire of other powers and countries to purchase its goods, the same happened with Italy and its human exports. In both cases, a slowdown in the receiving markets—due to whatever events—would lead to catastrophic results internally.

Italy's attempt to master the food supply problem through an increase in its industrial activity cannot lead to a definitive success because the shortage of natural resources in the motherland robs Italy of a great share of necessary competitiveness from the beginning.

As soon as the perceptions of a formal bourgeois national policy are overcome in Italy and replaced by an ethnic sense of responsibility, this state will also be forced to depart from its previous political perception in order to turn to a large-scale policy of space.

The natural area for Italian expansion is and remains the land bordering the Mediterranean Sea. The more today's Italy departs from its previous national unification policy and turns to an imperialistic one, the more it will follow the path of ancient Rome—not out of the arrogance of power but out of profound internal necessities.[325] If Germany seeks land today in eastern Europe, then this is not the sign of an exaggerated hunger for power, but only the result of the nation's shortage of land. And if Italy seeks to expand its influence today on the perimeter of the Mediterranean basin, and ultimately wishes to establish colonies,[326] then this is likewise only the natural representation of its interests, triggered by a difficult situation. If the German policy of the prewar period had not been stricken with complete blindness, then it would have had to have supported and promoted this development by all possible means, not only because it would have meant a natural strengthening of our ally, but because it might have offered the only possibility of pulling Italy's interest away from the Adriatic and thus reducing friction with Austria-Hungary. What is more, though, such a policy would have solidified the most natural antagonism that can ever exist—namely, that between Italy and France—and thus again had the favorable effect of strengthening the Triple Alliance.

It was unfortunate for Germany not only that the Reich leadership completely failed back then, but above all that public opinion, led by insane German nationalist patriots and foreign policy visionaries, opposed Italy. Especially also because Austria detected something unfriendly in the Italian actions in Tripolitania. But at that time it was part of the political wisdom of our nationalist bourgeoisie to back every stupidity or perfidy of Viennese diplomacy— yes, when possible, even to undertake it ourselves—in order to best demonstrate to the world the inner harmony and cohesiveness of this heartfelt alliance.

Now Austria-Hungary has been obliterated. But Germany has less cause than ever to regret an Italian development that must one day inevitably end at the expense of France. Because the more today's Italy considers its highest ethnic duty, and the more it accordingly moves toward the Roman concept of a policy of space, the more it must come into conflict with the fiercest competitor in the Mediterranean: France. France will never tolerate Italy becoming a supreme power in the Mediterranean. It will attempt to prevent this either by its own strength alone or through a system of alliances. It will lay obstacles in the path of Italian development wherever possible, and ultimately it will not hesitate to resort to force either.[327] And the so-called kinship between the two Latin nations will change nothing in that regard, as their relation is no closer than that of England and Germany.

In[328] addition, to the degree that the strength of France's own people decreases, this state turns to the utilization of its reservoir of blacks. This brings up a danger of unimaginable proportions for Europe. The idea that French Negroes—as cultural watchdogs against the Germans along the Rhine—could poison white blood is so monstrous that it would have seemed altogether impossible a few decades ago. Certainly France itself will suffer the greatest detriment from this blood pollution, but only if the other European nations remain conscious of the value of their white race. From a purely military perspective, France can very easily supplement its European formations and, as the Great War showed, also deploy them effectively. In the end, this completely non-French black army even affords a certain protection against communist demonstrations, as it will be easier to maintain slavish obedience in all situations in an army that is not at all related by blood to the French people. But this development contains the greatest danger for Italy, first and foremost. If the Italian people wishes to shape its future according to its own interests, it will one day have the black armies, mobilized by France, as its enemy. It cannot be remotely in Italy's interest to maintain an enmity with Germany—an enmity that even in the best case can contribute nothing advantageous toward the organization of Italian life in the future. On the contrary, if one state can definitely bury the wartime enmity, it is Italy. Italy has no interest of its own in further oppression of Germany, if both states wish to pursue their most natural tasks for the future.

Bismarck already recognized this fortunate coincidence. More than once he assessed the German and Italian interests as being completely parallel.[329] It is he who already indicates that the Italy of the future will have to seek its development on the perimeter of the Mediterranean Sea, and it is also he who further establishes the harmony of the Italian interests with the German ones by emphasizing that only France can think of disrupting this arrangement of the Italian life, whereas Germany, from its point of view, must only welcome it. He truly sees no necessary cause, ever, for estrangement or especially animosity between Italy and Germany. If Bismarck, instead of Bethmann Hollweg,[330] had guided Germany's fate before the Great War, this terrible enmity due only to Austria would [not] never have arisen.

It is certain—even more than in the case of England—that a German continental expansion in northern Europe poses no threat to Italy and thus can give no cause for Italian alienation from Germany. On the other hand, Italy's most natural interests argue against any further augmentation of France's hegemony in Europe.

But for this reason Italy, above all, would come into consideration for an alliance relationship with Germany.

Since fascism in Italy brought a new concept of state, and with it a new will, into the life of the Italian people, the hostility of France has already become obvious. Through a whole system of alliances, France is attempting to strengthen itself not only for the possible conflict with Italy but also to cut off and strangulate Italy's possible friends.[331] The French goal is clear: a French alignment of states should be formed that reaches from Paris via Warsaw, Prague and Vienna to Belgrade. The attempt to incorporate Austria into this system is not at all as hopeless as it might appear at first glance.[332] Considering the dominating character that Vienna, a city of two million, exerts on Austria, which encompasses only six million people altogether,[333] the policies of this country will always be determined first and foremost by Vienna. To the cosmopolitan [character] nature of Vienna, which in the last decade has expressed itself ever more clearly, an alliance with Paris is in principle much more likely than one with Italy. The manipulation of public opinion guaranteed by the Vienna press is already providing for this. But this activity has threatened to become particularly effective ever since the press, with the help of the South Tyrolean clamor, succeeded in agitating the bourgeois nationalist rural people who are completely without instinct against Italy as well. This brings up a danger of unimaginable proportions. Because with a consistently implemented campaign of press agitation, carried out for many years, no people can be brought to make the most unbelievable and in reality truly suicidal decisions more easily than the German people.

But if France succeeds in incorporating Austria into the chain of its "friendship," then Italy will one day be forced into a two-front war, or it will have to again renounce a true representation of the interests of the Italian people. In both cases the danger exists for Germany that a possible ally would be definitively eliminated for an unforeseeable length of time and France would thus become ever more the master of Europe's fate.

One can cherish no illusions about what this will mean for Germany. Our bourgeois nationalist border politicians and patriotic association protesters will then have their hands full trying repeatedly—in the name of national honor—to eliminate the traces of the mistreatment they will have to endure from France, thanks to their farsighted policies.

Since the time the National Socialist movement has dealt with foreign policy ideas, I have, under consideration of all the cited motives, attempted to mold it into the bearer of a clear foreign policy goal. The objection that this is primarily the task of the government is raised wrongly in a state whose official government is descended from the ranks of parties that neither know Germany nor desire an auspicious future for this Germany. Since those responsible for arranging the November outrage have become eligible to be part of the government, the interests of the German nation will no longer be represented, but only the interests of the countries mistreating it. One cannot very well expect German vital necessities to be promoted by people for whom their own fatherland and nation are only means to an end, and which, when necessary, will be shamelessly sacrificed for their own personal advantage. Yes, in truth, the so often observable self-preservation drive of these people and parties alone argues against any revitalization of the German nation, because the fight for freedom on behalf of German honor would inevitably mobilize forces that would lead to the downfall and destruction of the previous desecrators of German honor.

There is no fight for freedom without a general national renewal. But a renewal of the national conscience and the national honor is unthinkable without bringing to judgment those responsible for the previous dishonoring. The naked self-preservation drive will force these depraved elements and their parties to thwart all steps that could lead to a true rebirth of our people. And the apparent lunacy of some acts of these Herostratuses[334] of our people becomes, as soon as the inner motives are recognized, a purposeful, skillful—if also infamous and sordid—operation.

At such a time, because public life is being shaped by parties of this type and represented by individuals of the most inferior character, it is the duty of a national reform movement to follow its own foreign policy path as well—a path that someday in all reason and probability must lead to the success and happiness of the fatherland. So to the extent that this objection, pursuing a policy that does not correspond to the official foreign policy, comes from the Marxist-Democratic-Center side, it can be dispatched with appropriate disdain. When bourgeois nationalist and so-called patriotic circles raise it, then it is really only the expression and symbol of an attitude of playing around in associations, which always only exercises itself in protests and which cannot seriously grasp that another movement possesses the indestructible will to come to power one day and to undertake the necessary education of this power now, in anticipation of this actuality.

Since 1920, I have attempted—by all means and with great persistence—to familiarize the National Socialist movement with the idea of an alliance between Germany, Italy, and England.[335] This was very difficult, particularly in the first years after the war, because the "God punish England" attitude had initially robbed our people of all capability of clear and levelheaded thinking in the foreign policy area, and continued to hold it captive.

The situation of the young movement was also extremely difficult vis-à-vis Italy, especially after the leadership of the brilliant statesman Benito Mussolini[336] instituted an unheard of reorganization of the Italian people, which drew protest from all the states controlled by international freemasonry. Because while until 1922 the shapers of German public opinion took absolutely no notice of the suffering of the people separated from Germany[337]— by these politicians' misdeeds—they now suddenly began [on] to honor South Tyrol with their attention. With all the resources of clever journalism and false dialectics, the South Tyrolean problem was magnified into a question of extraordinary significance, so that in the end Italy was demonized in Germany and Austria unlike any of the other victorious states. If the National Socialist movement wanted to represent its foreign policy mission honestly—carried by the conviction of its absolute necessity—then it could not flinch from taking up the fight against this system of lies and confusion. In doing so it could not rely upon any allies, but rather had to be guided by the idea that it is better to forego cheap popularity than to act against a recognized truth, a present necessity, and the voice of one's own conscience. Even if one were to be defeated, this would still be more honorable than participating in a recognized crime.

In 1920, when I spoke of the possibility of a future association with Italy, all of the preconditions for this actually seemed to be absent, at least initially. Italy was in the circle of victorious states and shared in the advantages (actual or also only supposed) of this situation.[338] In 1919 and 1920 there seemed to be absolutely no prospect that the internal structure of the Entente would loosen in the foreseeable future. The powerful international coalition still set great store on demonstrating that it was an internally cohesive guarantor of victory and thus also of peace. The difficulties that appeared already during the drafting of the peace treaties did not come to the attention of the wider public, as clever management was always able to sustain the impression—at least outwardly—of complete unity. This collective action was based on the public opinion achieved through generally similar war propaganda, but also on the still uncertain fear of the German giant. Only gradu-

ally did the outside world gain insight into the magnitude of
Germany's internal decay. Another reason also contributed to the
seemingly indissoluble cohesion of the victorious states: The individual states' hopes of in this way not being passed over in the distribution of the booty. Finally, there was also the fear that if a state
really had withdrawn back then, the fate of Germany would nevertheless not have run a different course, but the beneficiary of our
collapse would then perhaps have been France alone. Because in
Paris, of course, they did not consider bringing about a change in
the anti-German attitude activated by the war. "Peace, for me, is
the continuation of the war."[339] With this sentence, the old, white-
haired Clemenceau[340] expressed the true aims of the French people.

This at least apparent internal cohesion of the coalition of victors with the French-inspired immovable goal of still totally destroying Germany was confronted by a complete lack of purpose in
German intentions. Next to the sordid villainy of those who in their
own land, against all truth and against their own knowledge, laid
the blame for the war on Germany and impertinently [the] derived
from that the justification for the enemy extortion, stood a nationalist side—in part intimidated, in part uncertain—that believed the
nation, after the collapse, could now be helped by a most painful
reconstruction of the past. We lost the war due to a lack of nationalist fervor against our enemies. It was the opinion of the nationalist circles, therefore, that we should, more than ever, make up for
this disastrous shortcoming and in peacetime anchor hatred against
the former adversaries. It was noteworthy that from the beginning
this hatred was concentrated more against England, and later Italy,
than against France. AgainstEngland because thanks to the lulling
policy of Bethmann Hollweg, people did not believe—up until the
final hour—in a war with England, and thus saw its entry as an
extraordinarily dishonorable crime against good faith.[341] In the case
of Italy, the hatred was more understandable in view of the political thoughtlessness of our German people. People were so trapped
by the official governmental circles in the haze and fog of the Triple

Alliance that even the nonintervention of Italy on behalf of Austria-Hungary and Germany was seen as a breach of trust. The later alignment of the Italian people with our enemies was seen, however, as endless perfidy. This cumulative hatred then released itself in the true bourgeois-nationalist curse and battle cry: "God punish England." Now, because dear God is just as much with the stronger and more resolute as also, preferably, with the more intelligent, he apparently declined this punishment. Nevertheless, at least during the war, the whipping up of our nationalist passion by all possible means was not only allowed but demanded as a matter of course. The bad thing was that although the passion was never driven too high with us, we nevertheless lost sight of real truths. In politics there is no absolute justice, and thus it was wrong during the war—especially in response to Italy's entry into the international coalition—to draw no other conclusion than only flaming rage and indignation. Because instead we should have had, more than ever, the obligation to continuously examine the options under the circumstances, in order to reach those decisions that could possibly rescue the threatened German nation. Because with Italy's entry into the Entente front, it was inevitable that the military situation would become much more difficult—not only as a result of the increase in weaponry that the Entente gained,[342] but much more as a result of the boost in morale, especially for France, provided by the appearance of such a power on the side of the developing international coalition. The political leadership of the nation at that time should have been duty bound to decide to end the two- and three-front war, cost what it may. Germany was not responsible for preserving the corrupt, careless Austrian state [sic]. The German soldier did not fight for the territorial power policies of the Habsburg royal house either. At most, our nonfighting cheerleaders might have had that in mind, but not those spilling their blood on the front. The suffering and hardship of the German musketeers was already overwhelming in 1915. One could demand this suffering for the future and preservation of our German people, but not to rescue the Habsburg great-power mania. It was a monstrous idea to allow the blood of millions of German soldiers to be shed in a hopeless war, only to preserve the state of a dynasty whose own dynastic interests have been anti-German for centuries. The full extent of this insanity is only understood when one considers that the best German blood had to be shed so that, at best ideally, the Habsburgs could then in peace again secure the possibility of denationalizing the German people. For this scandalous lunacy we not only had to accept the most enormous casualties; no, we were then even obligated again and again to fill with German flesh and blood the gaps that betrayal and corruption had torn in our distinguished ally's front. And we made these sacrifices for a dynasty that was ready to abandon its all-sacrificing ally at the first opportunity. And which it then later also did. Our bourgeois nationalist patriots, however, say as little about that betrayal as they do about the ongoing betrayal of the Austrian fighting peoples—allied with us—of Slavic nationality, who crossed over to the enemy regiment by regiment and brigade by brigade[343] in order in the end to take part in the war (even in their own legions)[344] against those who were thrown into this unspeakable calamity only through the actions of their own state. Austria-Hungary would never voluntarily have taken part in a war that concerned Germany. The fact that people here and there perhaps truly believed to have, in the Triple Alliance, a protection based on reciprocity can only be attributed to the boundless ignorance that generally prevailed in Germany with regard to the Austrian circumstances. It would have caused the sorest disappointment for Germany if the Great War had broken out as the result of an issue affecting Germany. The Austrian state—with its Slavic majority and Habsburg dynasty fundamentally anti-German and hostile to the Reich—would never have taken up arms to protect and assist Germany against the rest of the world, as Germany stupidly did. Actually, Germany only had to fulfill a single obligation to Austria-Hungary: to use all possible means to save the German people in this state and to eliminate the depraved, most guilt-burdened dynasty the German people has ever had to endure.

The entry of Italy into the Great War should have been the occasion for Germany to fundamentally revise its stance toward Austria-Hungary. It is not a wise and capable political action or the outflow of wise and capable political leadership to find no other response in such a situation than sullen rage and impotent fierceness. Such a thing is usually damaging even in private life; in political life, however, it is worse than a crime. It is a stupidity.

And even if this attempt to change the previous German attitude had not been successful, then at least it would have absolved the nation's political leadership of the guilt of not having attempted it. In any case, Germany had to attempt to end the two-front war after Italy's entry into the Great War. It should then have aimed for a separate peace with Russia,[345] not only based on a relinquishment of any advantage of the previous successes gained by German arms in the east, but even, if necessary, by sacrificing Austria-Hungary. Only the complete dissociation of German policy from the task of saving the Austrian state, and its exclusive concentration on the task of helping the German people, could still grant any conceivable prospect of success.

In addition, with the breakup of Austria-Hungary, the incorporation of nine million German Austrians[346] into the Reich would have been a more valuable result for the history and for the future of our people than the gain—of dubious consequence—of a few French coal or iron-ore mines.[347] But it must repeatedly be emphasized that the task of German foreign policy, even a mere bourgeois nationalist foreign policy, would not have been to preserve the Habsburg state but exclusively only to save the German nation, including the nine million Germans in Austria. And nothing else—absolutely nothing else.

The reaction of the German Reich leadership to the new situation created by Italy's entry into the Great War was, as is generally known, quite different. They tried, now more than ever, to save the Austrian state (whose Slavic confederation citizens were deserting) by committing even more German blood and, at home, calling down the vengeance of heaven upon the faithless erstwhile allies. But to exclude any possibility of ending the two-front war, they allowed themselves to be maneuvered by the artful and cunning Viennese diplomacy into establishing the Polish state. In this way, any hope of coming to an understanding with Russia, which naturally would have had a negative impact on Austria-Hungary, was cleverly eliminated by the Habsburgs. The German soldier from Bavaria and Pomerania, Westphalia, Thuringia, and East Prussia, from Brandenburg, Saxony, and the Rhine would then have gained the high honor of giving his life—in the most terrible, bloodiest battles in the history of the world—by the hundreds of thousands [for the formation], not to save the German nation but to form a Polish state, which, with a favorable end to the Great War, would have given the Habsburgs a titular leader and which would then have been an eternal enemy of Germany.[348]

Bourgeois nationalist state policy. But if this reaction to the Italian step was unpardonable insanity during the war, then the maintenance of this attitude in reaction to the Italian step after the war was an even greater capital stupidity.

Certainly Italy was in the coalition of victorious states after the war as well, and thus also on the side of France. But this was understandable, because Italy did not enter the war out of pro-French feelings. The decisive force that drove the Italian people to this was nothing but hatred against Austria and the visible opportunity to advance Italian interests. This was the reason for the Italian action, and not some fanciful emotional feeling for France. Now, as a German one can sense with deepest pain the extensive consequences that Italy drew from the collapse of its hated enemy of a hundred years; but cannot take away from one the sense of healthy rationality. Fortune has shifted. Once Austria had more than 800,000 Italians under its rule, and now 200,000 Austrians came under the rule of Italy. The cause of our pain is the fact that these 200,000 that interest us are of German nationality.

The end of the perennial latent Austrian-Italian conflict has achieved the future goals of neither a nationally nor an ethnically conceived Italian policy. On the contrary, the enormous surge in the Italian people's self-confidence and awareness of power, brought about by the war and especially by fascism, will only increase its strength to pursue greater goals. But that will cause the natural clash of Italian and French interests to become increasingly apparent. And we could already count on that and hope for it in the years 1920 [*sic*]. Actually, the very first traces of internal disharmony between the two states appeared even then. While the southern Slavic instinct to further curtail the German element in Austria was sure of French sympathy, the Italian attitude—already at the time of the liberation of Carinthia from the Slavs[349]—was, at least toward the German people, one of goodwill. This internal reversal vis-à-vis Germany was also apparent in the behavior of Italian commissions in Germany itself, most clearly during the battles in Upper Silesia.[350] One could, in any case, identify the beginning of a—if initially only slight—separation between the two Latin nations. According to all human logic and reason, and based on all previous historical experience, this separation must continue to grow and must one day end with open fighting. Italy, whether it wants to or not, will be forced to fight against France for the existence and future of its state, just like Germany itself. In doing so, it is not necessary that France always be in the forefront of the action. But it will pull the strings of those it has cleverly brought into financial and military dependence on it, or those with whom it appears allied due to parallel interests. The Italian-French conflict can ultimately be initiated in the Balkans just as well as it can, perhaps, find its end in the plains of Lombardy.

In view of this compelling probability of future hostility between Italy and France, it was Italy, above all, that seemed already in 1920 to be a potential future ally for Germany. This probability grew into a certainty when, with the victory of fascism, the feeble

Italian government, in the end still subject to international influences, was eliminated and in its place stepped a government that had attached to its banners the rallying cry of the exclusive representation of Italian interests. A weak Italian democratic bourgeois government could perhaps maintain a contrived relationship with France if Italy's true tasks for the future were disregarded; however, a nationally conscious and responsible Italian government could never do so. On the day that the fasces became the symbol of the Italian state,[351] the struggle of the third Rome for the future of the Italian people obtained its historical declaration. One of the two Latin nations will have to vacate its position on the Mediterranean Sea, while the other will gain dominance as the prize in this struggle.

As a nationally conscious and rationally thinking German, I have the firm hope and the strongest wish that this might be Italy and not France.

But this will mean that my behavior toward Italy will be motivated by anticipation of the future and not by fruitless memories of the war.

As a sign on the troop transport railroad cars, the statement "Declarations of war are received here" was a good indication of the confidence in victory of the only [*unique?*] old army. As a political avowal, however, an insane stupidity. But it is even more insane to take the position today that no state that took part in the Great War on the enemy's side and that participated in using the Great War to our disadvantage can be considered as a possible ally. When Marxists, Democrats, and Centrists make such an idea the leitmotiv of their political action, then this is clear because this depraved coalition never wishes to see a German revitalization at all. But when nationalist bourgeois and patriotic circles adopt such ideas, then that exceeds all limits. Because just name for me the one power that could come into consideration as an ally in Europe and that has not enriched itself territorially at our expense or the expense of our former allies. From that standpoint, France is immediately eliminated because it robbed us of Alsace-Lorraine and wishes to rob the Rhineland; Belgium, because it possesses Eupen and Malmedy; England, because although it does not necessarily possess our colonies, it does administer most of them—but every child knows what that means in the life of nations. Denmark is eliminated because it took North Schleswig; Poland, because it possesses West Prussia and Upper Silesia and parts of East Prussia; Czechoslovakia because it is oppressing almost four million Germans; Romania, because it likewise annexed more than one million Germans; Yugoslavia, because it has nearly 600,000 Germans;[352] and Italy, because today it calls South Tyrol its own.[353]

Thus, the alliance possibilities in Europe are all impossible for our nationalist bourgeois and patriotic circles. But they do not need that anyway, as the flood of their protests and the din of their cheers will smother some of the outside world's resistance, and some will cave in. And then, without any allies—yes, also without any weapons—supported only by their firmly protesting eloquence, they will take back the stolen areas and have dear God punish England belatedly, but chastise Italy and abandon it to the due disdain of the entire world—provided they are not first hanged from the lampposts by their own momentary foreign policy allies, the Bolshevikists [*sic*] and Marxist Jews.

It is noteworthy that our nationalist circles of bourgeois and patriotic origin are not even conscious of the fact that the strongest evidence of the incorrectness of their foreign policy stance lies in the agreement of the Marxists, Democrats, and Centrists, but especially in the agreement of the Jews. But one must know our German bourgeoisie in particular in order to know immediately why this is so. They are all exceedingly happy to have found at least one issue that seems to create the supposed unity of the German people. And it can just as well concern some foolishness. It is nevertheless immensely pleasant for a courageous bourgeois and patriotic politician to be able to speak in nationalist fighting tones without immediately receiving a box on the ear from the nearest communist for it. But the fact that they are spared this only because their political concept is just as ineffective from the nationalist perspective as it is useful from the Jewish-Marxist perspective either escapes these people or is concealed deep inside. The scale that the corruption of lies and cowardice has reached among us is shocking.

[B]

In 1920, when I took up the movement's foreign policy position toward Italy,[354] I initially encountered a complete lack of understanding in nationalist circles as well as in so-called patriotic ones. It was simply incomprehensible to these people that one could—contrary to the general obligation of continual protest—accept a political idea that for all practical purposes meant the internal termination of one of the enmities of the Great War. The nationalist circles could not understand at all why I wanted to place the focus of national activity not on protests—raised to the skies in front of the Feldherrnhalle in Munich or somewhere else, first against Paris, then again against London, or also against Rome—but rather on the elimination of those responsible initially within Germany for the collapse. About the dictated peace of Paris, a flaming protest rally against Paris took place in Munich as well; although it could not have caused Mr. Clemenceau much concern, it prompted me to map out very clearly the National Socialist position against all these protests.[355] France only did what every German could have known and should have known. If I were French myself, I would naturally have stood behind Clemenceau. Continually barking at a superior enemy from afar is just as shameful as it is foolish. The nationalist opposition of these patriotic circles should instead have bared its teeth in Berlin at those responsible and guilty for the terrible catastrophe of our collapse. But it was more convenient to call out curses against Paris—curses whose realization was impossible, in light of the actual circumstances—than to act against Berlin with deeds.

This was also particularly true of those representatives of Bavarian state policy who had already sufficiently revealed the character of their brilliance through the fact of their previous achievements. Because precisely these men—who continually pretended to want to protect Bavarian sovereign rights, and thus were also thinking of the preservation of the rights to conduct foreign policy[356]—should, above all, have been obligated to actively represent a possible foreign policy in such a way that Bavaria would inevitably have gained the leadership of a nationalist opposition in Germany, understood in terms of truly far-reaching viewpoints. The Bavarian state, in view of the complete unreliability of the Reich policy or the intended negation of every real possibility of success, should have elevated itself to being the spokesman for a foreign policy that in all probability would one day have brought about the end of Germany's appalling isolation.

But even there, in these circles, people responded in a completely unthinking and stupid manner to the foreign policy concept of an association with Italy, which I advocated. Instead of becoming spokesmen and protectors of Germany's most critical future national interests in such a noble way, they would rather squint from time to time with one eye toward Paris and affirm, raising the other toward heaven, their loyal attitude to the Reich on the one hand, but on the other their determination to save Bavaria by letting the Bolshevists ruin the north. Yes, yes, the Bavarian state entrusted the representation of its sovereign rights to particularly great intellectual phenomena.

Considering such a general mentality, no one can be surprised that my foreign policy concept was, from the first, if not directly dismissed then at least met with complete incomprehension. Quite frankly, I did not expect anything else at the time. I still took the general war psychosis into account and attempted only to instill levelheaded foreign policy thinking into my own movement.

At that time, I did not yet have to suffer any open attacks because of my policy on Italy. The reason was likely that, on the one hand, people did not consider it at all dangerous at that moment, and that, on the other hand, Italy itself had a government subject to international influence. Yes, in the background it was perhaps even hoped that this Italy would succumb to the Bolshevik plague, and then it would have been very welcome as an ally, at least for our left-wing circles.

In addition, from the left one could not very well at that time take a position against the elimination of a wartime enmity, because in this camp people were in any case continually attempting to eradicate the ugly sentiment of war hatred, which was degrading for Germany and thus unjustifiable. From within these circles it would not have been easy to raise an objection against me on account of a foreign policy concept that would have required at least the elimination of the war hatred between Germany and Italy as a precondition for its realization.

But I must again emphasize that perhaps the primary reason I found so little active resistance was due to my opponents' assumption of the harmlessness, unfeasibility, and thus also innocuousness of my activities.

This situation changed almost at once when Mussolini undertook the march on Rome. As if a spell had been cast, from this point on the entire Jewish press began a barrage of poisoning and slander against Italy. And it was not until after 1922 that the South Tyrolean question was posed and—whether the South Tyroleans wanted this themselves or not—turned into the focal point of German-Italian relations. It did not take long before even the Marxists became representatives of a nationalist opposition, and one could now experience the unique spectacle of Jews and ethnic Germans, Social Democrats and members of the patriotic associations, communists and the nationalist bourgeoisie mentally crossing the Brenner arm in arm to reconquer this area—in immense battles, but without bloodshed. The fact that those super Bavarian representatives of the sovereign rights of the Bavarian state also took an active interest in the fight to liberate the land of Andreas Hofer—

those representatives whose intellectual forefathers, just over a hundred years ago, handed over the good Andreas Hofer[357] to the French and allowed him to be shot—gave this bold nationalist front a very special attraction.

Because the pack of Jewish journalists and the nationalist bourgeois and patriotic idiots that follow them have now truly succeeded in inflating the South Tyrolean problem to the magnitude of a vital issue for the German nation, I am prompted to comment on this in detail.

The old Austrian state, as already emphasized, had just over 850,000 Italians within its borders. The proportion of nationalities established by the Austrian census is not entirely accurate. They did not count the individual's nationality, but only the language he specified as the one he commonly spoke. It is obvious that this cannot provide a completely clear picture, but one of the weaknesses of the nationalist bourgeoisie is that it willingly allows itself to be deceived about the true situation. If one does not find out about something, or at least does not speak about it openly, then it does not exist. A very large share of the Italians—or, more accurately, people who commonly spoke Italian—identified on the basis of this procedure lived in Tyrol. According to the results of the 1910 census, Tyrol had a population of …[358], of which … percent identified themselves as speaking Italian; the rest were German or some also Ladin. Consequently, around … Italians lived in the archduchy of Tyrol. Because this total number is within the area occupied by Italians today, the ratio of Germans to Italians in the entire Tyrolean area occupied by Italy is therefore one of … Germans to … Italians.

It is necessary to establish this because in Germany, due to the dishonesty of our press, quite a few people have absolutely no idea that the area referred to by the term South Tyrol is actually populated by two-thirds Italians and one-third Germans. So anyone who seriously advocates the reconquest of South Tyrol would only change the situation by bringing 400,000 Italians under German rule instead of 200,000 Germans under Italian rule.[359]

Now, the Germans in South Tyrol are predominantly concentrated in the northern part, while Italian people inhabit the southern part. So if someone wished to find a nationally equitable solution, then he would first have to completely eliminate the term South Tyrol from the general discussion. Because on moral grounds we cannot very well fight the Italians for taking an area in which in addition to 400,000 Italians there are also 200,000 Germans, if, in order to eliminate this injustice, we ourselves wish to regain this same area for Germany—thus, from a strictly moral standpoint, committing an even greater injustice than that committed by Italy.[360]

For this reason, the call for a reconquest of South Tyrol will reflect exactly the same moral failings as those currently detected in the Italian rule in South Tyrol. But this call therefore also loses its moral justification. Other viewpoints could be asserted that must then argue for the recovery of all of South Tyrol. Based on general, morally justifiable feelings, one could at most advocate regaining the part that is actually predominantly inhabited by Germans. This is a tightly circumscribed area of …[361] square kilometers. But even in this area there are about 190,000 Germans, 64,000 Italians and Ladins, and 24,000 other foreigners; the completely German area actually incorporates scarcely 160,000 Germans.

Now, there is hardly any current border that does not cut Germans off from the motherland like in South Tyrol. Yes, in Europe alone, no fewer than a total of …[362] million Germans are separated from the Reich. Of those, … million live under pronounced foreign rule and only … million—in German Austria and Switzerland—under circumstances that at least for the present do not threaten their nationality.

Here, in a great many cases, it is a matter of completely different numerical complexes[363] than our people against South Tyrol [*sic*].

As terrible this fact is for our people, equally guilty for it are those who raise their clamor about South Tyrol today. But in any case one cannot, even by adopting a purely bourgeois border policy, simply make the fate of the entire rest of the Reich dependent upon the interests of these lost areas, or even on the wishes of one of them.

Because something must first be rejected most rigorously: there is no sacred German people in South Tyrol, as the members of the patriotic associations prattle on about. Rather, whatever must be considered as belonging to the German people must be held equally sacred. It is not acceptable to value a South Tyrolean more highly than a Silesian, an East Prussian, or a West Prussian who is oppressed under Polish rule. It is also not appropriate to view a German in Czechoslovakia as more valuable than a German in the Saar area or also in Alsace-Lorraine. The right to rank the German people in the separated regions according to particular values could at best arise from an analytical examination of their respective decisive and dominating basic racial values. But it is precisely this measure that the grand protest union applies the least to Italy. And for the Tyroleans in the currently separated areas, it would certainly yield no higher value than, say, for an East or West Prussian.[364]

Now, the foreign policy task of the German people cannot be determined by the interests of one of the areas separated from the Reich. Because in reality these interests will not be served in that way, as practical assistance presupposes the regained strength of the motherland. For this reason, the only viewpoint that can be considered for the foreign policy position is the one that is the swiftest and soonest restoration of the independence and freedom of the remainder of the nation assembled into a state.

In other words: Even if German foreign policy were to acknowledge no other goal than the rescue of the "sacred people in South Tyrol"—meaning the 190,000 Germans that could actually come into consideration—then the precondition for this would first be the achievement of Germany's political independence as well as the acquisition of military power resources. Because it should be fairly clear that the Austrian protest state will not wrest South Tyrol away from the Italians. But it must also be equally clear, then, that even if German foreign policy were to pursue no other goal than the actual liberation of South Tyrol, it must more than ever allow its actions to be determined by the viewpoints and motives that will provide the preconditions for regaining political and military power resources. So for this reason alone, we should certainly not make South Tyrol the focal point of foreign policy considerations; rather, we should instead allow [*ourselves*] to be governed and led more than ever by those ideas that allow the currently existing international coalition, aimed against Germany, to break up. Because ultimately, Germany cannot give South Tyrol back to the German people by rattling off a Tibetan prayer wheel of protests and indignation, but by applying the sword.

So if Germany were to possess this goal itself, it would nevertheless again and again—and then more than ever—have to seek an ally that would assist Germany in gaining power. Now, one could say that in this case France could come into consideration. But as a National Socialist I oppose that most resolutely.

It could be that France would declare itself ready to let Germany march as an auxiliary against Italy—yes, it could even be that we would then graciously be awarded South Tyrol in recognition of our casualties and as a small plaster for our wounds; but what would such a victory mean for Germany? Could our people then perhaps live, due to the possession of 200,000 additional South Tyroleans? Or do people not believe that France, as soon as it had defeated its Latin competitor on the Mediterranean with German military assistance, would turn against Germany more than ever? That come what may, it would more than ever pursue its old political goal of breaking Germany up?

No, if Germany has any choice at all between France and Italy, then according to all human reason only Italy can come into consideration for Germany. Because a victory with France over Italy brings us South Tyrol and also a stronger France as an enemy afterward. A German victory over France, with the help of Italy, brings us Alsace-Lorraine as the least important gain, and as the most important the freedom to carry out a truly large-scale policy of space.[365]

And in the long run, it is that alone—not South Tyrol—that will enable Germany to live in the future. But it is simply not acceptable to pick out one of all the separated areas, the least vital one, at that, and jeopardize all the interests of a people of seventy million—yes, simply renouncing its future—so that disastrous, fanciful German jingoism can be gratified for the moment. And all of this on account of a pure phantom, because in reality South Tyrol will not be helped by that any more than it is now.

The National Socialist movement must educate the German people so that it does not balk at suffering casualties to further the arrangement of its life. But by the same token, our people must be educated in such a way that such casualties can never again—at least in the foreseeable future—take place on behalf of phantoms.

Our protest patriots and members of the patriotic associations can kindly say, however, how they envision the reconquest of South Tyrol without the force of arms. They can muster up the honesty to admit whether they seriously believe that Italy, simply worn down by all the speeches and protests, will one day give up South Tyrol, or whether they too are not convinced that it will take the duress of a military decision to bring a nationally aware state to again sacrifice an area for which it fought for four years. They should not always say that we or I would have abandoned South Tyrol.[366] These infamous liars know very well that, at least with respect to me personally, during the time in which the fate of South Tyrol was being decided I was fighting on the front[367]—something that more than a few of today's protesters failed to do back then. That, however, during this same time, the forces that our patriotic associations and our nationalist bourgeoisie make joint foreign policy with today and agitate against Italy used every possible means to sabotage the victory, that internationalist Marxism, the Democrats, and the Center already before the war, neglected nothing to weaken and paralyze the military power of our people, and that finally, during the war, they organized a revolution that had to lead to the collapse of the German homeland and thus the German army.

Because of these people's actions and the accursed weakness and powerlessness of our current bourgeois masters of protest, South Tyrol was also lost to the German people. It is a pathetic misrepresentation when these so-called nationalist patriots talk about an abandonment of South Tyrol today. No, dear gentlemen, do not twist and turn so spinelessly around the correct word. Are you not too cowardly to state that today it could only be a question of conquering South Tyrol? Because the abandonment, my gentlemen nationalist protesters, was carried out by your eminent allies at the time, the Marxist traitors of that time, in due form according to the law. And the only ones who had the courage to openly criticize this crime at the time were not you, dear sirs, nationalist association members and bourgeois politicians, but the little National Socialist movement, and that was primarily I myself. Yes, indeed, gentlemen. When no one in Germany had any idea of your existence because of your silence, and you had crept into your mouse holes, then I emerged in 1919 and 1920 to oppose the disgrace of the signing of the peace treaties.[368] And not in secret, behind four walls, but publicly. But you were so cowardly back then that you did not even dare to come to our meetings, for fear of being thrashed by your current foreign policy allies, the Marxist street thugs.

The men who signed the peace treaty of St. Germain[369] were no more National Socialists than those who signed the treaty of Versailles. They were members of the parties for whom this signing was only the final crowning act of their decades-long treason. Anyone who wishes to change anything about the fate of South Tyrol today can no longer renounce it, because it was already formally renounced once by today's protesters; rather, he could at best only reconquer it.

But I turn against this most fanatically and oppose this effort most intensely, and I will fight with the most extreme fanaticism against the men who attempt to draw our people into this bloody and insane adventure.[370] I did not get to know war from hearsay only. Nor was I one of those who had anything to order or command in this war. I was just an ordinary soldier who was ordered around for four and a half years but who nevertheless fulfilled his duty honestly and faithfully. But because of that I had the good fortune to learn about war the way it is, and not [*the way*] people wish to see it. I was for the war, until the final hour of this war—even as a regular soldier, who knew only its dark side—because I was convinced that our people could be saved only through victory. But because there is now a peace that others are evilly responsible for, I utterly oppose a war that would not benefit the German people, but only those who already sacrilegiously sold the blood of our people for their own interests. I am convinced that I would not lack the resolve to accept the responsibility for casualties among the German people either,[371] if necessary, but I resist allowing even a single German to be dragged onto a battlefield from whose blood only fools or criminals feed their plans. Anyone who thinks about the shocking horrors and terrible misery of a modern war, or who considers the infinite strain on the nerves of a people, must be frightened by the thought that such a sacrifice could be demanded for a result that, in the best case, could never be commensurate with these casualties. And I also know that if the South Tyrolean people, insofar as it has a German mentality, were collected today along a single front, and the hundreds and hundreds of thousands of dead which the fight on the South Tyroleans' behalf would impose upon our people were to appear before the eyes of these spectators, then three hundred thousand hands would be raised to heaven to avert this battle, and the foreign policy of the National Socialists would be justified.

But the terrible thing about it all is that people play around with these awful possibilities without even thinking about wanting to help the South Tyroleans.

The fight for South Tyrol will be led today by those who once abandoned all of Germany to ruin, and South Tyrol is also for them only a means to an end, that they will use with stone-cold unscrupulousness in order to be able to gratify their villainous anti-German—in the truest sense of the word—instincts. What prompts them to stir up the German public, with the help of South Tyrol, is hatred for today's nationally aware Italy, and in particular hatred for the new national concept of this country, and above all hatred for the outstanding Italian statesman.[372] Because how indifferent these elements really are toward the German people. While they lament the fate of South Tyrol with crocodile tears in their eyes, they drive all of Germany toward a fate that is worse than that of the separated areas. While they protest against Italy in the name of national culture, they pollute the culture of the German nation from within, corroding our entire cultural feeling, poisoning the instincts of our people, and destroying even the achievements of the past. Does an age have a moral right to act against today's Italy in the name of culture, or to defend the German culture from it, when internally this age is pushing our entire theater, literature, and fine arts down to the level of pigs?[373] The gentlemen of the Bavarian People's Party, the German Nationalists, and even the Marxist culture-desecrators are concerned about the German culture of the South Tyroleans, but they allow the culture of the homeland to be insulted undisturbed by the most pathetically shoddy work. They surrender the German stages to the racial disgrace of a *Jonny spielt auf*[374] and lament hypocritically about the suppression of the German cultural life in South Tyrol, while they themselves viciously persecute those who wanted to defend the German culture from conscious and deliberate destruction at home. Here the Bavarian People's Party incites the authorities against those who raise protest against the villainous desecration of our people's culture. What do they do, these concerned guardians of German culture in South Tyrol, in defense of German culture in Germany itself? They have allowed the theater to sink to the level of a brothel—to a place of demonstrated racial disgrace; they allow the cinema, by mocking decency and propriety, to destroy all the foundations of the life of our people; they watch the degeneration of our fine arts by cubism and dadaism; they themselves sponsor the creators of this base fraud or insanity;

they allow German literature [on the] to sink into mud and filth and surrender the entire intellectual life of our people to the internationalist Jews. And this same miserable pack then has the impertinence to speak up on behalf of German culture in South Tyrol; but their only goal in doing so, naturally, is to incite two civilized peoples in order to beat them down more easily in the end to the level of their own cultureless pitifulness.

But that is how it is in everything.

They complain about the persecution of the Germans in South Tyrol, and these are the same people who in Germany violently oppose anyone who has a different understanding of being a nationalist than the surrender of his people without a fight to syphilitization by Jews and Negroes. These same people who call for freedom of conscience for the Germans in South Tyrol are oppressed most horribly in Germany itself. Never has the freedom to express one's nationalist sentiments been so stifled in Germany as under the rule of this dishonest party mob that presumes to take up the cudgels for the rights of conscience and national freedom in South Tyrol of all places. They moan about every wrong inflicted upon a German in South Tyrol but keep silent about the murders that these Marxist street thugs in Germany commit every month against the nationalist element—and the whole clean nationalist bourgeoisie, including the patriotic protesters, keeps silent with them. In a single year—that is, only five months of this year have elapsed—from the ranks of the National Socialist movement alone, nine people were killed, some under brutal circumstances, and more than six hundred injured.[375] This whole dishonest lot is silent about that, but how they would howl if even only one such act were committed by the fascists against the German people in South Tyrol. How they would call upon the whole world to revolt if even one German in South Tyrol were butchered under circumstances similar to the way the murderous Marxist rabble operates in Germany; however, this would not provoke the outrage of this clean phalanx for saving the German people. And how these same people, who protested most ceremoniously against the official persecution of the Germans in South Tyrol, have persecuted Germans "inconvenient" for them in the Reich itself. How the men who first gave their blood for Germany—starting with the submarine heroes[376] and continuing on to the saviors of Upper Silesia[377]—were dragged in chains before the courts and ultimately sentenced to prison terms, and all because they risked their lives hundreds and hundreds of times out of fervent love for the fatherland, while these pitiful protesting riff-raff crept away to some hiding place. You can add up the prison sentences that were imposed in Germany for acts that in a nationally aware state would have been rewarded with highest honors.[378] If Italy arrests a German in South Tyrol today, then the entire German nationalist and Marxist newspaper pack immediately cries for help. But they completely ignore the fact that in Germany one can be imprisoned for months based on a denunciation alone, and that house searches, violations of the secrecy of letters, telephone wiretapping—all unconstitutional violations of personal freedom guaranteed by the civil rights of this state—are the order of the day.[379] And our so-called nationalist parties cannot say that this is only possible in Marxist Prussia. First, with regard to foreign policy, they are fraternizing arm in arm with these same Marxists today, and second, these same nationalist parties have the same interest in suppressing a truly self-aware nationalism. In "nationalist Bavaria," the deathly ill Dietrich Eckart[380] was thrown into so-called protective custody—despite medical evidence and without even a trace of any guilt except, at most, his incorruptible nationalist sentiments—and kept there so long that he eventually collapsed and died two days after his release.[381] And this was Bavaria's greatest poet; indeed, he was a nationalist German, and because he hadn't created a *Jonny spielt auf*, he didn't exist for these guardians of national culture. In the same way that these nationalist patriots first killed him, they are today silencing his works to death because he was, after all, only a German, and a good Bavarian besides, not an internationalist Jew contaminating Germany. If he had been, he would be sacred to this patriots' league, but this was how they acted upon their nationalist bourgeois sentiments, in accordance with the openly expressed appeal in the Munich police headquarters: "Die, nationalist pig." But these are the same consciously German elements that mobilize the outrage of the world if a German is even only stupidly arrested in Italy.

When a few Germans were expelled from South Tyrol, these same people again stirred up the greatest outrage among the entire German people, but they only forget to add that Germans are harassed the most in Germany itself. "Nationalist Bavaria," under a bourgeois nationalist government, expelled dozens of Germans who, due to their uncompromising nationalism, simply did not suit the rotten bourgeois ruling stratum politically. Then suddenly people no longer saw in him the German Austrians' brother, but only the foreigner. And it did not stop with the expulsion of so-called foreign Germans. No, these same bourgeois nationalist hypocrites who hurled flaming protests against Italy for expelling a German from South Tyrol and deporting him to a different province, expelled from Bavaria dozens of Germans with German citizenship who fought for four and a half years in the German army, were seriously wounded, and received the highest honors.[382] Yes, this is what they look like, these bourgeois nationalist hypocrites who now rant in indignation at Italy while they themselves have heaped disgrace after disgrace upon themselves among their own people.

They lament about the denationalization in Italy while they denationalize the German people in their own homeland. They fight against anyone who opposes the contamination of our German blood; yes, they persecute in the most brazen and reckless manner those Germans who resist the de-Germanization, niggerization, and Judaization of our people—staged and sponsored by these hypocrites in the large cities—and attempt to have them imprisoned by dishonestly accusing them of endangering religious institutions.[383]

When an Italian Exaldo[384] damaged the Empress Elizabeth monument in Meran, they raised a fierce clamor and could not calm down, even though an Italian court sentenced the perpetrator to two months in prison. But they are not interested in the fact that the monuments and memorials to the past greatness of our people are continually defiled in Germany itself. It is all the same to them that in France almost all the monuments commemorating Germany in Alsace-Lorraine have been destroyed, and they are not upset that the Poles systematically lay waste to anything that even reminds them of the German name—yes, that in these months the Bismarck tower in Bromberg was quite officially demolished,[385] all this leaves them cold, these fighters for the national honor of our people. But woe if something like that were to happen in South Tyrol. Because that has suddenly become sacred ground to them. But the fatherland itself—our homeland—it can go to hell.

Certainly, in South Tyrol as well there has been more than one unwise action on the part of the Italians, and the attempt to systematically denationalize the German element is as unwise as its results are questionable; but those people have no right to protest against it when they are to some extent to blame for it all and when they also do not actually comprehend their people's national honor at all; instead the only ones who would have this right are those who have truly fought for German interests and German honor. In Germany, that was only the National Socialist movement.

The whole inner dishonesty of the agitation against Italy becomes obvious, however, when one compares the Italians' actions with the deeds committed against Germany by the French, Poles, Belgians, Czechs, Romanians, and [Kingdom of the] South Slavs. They do not care at all that France has expelled more than a quarter million Germans from Alsace-Lorraine[386]—more people than the entire population of South Tyrol [*sic*]. And the fact that the French are today attempting to eradicate every trace of Germanness in Alsace-Lorraine does not prevent these people from fraternizing with the French, even when the Parisians constantly respond with a box on the ears. That the Belgians persecute the German element with an unparalleled fanaticism, and that the Poles slaughtered more than seventeen thousand Germans, sometimes under downright brutish circumstances,[387] is no cause for excitement. That they expelled finite[388] tens of thousands, scarcely dressed, from their homes and drove them across the border[389]—these are all things that are unable to raise the ire of our bourgeois and patriotic protest swindlers. Anyone who wants to learn the true disposition of this pack only needs to remember the way in which the fugitives were met back then. Back then their hearts did not bleed for them [as little as these do today] when the tens of thousands of unfortunate displaced persons again found themselves on the soil of their beloved homeland, some in formal concentration camps,[390] and were now shifted from place to place like gypsies. I can still see before me the time when the first fugitives from the Ruhr came to Germany[391] and were shifted from police headquarters to police headquarters as if they were dangerous criminals. No, then their hearts did not bleed, these advocates and defenders of the German people in South Tyrol; but if a single German in South Tyrol itself is expelled by the Italians, or if he is wronged in some other way, then they tremble with righteous indignation and outrage over this unique disgrace to culture and over this greatest barbarity that the world has ever seen. Then they say: "The German people has never been oppressed anywhere with such appalling and tyrannical methods as in this country." Yes, but with one exception—namely, in Germany itself, through your own tyranny.

South Tyrol—or, more accurately, the Germans in South Tyrol—must not be lost to the German people, but in Germany itself, through their disgraceful policy of non-national dishonesty, general corruption, and subservience to the masters of international finance, they have killed more than twice as many people as the entire German population of South Tyrol numbers. They are silent about the seventeen to twenty-two thousand people[392] driven to suicide each year, on average, by their catastrophic policies in the last few years, although this number, with children, would in just ten years likewise account for more than [*sic*] the entire German population of South Tyrol.[393] They support emigration, and the increasing emigration levels are seen by this nationalist bourgeoisie of Herr Stresemann as an enormous foreign policy success, and yet this means that every four years Germany loses more people than all of South Tyrol's inhabitants of German nationality. With abortions and birth control, the number they murder each year is almost twice as high as the German population in South Tyrol. And this pack then claims the moral right to speak for the interests of the German people abroad.

Or this nationalist, official Germany complains about the de-Germanizing of our language in South Tyrol, but in Germany itself the German names in Czechoslovakia, Alsace-Lorraine, and so on are de-Germanized by official means. Yes, official travel guides are published in which even our German city names in Germany are Czechified for the sake of the Czechs. That is all fine, but the fact that the Italians have changed the sacred name of Brenner to Brennero is reason to provoke the most fervent resistance. And one has to have seen that, when a bourgeois patriot like that begins to seethe although one knows very well that it is all just comedy. Feigning nationalist passion suits our unemotional, rotten bourgeoisie just as well as when an old whore imitates love. It is all just artificial window dressing, and the worst is when such agitation comes from Austria. The black and yellow[394] legitimist element, which was previously completely indifferent to the Germans in Tyrol, now joins in the sacred nationalist outrage. That sort of thing then electrifies all the bourgeois associations, especially when they then hear that the Jews are participating as well. That is to say, they themselves only protest because they know that this time, as an exception, they can scream out their nationalist sentiments quite loudly without being sacked by the Jews controlling the press. On the contrary: It is lovely for an upright nationalist bourgeois man to appeal for the nationalist struggle and even be praised for it [by] Itzig Veitel Abrahamsohn. Yes, even more. The Jewish gazettes scream as well, and thus for the first time the true bourgeois nationalist German unity front is established from Krotoszyn[395] to Vienna to Innsbruck.

And our politically stupid German people allows itself to be taken in by this whole act in the same way that German diplomacy and our German people once allowed themselves to be snared and abused by the Habsburgs.

Germany has already once before allowed its foreign policy to be determined exclusively by Austrian interests. The penalty for that was appalling. Woe unto the young German nationalist movement if it allows its future policies to be determined by the theatrical babblers of the rotting bourgeois element, or even by the Marxist enemies of Germany. And woe unto it if it again obtains its directives from Vienna, in complete misjudgment of the true driving forces of the Austrian state. It will be the task of the National Socialist movement to prepare an end for this sham uproar and to choose sober reason to govern future German foreign policy.

But Italy also carries some responsibility for this whole development. I would find it dumb and politically immature to criticize the Italian state for pushing the border to the Brenner at the time of the Austrian collapse. The motives that guided it at the time were no baser that the motives that [indefinite] once guided the bourgeois annexationist politicians, including Herr Stresemann and Herr Erzberger, to strengthen the German border with the Belgian Maas fortifications.[396] A responsibly [and] thinking and acting state government will always strive to find strategically natural and secure borders. Italy certainly did not annex South Tyrol in order to gain possession of a few hundred thousand Germans; the Italians would certainly have preferred it if only Italians lived in this area instead of these Germans. Because actually, it was above all never [*sic*] strategic considerations that caused them to place the border over the Brenner. But no state would have acted differently in a similar situation. It is therefore pointless to make accusations about this border configuration, as ultimately every state determines its natural borders according to its own interests, not those of others. But although the possession of the Brenner may serve military interests and strategic purposes, it is inconsequential whether two hundred

thousand Germans live within this strategically established and secured border or not when the state itself encompasses forty-two
million people[397] and there is no militarily powerful enemy on this
particular border at all. It would have been wiser to spare these two
hundred thousand Germans any coercion, rather than attempting
[*to*] instill an attitude in them by force. The results of such an inducement, based on experience, usually seem to be worthless. One
also cannot exterminate a people in twenty or thirty years, regardless of the methods one employs and whether one wishes to do
this or not. The Italians will reply, with a certain appearance of right,
that this was initially not the intent either, but that it developed naturally and inevitably as a result of the provocative attempts at continual interference in domestic Italian affairs on the part of external Austrian or German forces and the repercussions this caused
among the South Tyroleans themselves. This is correct, because the
Italians actually did initially accommodate the Germans in South
Tyrol very decently and loyally. But as soon as fascism came to power
in Italy, agitation against Italy began in Germany and Austria, for
reasons of principle, and now led to increasing bad temper on both
sides—which in South Tyrol ultimately had to lead to the consequences that we see before us today. The most disastrous part of
that was the activity of the Andreas Hofer League,[398] which, instead
of recommending prudence to the Germans in South Tyrol and
making it clear to them that their mission was to build a bridge between Germany and Italy,[399] awakened hopes among the South
Tyroleans that were outside the realm of all feasibility but which
had to lead to provocation and thus to unintended measures. If
measures got carried to extremes, this league can be credited as one
of the primary reasons. Anyone who has had the opportunity, as I
have, to get to know important members of this association as
people as well, must be amazed at the irresponsibility with which
an organization whose truly active forces are so limited nevertheless manages to do disastrous harm. Because when I look at some
of these leading minds—and I am thinking of one in particular,

whose office is in the Munich police headquarters[400]—then one becomes worried at the thought that people who would never put themselves in danger provoke a development that, as its final consequence, must end with a bloody conflict.

It is also true that no understanding can be reached over South Tyrol with the real manipulators of this anti-Italian agitation because these elements are just as indifferent to South Tyrol itself as they are to the German people in general; rather, to them South Tyrol is nothing more than a suitable means to cause confusion and turn public opinion, especially in Germany, against Italy. Because that is what these characters have in mind. And thus the Italian objection also has a certain justification that regardless of how the Germans are treated in South Tyrol, these people would always, because they want to, find some suitable cause for their agitation. But precisely because certain elements in Germany today, just as in Italy, have an interest in using every possible means to thwart an understanding between the two nations, wisdom would oblige one to deprive them of these means to the extent possible, even at the risk that they will then naturally continue searching all the same. The alternative would only make sense if there were absolutely no one in Germany with the courage to argue for an understanding in the face of this agitation. But that is not the case. On the contrary, the more today's Italy attempts to avoid all imprudent incidents itself, the easier it becomes for Italy's friends in Germany to expose the agitators here, reveal the hypocrisy of their arguments, and halt their activities that are poisoning our people. But if people in Italy really believe that no accommodation can be reached amid the clamor and the demands of foreign organizations, because this would seem more like a capitulation and might only increase the arrogance of these elements, then ways could be found to attribute such an accommodation strictly to those who not only are not involved in this agitation, but who, on the contrary, as supporters of an understanding between Italy and Germany, themselves lead the fiercest battle against the poisoners of public opinion in Germany.

The foreign policy goal of the National Socialist movement is concerned neither with economic policy nor a bourgeois border policy. Our goal of obtaining space for our people will establish a pattern of development for the German people that will never need to bring it into conflict with Italy in the future either. We will also never sacrifice the blood of our people to achieve minor border corrections, but only to gain space for the further expansion and feeding of our people. This goal pushes us toward the east. What the Mediterranean Sea is for Italy, the eastern shore of the Baltic is for Germany. Germany's mortal enemy in any further development—yes, even for the mere preservation of the unity of our Reich—is France, which is likewise the mortal enemy of Italy. The National Socialist movement will never sink to superficial, shallow jingoism. It will not rattle the saber. Its leaders have, almost without exception, come to know war as it is in reality and in truth. It will thus also never spill blood for goals other than those that benefit the entire future development of our people. It thus also refuses to provoke a war with Italy on account of a ridiculous—given the German fragmentation in Europe—border correction. On the contrary, it wishes the disastrous Germanic drive to the south to end forever, and the representation of our interests to take place in the direction that would make it possible for our people to overcome its shortage of space. But by releasing Germany from its current period of enslavement and servitude, we are also fighting above all for the restoration of and thus on behalf of German honor.

If the Italy of today believes that changing various measures in South Tyrol could be perceived as a capitulation in the face of foreign interference, but without leading to a desired understanding in the end anyway, then its reorientation may take place—and also be openly attributed exclusively to those who, within Germany itself, are advocates for an understanding with Italy and who do not merely refuse to be identified with the agitators against such a thing [understanding] but who have even fought the fiercest battle against these elements for years and who acknowledge as self-evident the sovereign rights of the Italian state.

Just as it is not a matter of indifference to Germany whether it acquires Italy as a friend, it is similarly no matter of indifference to Italy. Just as fascism gave the Italian people new value, the value of the German people cannot be calculated for the future based on its current expressions of life, but on the strengths that it so often demonstrated in its previous history and that it perhaps can show again already tomorrow.

Just as for Germany, the friendship of Italy is worth a sacrifice, so the friendship of Germany is worth just as much to Italy. It would be fortunate for both peoples if the powers that carry this awareness in the two countries could reach an understanding.

So although the anti-Italian agitation in Germany is very much to blame for the disastrous hostility, the same amount of responsibility also lies on Italy's side, as it did not attempt to remove the means as far as possible from these agitators, given the fact that in Germany itself people were fighting against this agitation.[401]

If the cleverness of the fascist regime one day manages to turn sixty-five million Germans into friends of Italy, then this is worth more than if two hundred thousand are educated to be bad Italians.

Italian advocacy to forbid the union of Austria with Germany was not right either.[402] The very fact that it was primarily France that argued for this prohibition should have led to the opposite response in Rome. Because France does not take this step to be of use to Italy either, but rather in the hope of also being able to inflict damage on it in this way. There are two primary reasons that induced France to push through the annexation prohibition: First, because the French wanted in this way to prevent a strengthening of Germany, and second, because they are convinced that they can one day gain the Austrian state as a member of the French European alliance. In Rome, however, one can harbor no illusions that the French influence is significantly more decisive in Vienna than even the German, not to mention the Italian. The French attempt to transfer the League of Nations to Vienna if possible[403] arises only from the aim of strengthening the cosmopolitan character of this city and bringing it into relation with that country whose essence and culture finds a stronger resonance in the current Viennese atmosphere than the essence of the German Reich does.

Although the annexationist leanings of the Austrian provinces are meant seriously, they were not taken seriously in Vienna. On the contrary, when the annexation idea was really considered in Vienna, then it was always only to eliminate some financial difficulty, because then France was much readier to assist the little borrowing state. But to the extent that there is an internal consolidation of the Austrian Federal State and Vienna regains its full dominant position, this annexation idea will gradually evaporate. In addition, political developments in Vienna are assuming an increasingly anti-Italian and especially antifascist character, while Austro-Marxism has never from the beginning made any secret of its sympathies for France.

So because annexation was fortunately prevented back then, in part due to Italian help, the French alliance system will one day insert the missing member between Prague and Yugoslavia.

But for Italy, the prevention of Austrian union with Germany was wrong also for psychological reasons. The smaller the splintered Austrian state remained, the more limited, naturally, were its foreign policy aims as well. One cannot expect a far-reaching territorial policy objective from a state entity that has barely ...[404] square kilometers of land area with less than ... million inhabitants. If German Austria had been annexed to Germany in 1919–[19]20, the drift of its political thinking would gradually have been determined by the great, and at least possible, political goals of Germany, a people of almost seventy million. Because this was prevented back then, even the direction of foreign policy thinking was turned away from larger goals and restricted to small ideas of reconstructing old Austria. Only in this way was it possible for the South Tyrolean question to have developed such significance. Because as small as the Austrian state was, it was at least big enough to become the bearer of a foreign policy idea that not only corresponded to its smallness but was also, on the other hand, gradually able to poison the political thinking of all of Germany. The more limited the political ideas of the Austrian state become due to the contraction of its territory, the more they will result in problems that could very likely be important for this state, but which, for the German nation, cannot be seen as decisive for the formation of German foreign policy.

Italy should argue for Austria's annexation to Germany, if only to thwart the French alliance system in Europe. But it should also do this to give the German border policy faction other tasks as a result of its incorporation into a large Reich.

In addition, the reasons that once induced Italy to oppose the annexation are not entirely obvious. Neither the current Austria nor the current Germany could come into consideration as a military adversary for Italy at the present. But if France succeeds in creating a general anti-Italian alliance in Europe, and Austria and Germany take part in this alliance, then it would not make any difference at all in the military situation if Austria is now independent or if it is part of Germany. And one cannot really speak of true independence for such a small entity in any case. [They will always] Austria will always be tied to the apron strings of some great power. Switzerland cannot prove the opposite at all, because as a state, albeit based on tourism, it nevertheless possesses its own possibility to support its life. This is impossible for Austria due to the imbalance between the country's capital and the size of the total population. But regardless what attitude this Austria itself adopts toward Italy, the fact of its existence alone already eases the strategic military situation of Czechoslovakia, which one day, in one way or another, can make its presence known to Hungary, the natural ally of Italy.

Military and political reasons would argue that the Italians should view the annexation prohibition as at least meaningless, if not even expedient [*sic*].[405]

[C]

I cannot conclude this chapter[406] without now establishing in detail who actually bears the guilt for the fact that there is a South Tyrolean question at all.

For us National Socialists, the decision has been made legally and at least I oppose most forcefully the dragging of millions of Germans onto a battlefield and allowing them to bleed there for France's interests, without obtaining a result for Germany that is in any way commensurate with the casualties. I also refuse to acknowledge the standpoint of national honor as decisive here, because according to this viewpoint I would then still have to march first against France, which, in all of its actions, violated German honor quite differently than Italy did. In the introduction[407] to this book I have [not d] already addressed the possibility of making the concept of national honor the foundation of foreign policy, and thus do not need to comment on that further here. When our protesting associations now attempt to portray our attitude as a betrayal or abandonment of South Tyrol [*sic*], then this could only be true if without this stance South Tyrol either would not have been lost at all or would be on the point of reverting back to the other Tyrol in the foreseeable future.

I thus feel compelled in this discussion to establish once again very precisely who betrayed South Tyrol and through whose measures it was lost to [Austria] Germany.

1. South Tyrol was betrayed and lost through the actions of those parties that worked throughout peacetime to weaken or completely refuse the armaments that the German people needed to assert itself in Europe and thereby robbed the German people of the strength needed in the critical hour for victory and thus also for the preservation of South Tyrol.

2. [*South Tyrol was lost by*] those parties that worked throughout peacetime to undermine the moral and ethical foundations of our people and, above all, to destroy belief in the right to self-defense.

3. South Tyrol was also betrayed by those so-called state-support-ing and nationalist parties that watched these events indifferently, or at least without serious opposition. They are, albeit indirectly, also partially responsible for the military weakening of our people.

4. South Tyrol was betrayed and lost through the actions of those political parties that debased the German people to the role of henchman in the Habsburgs' great-power notion; that saw the task of the German nation as preserving the Austrian state in-stead of propounding for German foreign policy the goal of the national unification of our people; that for this reason, in peace-time already, watched—yes, assisted in—the systematic, decades-long de-Germanizing work of the Habsburgs; and that are thus also complicit in the failure to solve the Austrian question, either by Germany itself or at least with decisive German participation. In such a case, South Tyrol would certainly have been preserved for the German people.

5. South Tyrol was lost as a result of the general aimlessness of German foreign policy. In 1914, this aimlessness also extended to the establishment of sensible war aims—or it impeded their adoption.

6. South Tyrol was betrayed by all those who, throughout the course of the war, did not contribute their utmost to the strength-ening of the German defensive and offensive power, as well as by those parties that purposely paralyzed the German defensive power and also those that tolerated this paralysis.

7. South Tyrol was lost as a result of the inability, even during the war, to reorient German foreign policy and save the German people in the Austrian state by renouncing the preservation of the Habsburg great power.

8. South Tyrol was lost and betrayed by the actions of those who, during the war—under the pretence of hoping for peace with-out victory[408]—broke the German people's moral power of resis-tance and, instead of a demonstration of the will to fight, brought about a peace resolution that was disastrous for Germany.[409]

9. South Tyrol was lost through the betrayal of those parties and men who, during the war still, infatuated the German people by lying about the Entente's lack of imperialistic aims, drew the people away from the absolute necessity of resistance, and ultimately allowed them to believe the Entente more than the German voices of warning.

10. South Tyrol was also lost by those who, from within Germany, caused the attrition of the front, and by the contamination of German thinking with the sham declarations of Woodrow Wilson.[410]

11. South Tyrol was betrayed and lost through the actions of the parties and men who—from conscientious objection to the organization of munitions strikes[411]—robbed the army of the perception that its fight and its victory were unyieldingly necessary.

12. South Tyrol was betrayed and lost through the organization and execution of the November crime as well as through the pathetic and cowardly toleration of this ignominy by the so-called state-supporting nationalist forces.

13. South Tyrol was lost and betrayed through the shameless actions of those men and parties that sullied German honor after the collapse and destroyed our people's reputation in the world, thereby first awakening our enemies' courage to make such extensive demands. It was also lost through the pathetic cowardice of the nationalist bourgeois parties and patriotic associations, which all capitulated dishonorably when faced with the terror of the baseness and perfidy.

14. Finally, South Tyrol was betrayed and lost through the signing of the peace treaties,[412] and thereby through the legal acknowledgment of the loss of this area as well.

All the German parties are responsible for all of this. Some of them destroyed Germany consciously and deliberately, and the others—with their proverbial incompetence and shocking cowardice—not only did not do anything to impede the annihilators of the German future, but instead, through the incompetence of their domestic and foreign policy leadership, actually played into the hands of these enemies of our people. Never has a people been ruined through such a combination of baseness, perfidy, cowardice, and stupidity as the German people has.

Insight into the foreign policy actions and operations of this old Germany is provided in these days[413] by the publication of the war memoirs of the head of the American intelligence service, Mr. Flynn.[414]

I permit a bourgeois-democratic organ to speak on this only to provide broader understanding:[415]

[How America Entered the War
Flynn Publishes from within the Diplomatic Intelligence Service
by F. W. Elven,[416] *representative of the* Münchner Neuesten Nachtrichten

Cincinnati, mid-June

In the weekly Liberty, *much read here, William J. Flynn publishes some of his recollections of the war. During the war, Flynn was head of the United States Secret Service. This agency spans the entire country and is splendidly organized. In peacetime it is primarily responsible for the personal protection of the president. Anything else in the federal capital that is in need of protection—or believes itself to be—also enjoys its care. It monitors all dubious elements that are under suspicion of being associated in any way with political activities directed against the state and its officials. During the war its primary responsibility was to monitor those who had attracted attention to themselves as greater or lesser enemies of the war, or also those who were only under suspicion of disagreeing with the Wilsonian war policy. Germans also enjoyed its special consideration, and many of them walked into the traps that were laid everywhere at the time by the federal intelligence service.*

But from Flynn's recollections one learns that the Secret Service was given an important assignment even before our entry into the war. In 1915, a full two years before the declaration of war, the most proficient telephone expert was ordered to Washington and instructed to arrange the telephone lines leading to the German and Austrian embassies in such a way that Secret Service agents could eavesdrop on every discussion that anyone held with the ambassadors and their staff and every conversation that left the embassy premises. A room was set up with which all the lines were ingeniously connected, so that not a single conversation could be lost. Secret agents sat in this room day and night, listening to the eavesdropped conversations and dictating them to stenographers sitting nearby. Every evening the head of the Secret Service—i.e., the author of the article in the weekly Liberty—*received the stenographic transcripts of all conversations held in the last twenty-four hours, so he was able to communicate everything important to the State Department [sic] and President Wilson that same night.*

Note the time: This arrangement was created at the beginning of 1915, so at a time when the United States was still living at peace with Germany and Austria-Hungary, and Wilson did not tire of affirming that he harbored no hostile intentions against Germany. It was also a time when the then German ambassador in Washington, Count Bernstorff,[417] missed no opportunity to acknowledge Wilson's friendly attitude and amicable feelings toward Germany and the German people. It was at this same time that Wilson instructed his confidant Baruch[418] to gradually begin mobilizing industry for war—so the time in which it was becoming increasingly apparent (as the American historian Harry Elmer Barnes[419] also states in his book on the origins of the Great War) that Wilson was determined to enter the war and only delayed the execution of his bellicose plans because public opinion still had to be won over.

Flynn's publication must finally put an end to the foolish talk about Wilson being pushed into war against his will by the German submarine warfare. The tapping of the telephone lines leading to the German embassy was done with his knowledge. One learns that from Flynn's publication as well. The author adds that the material collected against Germany in this way contributed significantly to the final rupture. Which can only mean that this material gave Wilson the means to win over public opinion for the war that he had long planned. And this material was in fact admirably suited for that purpose. The publication confirms completely what unfortunately always should have been said: that Germany was represented in Washington at that time in manner that was downright unbelievably incompetent and unbelievably undignified. When one hears that Flynn writes in one passage that the daily stenographic reports prepared for him would have contained enough material to keep a divorce lawyer busy for months, then one obtains a rough idea of what was taking place.

The Secret Service kept trusted female associates in Washington and New York; these women were to sound out the staff of the German embassy, including Bernstorff, when something important occurred. One of these kept a fine apartment where the gentlemen met their ladies and where occasionally Secretary of State Lansing[420] also dropped in to hear what was new. On New Year's Day 1916, when the news of the sinking of the steamer Persia[421] became known in the capital, Bernstorff called five women in turn to pay them sweet compliments and receive similar compliments from them, although due to the mood left in the State Department and the White House by the news of the Persia's sinking, there could truly have been no lack of serious occupation.

One of the women complimented Bernstorff by saying that he was a great lover and always would be, even when he was a hundred years old. The other men from the embassy were no different. One, whom Flynn referred to as the best diplomat in the embassy, had a female friend in New York, a married woman, with whom he had daily telephone conversations— which cost the German Reich twenty dollars each time—and whom he visited frequently. He told her everything that happened, and she then made sure that it reached the appropriate authorities. Quite ordinary remarks about Wilson and his wife were also heard in the telephone conversations, and one can easily imagine that this did not make the White House sentiments toward Germany any friendlier.

From conversations that took place in early March 1916, one learns how little those in the German embassy knew the country and the people, and with what childish plans they occupied themselves. At that time Congress was considering a resolution proposal, submitted by Senator Gore,[422] to issue a warning to the American people about using armed merchant ships.[423] President Wilson fought the proposal most bitterly. He needed the loss of American lives in order to whip up anti-German sentiments.

Those in the German embassy knew that the proposal's prospects were not favorable, so they seriously considered the plan to buy Congress. But they did not know initially where they should get the money. On March 3 the Senate decided to table Gore's proposal temporarily. The vote in the House was to take place several days later. Therefore the plan to buy the House first was zealously pursued, but in this case at least Bernstorff was sensible enough to advise resolutely against the plan.

For anyone who has healthy German blood in his veins, reading Flynn's article must give rise to a great sense of indignation—not just on account of Wilson's insidious policy, but also and especially on account of the unbelievable stupidity with which those in the German embassy played into the hands of this policy. Wilson took in Bernstorff more and more every day. When Colonel House,[424] *his confidant, returned from his European trip in May 1916, Bernstorff traveled to New York to meet him there. Wilson, however, who had acted toward Bernstorff as if he had no objections to this encounter, secretly gave House instructions not to meet with the count and to avoid him at all costs. And that is how it happened. Bernstorff waited in vain in New York. Then he went to a nearby beach and allowed himself to be photographed in his swimsuit there with two female friends, in a very intimate position. The picture is included in Flynn's article. At that time it fell into the hands of the Russian ambassador Bakmateff,*[425] *who had it enlarged and sent it to London, where it was published by the newspapers with the caption "The dignified ambassador," and where it served the Allied propaganda admirably.]*

That is what the *Münchner Neuesten Nachtrichten* writes today. But the man who is characterized here was a typical representative of German foreign policy before the war, just as he is also a typical representative of the German foreign policy of the republic. This individual, who in any other state would be hanged by a national court of law, is Germany's representative at the League of Nations in Geneva.

These people carry the guilt and the responsibility for Germany's collapse and thus also for the loss of South Tyrol. And with them the blame falls on all parties and men who either caused such conditions or backed them or also even tacitly acquiesced or did not fight most forcefully against them.

But the men who today brazenly attempt to lie to the public again and who wish to designate others as responsible for the loss of South Tyrol must first give a detailed account of what they have done to preserve it.

For me personally, I can in any case declare with pride that from the time that I reached manhood I have advocated the strengthening of my people, and when the war came I fought for four and a half years on the German front in the West, and since the end of the war I have been fighting against those corrupt creatures whom Germany has to thank for this disaster. And that in this time I have made no compromises with the betrayers of the German fatherland, neither in terms of domestic policy nor foreign policy; rather, I have steadfastly proclaimed their destruction as the goal of my life's work and the task of the National Socialist movement.

I can endure the yapping of the cowardly bourgeois mutts and the members of the patriotic associations all the more calmly because I know only too well the average poltroons of this unutterably contemptible entity. They know me as well, and that is the reason for their clamor.

[CHAPTER XVI]

[Conclusion]

[A]

Today, as a National Socialist, I see Italy as the first possible ally of Germany that could step out of the old enemy coalition without this alliance meaning an immediate war for Germany—a war for which we would not be armed.

This alliance would, in my opinion, be of equal benefit to both Germany and Italy. Even when its direct benefit no longer existed, it would never become a detriment as long as both nations represent their own national interests, in the truest sense of the word. As long as Germany sees as its foremost foreign policy goal the preservation of the freedom and independence of our people, and intends to secure the necessities of daily life for this people, its foreign policy thinking will be determined by our people's need for space. And as long as that is the case, there can be no internal or external inducement for us to develop enmity with a state that does not present the least obstacle to us in this.

And as long as Italy wishes to serve its real vital interests as a true nation state, it will have to focus its political thoughts and actions on expanding Italy's territory, likewise obeying the need for space. The prouder and more independent, and the more nationalistic the Italian people becomes, the less its development will ever come into conflict with Germany.

These two countries' areas of interest are, most fortunately, so far apart that there is no natural area of friction.[426]

A nationally aware Germany and an equally proud Italy will one day—through their sincere, mutual friendship, based on common interests—also be able to heal the wounds left by the Great War.

South Tyrol will thus one day have an important mission to fulfill in the service of both peoples. When the Italians and Germans of this area, filled with responsibility for their own people, first recognize and understand the great problems that Italy and Germany have to solve, the minor day-to-day disagreements will seem less consequential in the face of the higher purpose of building a bridge of sincere mutual understanding across the former German-Italian border.

I know that this is just as impossible under the current government in Germany as it would be under a nonfascist one in Italy. Because the powers that determine Germany policy today do not desire a German revitalization, but rather our destruction. They likewise desire the destruction of the current fascist Italian state and will thus leave no stone unturned to reduce the two peoples to hatred and enmity. France would joyfully seize upon every such—even if just a thoughtless—comment and use it to its own advantage.

Only a National Socialist Germany will find the way to an ultimate understanding with fascist Italy and definitively eliminate the danger of military conflict between the two peoples. Because this old Europe was always an area that was controlled by political systems, and this will not change, at least in the foreseeable future. The general European democracy will either be replaced by a system [of] Jewish-Marxist Bolshevism, to which state after state falls victim, or by a system of free and unfettered nation states which, in the unrestricted play of forces, will impress upon Europe the stamp of their character according to their population and importance.

It is also not good for fascism as an idea to be isolated in Europe. Either the philosophy from which it is derived will become generally accepted or Italy will one day again become enslaved to the universal thinking of a different Europe.

[B]

So if one examines Germany's foreign policy options more closely, then only two states actually remain as potential valuable allies for the future: Italy and England. Italy's relationship with England itself is already a good one today[427] and, as I have already argued elsewhere, should hardly deteriorate in the near future. This has nothing to do with mutual liking, either; instead it is based, particularly on the Italian side, on a rational assessment of the actual power relations. Both states share an aversion to [*an*] excessive and unlimited French hegemony in Europe. Italy, because its most vital European interests will be threatened, and England, because a France that is dominant in Europe could pose a new threat to the currently no longer entirely unassailable naval and world dominance of the English.

The fact that Spain and Hungary can also already be assigned to this community of interests today—if only quietly—is based on Spain's objection to the French colonization activities in North Africa,[428] and Hungary's hostility toward Yugoslavia, which is supported by France.[429]

If Germany were to succeed in participating in a new coalition of states that would either lead to a shift in the weight distribution within the League of Nations itself or allow the development of the decisive power factors outside the League of Nations entirely, then the first domestic-policy precondition for a future energetic foreign-policy activity would be met. The disarmament—and thus defenselessness, for all intents and purposes—imposed upon us by the Treaty of Versailles could, even if only gradually, come to an end. This would only be possible if the previous coalition of victors itself were to break down on this issue, but never against the collective front of the coalition of former victorious states now constricting us, whether in alliance with Russia or even in association with other so-called oppressed states.[430]

In the distant future, one could then perhaps imagine a new association of nations—composed of individual states of superior national quality—that could then perhaps challenge the imminent overpowering of the world by the American union. Because it seems to me that the existence of England's world domination inflicts less suffering on the nations of today than would the emergence of an American one.

No pan-Europe can be summoned to solve this problem, however, but only a Europe with free and independent nation states whose areas of interest are kept apart and precisely defined.

But for Germany, only then can the time arrive—assured by a France pushed back within its limits and based on the renewed armed forces—to bring about the elimination of its shortage of space. But as soon as our people have grasped this great territorial goal in the East, Germany foreign policy will as a consequence achieve not only clarity but also stability which will enable us, at least in the foreseeable future, to avoid political insanities such as those that ensnared our people at the end into the Great War. And then we will finally have overcome the period of petty daily clamor and completely fruitless economic and border policies.

But Germany, also internally, will then have to move toward the greatest concentration of its power resources. It will have to recognize that armies and navies are not built and organized based on romantic ideas, but according to practical necessities. It will then naturally become clear that our primary task is the formation of a phenomenally strong land army, because our future does not actually lie on the water but in Europe.

Not until people completely recognize the significance of this statement—and, based on this recognition, end our peoples' shortage of land in the East [*sic*] in a large-scale manner—will German industry also cease to be a factor in the international disturbances that brought down a thousand dangers on our [*head*]. It will then at least serve the essential issue of satisfying our internal requirements. A people that no longer needs to shift its rural offspring to the large cities as factory workers [*sic*], but instead is able to settle them as independent farmers on their own land, will open up an internal market for German industry which will gradually withdraw and remove it from the frenzied struggle and the tussle for a so-called place in the sun in the rest of the world.[431]

The foreign policy task of the National Socialist movement is to prepare for this development and one day also implement it. The movement must also, from within its ideological philosophy, place foreign policy at the service of the reorganization of our people. Here as well, it must instill the basic principle that one does not fight for systems, but for a living people—flesh and blood—which must be preserved and which cannot lack daily bread, so that as a result of its physical health it may be spiritually healthy as well.

Just as it in its struggle for domestic policy reform it must, a thousand times, surmount resistance, lack of understanding, and malice, it will also have to clean up foreign policy—the deliberate treason of the Marxists just as much as the tangled mass of worthless, even harmful rhetoric and notions of our nationalist bourgeois world. The more limited the understanding is of the meaning of its struggle today, the more resounding its success will be one day.

[C]

The reason Italy, first and foremost, can come into consideration as a potential ally for Germany is connected to the fact that in this country—as the only one—domestic and foreign policy are determined by purely Italian national interests. It is only these Italian national interests, however, with which German interests do not conflict, and which, vice versa, do not run counter to German interests.

And this is important not only for factual reasons, but also for the following:

The war against Germany was waged by a most powerful international coalition in which only some of the states could have had a direct interest in the destruction of Germany. In more than a few countries, the transition to war took place through influences that did not in any way arise from—or even could benefit—the true intrinsic interests of these peoples. An enormous war propaganda campaign began to cloud the public opinion of these peoples and excite them for a war that could bring no advantage to some of these peoples, and sometimes ran completely contrary to their true interests.

The power that initiated this enormous war propaganda campaign was international Jewry.[432] Because although participation in the war—viewed from the standpoint of their own interests—may have been pointless for some of these nations, it was perfectly sensible and logical from the viewpoint of the interests of international Jewry.[433]

It is not my task here to provide a treatise on the Jewish question itself. This cannot be done within the scope of such a short, necessarily concise presentation. Only [so much] the following is to be said here, in the interests of better understanding:

The Jews, although they are a people whose core is not entirely uniform in terms of race, are nevertheless a people with certain essential particularities that distinguish it from all other peoples living on the earth. Judaism is not a religious community; rather, the religious ties between the Jews are in reality the current national constitution of the Jewish people. The Jew has never had his own territorially defined state like the Aryan states. Nonetheless, his religious community is a real state because it ensures the preservation, propagation, and future of the Jewish people. But this is the job of the state alone. The fact that no territorial boundaries underlie the Jewish state—as is the case with Aryan states—is associated with the fact that the essence of the Jewish people lacks the productive forces to build and sustain a territorial state.

Just as every people possesses, as the basic tendency of all its earthly actions has the obsession with preserving itself as its driving force, the same is true of the Jews. But here the struggle for survival takes various forms, corresponding to the entirely different natures of the Aryan peoples and the Jews. The basis of the Aryans' struggle for survival is the land, which is cultivated by them and which now provides the general basis for an economy that, in an internal cycle, satisfies their own requirements through the productive forces of their own people.

The Jewish people, because of its lack of productive capabilities, cannot carry out the territorially conceived formation of a state; instead, it needs the labor and creative activities of other nations to support its own existence. The existence of the Jew himself thus becomes a parasitic existence within the life of other peoples. The ultimate goal of the Jewish struggle for survival is the enslavement of productively active peoples. To reach this goal—which, in reality, the Jews' struggle for survival has represented throughout the ages—the Jew uses every weapon that is in accordance with the entirety of his character.

In terms of domestic policy, he fights within the individual peoples first for equality and then for superiority. Weapons assisting him in this are the attributes of shrewdness, cleverness, cunning, disguise, and so on, which are rooted in the character of his people. They are stratagems in his fight to preserve life, just like the stratagems of other peoples in military conflict.

In terms of foreign policy, he attempts to get the peoples into restlessness, divert them from their true interests, hurl them into wars with one another, and thus gradually—with the help of the power of money and propaganda—become their masters.

His ultimate aim is the denationalization and chaotic bastardization of the other peoples, the lowering of the racial level of the highest, and domination over this racial mush through the eradication of these peoples' intelligentsias and their replacement with the members of his own people.

The Jewish international struggle will therefore always end in bloody Bolshevization—that is to say, in truth, the destruction of the intellectual upper classes associated with the various peoples, so that he himself will be able to rise to mastery over the now leaderless humanity.

In this process, stupidity, cowardice, and wickedness play into his hands. Bastards provide him the first opening to break into a foreign ethnic community.

Jewish domination always ends with the decline of all culture and ultimately of the insanity of the Jew himself. Because he is a parasite on the peoples, and his victory means his own end just as much as the death of his victim.

With the collapse of the ancient world, the Jew faced young, in some cases still untainted, peoples who were secure in their racial instincts and who refused to be infiltrated by him. He was a stranger, and all his lies and disguises availed him little for nearly fifteen hundred years.

It was feudal rule and the princely regimes that first created the general situation that allowed him to join the struggle of an oppressed social class—yes, in a short time he made it his own. With the French Revolution he achieved equal civil rights. That built the bridge he could now stride across to capture political power within the ethnic communities.

The nineteenth century gives him a dominant position within the peoples' economy, due to the expansion of capital loans, founded on the concept of interest. Via the detour of stock, he finally obtains possession of a large portion of the production facilities, and with the help of the stock exchange he gradually becomes ruler not only of public economic life but ultimately also political life.

He supports this domination with the intellectual degradation of the peoples, assisted by Freemasonry and the work of the press which has become dependent upon him. He discovers in the newly rising fourth estate of the working class the potential force to destroy the bourgeois intellectual regime, just as the bourgeoisie was once the instrument to shatter feudal rule. Bourgeois stupidity, a shocking lack of principle, greed, and cowardice play into his hands in this. He formed the laborers' occupation into a special class, which he now asks to take up the fight against the national intelligentsia. Marxism becomes the intellectual father of the Bolshevik Revolution. It is the weapon of terror that the Jew now applies ruthlessly and brutally.

Around the turn of the century, the Jew's economic conquest of Europe is fairly complete; he now begins with securing it politically. That is to say, the first attempts to eradicate the national intelligentsia are undertaken in the form of revolutions.

He uses the European peoples' tension—most of which is attributable to their general need for space and the consequences that arise from it—to his advantage by systematically agitating for world war.

The goal is the destruction of inherently anti-Semitic Russia as well as the destruction of the German Reich, whose administration and army still provide resistance to the Jews. A further goal is the overthrow of those dynasties that have not yet been made subordinate to a Jewish-dependent and led democracy.

This goal in the Jewish struggle has at least to some degree been completely achieved. Czarism and Kaiserism [*sic*] in Germany have been eliminated. With the help of the Bolshevik Revolution, the Russian upper class and also the national intelligentsia were—with inhuman torture and barbarity—murdered and completely eradicated. The victims of this Jewish fight for dominance in Russia totaled twenty-eight to thirty million dead among the Russian people.[434] Fifteen times as many as the Great War cost Germany.[435] After the successful Revolution he [further] tore away all the ties of orderliness, morality, custom, and so on, abolished marriage as a higher institution,[436] and proclaimed in its place universal licentiousness with the goal that through disorderly bastardy, to breed a generally inferior human mush which itself is incapable of leadership and ultimately will no longer be able to do without the Jews as its only intellectual element.

Only the future will tell to what extent this has succeeded and to what extent the natural forces of reaction will now be able to bring about a change in this most terrible crime of all time against humanity.

At the moment he is attempting to steer the remaining states into the same situation. He is supported in his efforts and activities and backed by the bourgeois nationalist parties of the so-called nationalist patriotic associations, while the Marxists, the Democrats, and the so-called Christian Center appear as offensive combat troops.

The fiercest struggle over the victory of the Jews is currently taking place in Germany. Here it is the National Socialist movement alone that has taken up the fight against this execrable crime against humanity.

In all European states, the struggle for political power is currently being fought out—in some cases quietly, in some cases more violently—albeit often only under cover.

As in Russia, this struggle has now also been decided in France. There the Jew, benefiting from a number of circumstances, has entered into a joint venture with French national chauvinism. The Jewish stock exchange and French bayonets have since been allies.

The fight has not yet been decided in England. There the Jewish invasion is still confronted by old British tradition. The instincts of the Anglo-Saxons are still so acute and alive that one cannot speak of a complete Jewish victory; instead, the Jew is in some ways forced to adapt his own interests to those of the English.

If the Jew prevails in England, then English interests will recede into the background, just as in Germany today it is no longer

German but Jewish interests that dominate. If the British prevail, however, then a change in England's attitude toward Germany can still take place.

The struggle over Jewish dominance has been decided in Italy as well. In Italy, with the victory of fascism, the Italian people have won. Even though the Jew is forced to attempt to adapt himself to fascism in Italy today, his attitude toward fascism outside Italy reveals his real conception of it. Since that memorable day when the fascist legions moved to Rome, only Italy's own national interest has been dominant and decisive for the fate of the nation.[437]

For this reason, no other state is as well suited as Italy to be an ally of Germany. The fathomless stupidity and underhanded baseness of our so-called ethnic nationalists are reflected in the fact that they reject the only state that is governed nationalistically today and instead would rather, as true ethnic German nationalists, enter into an international coalition with the Jews. It is fortunate that these fools' time in Germany is ended,[438] and that thus the term *deutschvölkisch* (ethnic German nationalism) can be released from the entanglement of these petty and pitiful creatures. The term will gain infinitely from that.[439]

Appendix I

MUNICH
Centralverlag der NSDAP   Target No: 589
Thierschstr. 11[1]   Priority: 3

Remarks:

1.   This is a supplementary report.[2] Joseph Berg,[3] who lives at 35 Scheubner Richter Strasse, Munich, and was technical manager of this publishing house, gave us a manuscript of an allegedly unpublished work by Adolf Hitler. It was written over 15 years ago and locked up in a safe. Mr. Berg had strictest orders that the manuscript could neither be printed or shown to anybody. More information on this could be had through Mr. Berg.

2.   Mr. Berg also informed us that an evacuation place (Ausweichstelle) for books of the Verlag is in the Willibalds Burg nr. Eichstaedt.

Paul M. Leake
Capt. SC[4]

[1] This building was purchased by the Eher-Verlag in 1929, Dresler, p. 207.
[2] No prior report has been found.
[3] See the Introduction.
[4] Signal Corps.

Appendix II

Hitler's Speech of July 13, 1928
(published in the *Völkischer Beobachter* on July 18, 1928)

When we criticize the foreign policy activity of the current government, it is not mere carping, nor the desire to denigrate everything, but the awareness that one day we will carry the responsibility and that we will then give our ideas definite shape. The Social Democrats once criticized as well, but the critics of that time are in today's government and give cause for devastating criticism. They are afraid of it…Every well-founded criticism is countered with Bismarck's phrase: Politics is the art of the possible. People then say: We do what is possible, and consequently we are practicing statecraft. This conception of Bismarck's phrase, however, is a despicable misrepresentation. Bismarck believed that a specific, clearly identified goal was to be championed and fought for. But that is the basic difference between him and his successors, because they have absolutely no politically clear goal.

No people in the world has made so many sacrifices and given so much blood to ensure its continued existence as the German people. In doing so, however, it has fallen behind in terms of territory and population…The enormous blood sacrifices had negative effects because there was no clear foreign policy goal or domestic goal. We were also pulled into the Great War without a clear, definite goal…

The unification of Germany by Bismarck, which was welcomed because it made good sense, did not happen by itself because interest groups and traditions yielded only to force. Of course, this unification was not the final outcome of an agreement between all ethnic Germans; rather, it was only the great achievement of a Bismarck. Now his successors should have continued to expand instead of limiting themselves to the struggle to maintain the status quo. National political insight should have led to continued unification. When Cavour had united part of Italy, the idea of unification did not extinguish for one moment. In Germany, the current situation was supposed to last forever. But it was unfavorable from a military-geographic standpoint, and above all it lacked a sound food-supply basis. People forgot the most sensible thoughts, that the territory should be adjusted to fit the population size. The result was the industrialization of the nation, and the people became the drudges of the world.

The internal political conception of the state was limited to making the citizens speak a common state language. We do not believe, however, that a Czech or a Polack [*sic*] becomes German with language alone. When a Chinese person speaks German, he will do it with Chinese thoughts. A Jew speaks German and thereby conceals his Jewish thoughts. The language does not express the essence of a people; rather, it gradually depreciates the culture.

We thought about settlements in the east, to create land for bread; the bourgeoisie founded a Polish state. People wanted to annex iron and coal basins and establish new principalities, and for such foolish goals we sacrificed two million fellow nationals and a hundred years of German development.

It is so often said that pacifism opposes every war. Now, as long as one is fighting for bread, there is no pacifism. It only makes its appearance when one is fighting wars for others. Our colonial policy was not based on the idea of settling surplus population in the colonies; rather, it was only to serve the expansion of our economy. We too are against economic wars. Not a drop of blood for goals that are not in the interests of the people.

Feeding the people through increased industry and importing foodstuffs and raw materials with the revenue from the exported goods is a typically bourgeois idea. It is the cowardly pacifist view that hopes to avoid war in that way...A National Socialist territorial policy does not blind the people, because it knows that if you have no bread, don't complain—then the entire people must be mobilized to gain territory.

Emigration deprives a state of its most energetic individuals; the people gradually bleeds to death. Because of its racial value, the colony (here the area taken up by the emigrant) guides the destiny of the motherland. Reduced fertility decimates the highest achievements of a people, because the most valuable forces are not first- or second-born.

Today, as a result of the bourgeois-Marxist policy, we face the fact that 62 million are supposed to be fed from 460,000 square kilometers. The result is hunger and distress, 60,000 suicides per year,[440] 180,000 emigrants, and 300,000 unborn children—altogether an annual loss of around 500,000 people. If that continues for a hundred years or so, then racially we will be completely debased and degenerate.

It is said that we are without weapons. Yes, indeed. However, it is not weapons but will that is a people's strength…

If you give the people different leadership, you will experience wonders—if a people is still capable of carrying weapons at all. The current one is not capable of that…

The best weapon is the leadership, the spirit that is transmitted to the masses.

We cannot wage a war. Indeed, because we must first fight ourselves; we must first abolish the German slaves…

Gaining freedom, gaining land and territory: these are our goals.

We do not want border corrections. Ten or twenty kilometers will not improve the future of our nation. Those are never goals of a sound foreign policy.

We do not need to fabricate protests. My protest does not go to Paris, London, or Rome, where supplicants are sneered at, but against Berlin, as the foothill of Lebanon.

How do we release our people from its political isolation? Unless we dissolve the coalition of victors, all attempts will be futile.

To the extent that it pursues global power ambitions, England's goal is the elimination of every major power on the Continent. It achieved its goal with regard to Germany. In its place America appeared as an economic power. Consequently, war against Germany no longer makes sense. The new enemy is called America, and the close relationship is irrelevant in this situation, because opposing interests will always be fought out.

France's goal was and is the breakup of Germany, and has been for three hundred years. Germany is nevertheless attempting to go with France now. That is mistaken… Every attempt to reach understanding will fail, because Frenchmen of every shade say: Versailles is not open to discussion. We say: With Versailles there will be no recovery.

Russia, which once achieved statehood through Germans, is now led by international Jews. Regardless of this, an alliance would have no value, first because of the separation caused by Poland and second because of Russia's military and political inferiority...

One possibly ally is Italy. The entire bourgeois world objects to such a consideration. But it is precisely the objections of the Freemasons and Jews that proves to us the correctness of our view. People accuse Mussolini of excessive enthusiasm. Now, I have not yet gotten to know the great statesman (great in contrast to Gustav Stresemann), but I envy Italy because of him and regret that we do not have him. Italian and German interests do not conflict. It is foolishness, then, to ask if the Italians also have a pro-German disposition. They are as 100 percent Italian as I am 100 percent German. Our common interests are to be sought in our enmity with France—in common opposition. Italy must expand on the Mediterranean and thus comes automatically into conflict with France. Italy needs Africa to fill up. Is Italy imperialist then? Yes, thank God, because that means it is France's enemy. And the day will surely come when the two will confront each other as deadly enemies. Both are arming themselves. One bullet could make the conflict break out. France is also our enemy. But we must take the hand of every ally that we know is an enemy of France. The two powers will struggle for hegemony in the Mediterranean. I hope that Italy wins and France loses, because if France wins it will immediately turn on us, whereas Italy would then have to colonize and would be occupied with that.

The alliance idea cannot be based upon sympathies, but on motives of expedience.

People say that South Tyrol argues against an alliance with Italy. Now, Alsace-Lorraine, the Saar, and the Rhineland argue against one with France, the colonies against one with England, Silesia and West Prussia against one with Poland, Bohemia against one with Czechoslovakia, the Banat region against one with Yugoslavia, Transylvania against one with Romania—with whom should we join together then? With the oppressed peoples in India and Upper Egypt? Would South Tyrol be liberated by our failure to ally with Italy? Who betrayed South Tyrol? Those who betrayed everything...

Only Tyrol is holy land? Alsace...South Tyrol is being oppressed; in Germany they oppress even more. In South Tyrol there is persecution; in Germany the persecution is much worse. In the first five months of this year, the "German" terror brought us 9 dead and 670 injured. The German culture is being poisoned; who poisons it the most? In Berlin more Germans are being spiritually destroyed than South Tyrol has inhabitants, and more women and girls are being ruined than the total number of women and girls in South Tyrol. No one sees this. People incite the South Tyroleans and then abandon them, the same way it was done with the young nationalists in Germany.

We are consciously fighting against this hypocrisy. The point is not to liberate South Tyrol but to give life to Germany. The clamor has not helped South Tyrol; we should instead see it as the bridge between Germany and Italy—that would be of more use to the Tyroleans.

Advocacy for the German people in South Tyrol represents—also for the Jews—no more than hatred of fascism. If Freemasons ruled in Rome as they do in Paris, everyone would be quiet.

Our view will be more likely to improve the fortune of South Tyrol than the current official one. Only the necessity of entering into an alliance can bring Italy to change its conduct. (End)

NOTES

1 See Robert Harris, *Selling Hitler: The Story of the Hitler Diaries* (New York: Pantheon 1986).

2 Eberhard Jäckel and Axel Kuhn (eds.), *Hitler: Sämtliche Aufzeichnungen 1905–1924* (Stuttgart: Deutsche Verlags-Anstalt, 1980); Jäckel and Kuhn, "Zu einer Edition von Aufzeichnungen Hitlers," *Vierteljahrshefte für Zeitgeschichte* 29 (1981), pp. 304f.; Jäckel and Kuhn, "Neue Erkenntinisse zur Fälschung von Hitler-Dokumenten," *Vierteljahrshefte für Zeitgeschichte* 32 (1984), pp. 163–169. However, there are also additions; see Michael Kater, "In Pursuit of Hitler," *Canadian Journal of History* 16 (1981), p. 433.

3 Billy F. Price, *Adolf Hitler als Maler und Zeichner: Ein Werkkatalog der Ölgemälde, Aquarelle, Zeichnungen und Architekturskizzen* (Zug, Switzerland, 1983). See also on this topic Harris, *Selling Hitler*, p. 233.

4 (Düsseldorf: Droste), pp. 155f. Regarding Zoller, see the foreword by the editor of the French edition: Zoller, *Douze ans auprès d'Hitler* (Paris: René Julliard, 1949), pp. 7f. See also Christa Schroeder, *Er war mein Chef: Aus dem Nachlass der Sekretärin von Adolf Hitler*, ed. By Anton Joachimsthaler (Munich: Herbig, 1985), p. 192.

5 *Hitler's Table Talk 1941–1944*, translated by Norman Cameron and R. H. Stevens (London: Weidenfield and Nicolson, 1953), no. 148.

6 Gerhard Ritter (ed.), Henry Picker, *Hitlers Tischgespräche im Führerhauptquartier 1941–1942* (Bonn: Athenäum, 1951), no. 101.

7 Percy Ernst Schramm (ed.), Dr. Henry Picker, *Hitlers Tischgespräche im Führerhauptquartier 1941–1942* (Stuttgart: Seewald, 1965), p. 178; Werner Jochmann (ed.), *Adolf Hitler: Monologe im Führerhauptquartier 1941–1944. Die Aufzeichnungen Heinrich Heims* (Hamburg: Knaus, 1980), p. 280. Neither of these editions is complete, as they omit the pieces I found in Washington in 1951 (see Gerhard L. Weinberg, *Guide to Captured German Documents* (Montgomery, AL 1952, p. 55). The whole issue of the table talks, including the published notes from 1945, deserves a new thorough study.

8 According to the royalty register in the manuscript department of the Library of Congress in Washington, 10,000 copies were printed. Published in *Hitler: Reden, Schriften, Anordnungen. Februar 1925 bis Januar 1933*, Vol. I: *Die Wiedergründung der NSDAP, Februar 1925–Juni 1926*. Edited and annotated by Clemens Vollnhals (Munich: Kraus, 1992), doc. 100. (First references in-

clude complete citations for the individual volumes of this series; subsequently only volume and document numbers are used.)

9   Adolf Hitler, *Mein Kampf*, Vol. I: *Eine Abrechnung* (Munich: Eher, 1925). Vol. II: *Die nationalsozialistische Bewegung* (Munich: Eher, 1927). See on this topic "The Story of *Mein Kampf*" in *Wiener Library Bulletin* 6 (1952), pp. 31–32. Regarding the history of *Mein Kampf*, see also Reginald H. Phelps, "Die Autoren des Eher-Verlages," *Deutsche Rundschau* 81 (1955), pp. 30–34; Oron J. Hale, "Adolf Hitler: Taxpayer," *American Historical Review* LX (1955), pp. 830–852.

10   Hitler mentioned the 1938 testament in November 1941 and in May and July 1942; see Gerhard L. Weinberg, "Hitler's Private Testament of May 2, 1938," *Journal of Modern History* 27 (1955), pp. 415–419. The testament is the most extensive existing document known to have been handwritten by Hitler during his chancellorship.

11   Letter to the Institute of Contemporary History, September 12, 1958.

12   Adolf Dresler, *Geschichte des "Völkischen Beobachters" und des Zentralverlags der NSDAP, Franz Eher Nachfolger* (Munich: Eher, 1937), p. 89. Regarding Amann's role, see Oron J. Hale, *The Captive Press in the Third Reich* (Princeton: Princeton University Press, 1973).

13   Hitler had also dictated parts of *Mein Kampf* to Amann. Amann lost his left arm in 1931 in a hunting accident. The version orthographically corrected in this edition shows clearly that the text was dictated to the typist. In many places there is a space before a period or comma; the typist had already prepared himself for the next word and only then noticed that a period or comma was necessary. Regarding typed dictation, see also Zoller, *Adolf Hitler privat*, p. 14; Karl Wilhelm Krause, *Zehn Jahre Kammerdiener bei Hitler* (Hamburg: Hermann Laatzen, 1949), p. 42. The one-time existence of an additional copy of the present manuscript is evidenced by the fact that only pages 1–239 are original typescript, while pages 240–324, in contrast, are carbon copies (the difference is recognizable by examining the backs of the originals). Nothing is known about the fate of the second copy. Anton Joachimsthaler, the editor of Christa Schroeder's papers, suggests that this second copy is the document referred to in Schroeder, pp. 213–14.

14   Adolf Hitler, *L'expansion du IIIe Reich*, translated by Francis Brière (Paris: Plon, 1963).

15   *Hitler's Secret Book*, introduced by Telford Taylor, translated by Salvator Attanasio (New York: Grove, 1962). Review by Oron J. Hale in *Journal of Central European Affairs* 22 (1962), pp. 240–242. "The unauthorized English translation of the Hitler manuscript published by Grove Press is in many respects a burlesque imitation of the Weinberg edition. Whether it violates property rights may be legally debatable. But its appearance in such poor translation with inadequate editorial framework unfortunately precludes a

trustworthy scholarly edition in English. The translation is barely accept-able and shows signs of haste, while the introduction by Telford Taylor is an improvisation except insofar as the commentary and notes of Professor Weinberg are summarized or closely paraphrased." There is also an account of the physical history of the document by Sherrod E. East, *The American Archivist*, Oct. 1962, pp. 469–72.

[16] Albert Speer, *Spandaur Tagebücher* (Frankfurt a. M.: Ullstein, 1975), p. 533 (Oct. 22, 1960). Speer also claimed this in his memoirs, written after the appearance of the *Second Book*. See Speer, *Erinnerungen* (Berlin: Ullstein, 1969), p. 100.

[17] See Martin Broszat, "Betrachtungen zu Hitlers Zweitem Buch," *Vierteljahrshefte für Zeitgeschichte* 9 (1961), pp. 417–429; Enzo Collotti, "Il 'secondo libro' di Hitler," *Studi Storici* 3 (1962), pp. 161-167.

[18] Hess to the *Gauleitung Hannover-Nord* of the NSDAP, June 26, 1928, with notation of receipt June 28, 1928; Niedersächsischen Hauptstaatsarchiv Hannover, *Des.* 310 I A 19. Letter from Albrecht Tyrell to Gerhard L. Weinberg, dated April 6, 1968. Regarding Hitler's absence from Munich at the end of June 1928, see the letter from Rudolf Hess to Hans Frank, June 20, 1928; BA, *Slg.* Schumacher 236.

[19] Speculation in the Grove Press edition that the document originated in May 1928 was due to a translation error.

[20] The cause of the translation error mentioned in the previous note can be found here. The translator confused plural with singular, and the author of the introduction relied on the inadequate translation.

[21] Text in: *Hitler: Reden, Schriften, Anordnungen. Februar 1928 bis Januar 1933*, Vol. III: *Zwischen den Reichstagswahlen, Juli 1928–Februar 1929*, part I: *Juli 1928– Februar 1929*. Edited and annotated by Bärbel Dusik and Klaus A. Lankheit with the collaboration of Christian Hartmann (Munich: Saur, 1994), doc. 2. A translation can be found in Appendix II.

[22] See Walter Werner Pese, "Hitler und Italien 1920-1926," *Vierteljahrshefte für Zeitgeschichte* 3 (1955), pp. 113-126; Edgar R. Rosen, "Mussolini und Deutschland 1922–1923," *Vierteljahrshefte für Zeitgeschichte* 5 (1957), pp. 17–41. Significant on this topic: Kurt G. W. Lüdecke, *I Knew Hitler: The Story of a Nazi Who Escaped the Blood Purge* (New York: Scribners, 1937), pp. 69, 77, 135.

[23] See Jäckel and Kuhn, *Hitler*, p. 728. Also ibid., pp. 730f. and 733, as well as Günter Schubert, *Anfänge nationalsozialistischer Aussenpolitik* (Cologne: Verlag Wissenschaft und Politik, 1963), pp. 76f.

[24] See Gerhard L. Weinberg, *The Foreign Policy of Hitler's Germany: Diplomatic Revolution in Europe 1933–1936* (Chicago: Univ. of Chicago Press, 1970), pp. 16ff; Karl Heinz Ritschel, *Diplomatie um Südtirol* (Stuttgart: Seewald, 1966), pp. 104ff.

[25] Chapter 13: "Deutsche Bündispolitik nach dem Kriege" (German Alliance Policy After the War). See *Mein Kampf*, Vol. II, pp. 261–300.

[26] As far as I know, research has not focused on the preface. In the preface, Hitler also speaks of the (unfulfilled) intent to publish the fourteenth chapter on German-Russian relations, "Ostorientierung oder Ostpolitik" (Eastern Orientation or Eastern Policy), as a special reprint. In the present manuscript he also addresses this question. See *Mein Kampf*, Vol. II, pp. 301–331.

[27] (Munich: Eher) *Vorwort* (preface) dated August 1927.

[28] Note the relevant comment in the fine new biography by Ian Kershaw, *Hitler 1898–1936: Hubris* (New York: Norton, 1999), pp. 291–92

[29] Text in: *Hitler: Reden, Schriften, Anordnungen. Februar 1925 bis Januar 1933*, Vol. II: *Vom Weimarer Parteitag bis zur Reichstagswahl, Juli 1926–Mai 1928*, part 1: *Juli 1926–Juli 1927*. Edited and annotated by Bärbel Dusik (Munich: Saur, 1992), doc. 92.

[30] This letter, printed as a pamphlet by Lindemann and Lüdecke in Berlin in 1930, is listed as No. 1150 in the Wiener Library Catalogue Series No. 2, *From Weimar to Hitler, Germany 1918–1933* (London: Valentine, Mitchell, 1951).

[31] See the *Liste des schädlichen und unerwünschten Schrifttums* as of December 31, 1938 (Leipzig: Ernst Hedrich Nachf., 1939), p. 44.

[32] Text in: *Hitler: Reden, Schriften, Anordnungen. Februar 1925 bis Januar 1933*, Vol. II: *Vom Weimarer Parteitag bis zur Reichstagswahl, Juli 1926–Mai 1928*, part 2: *August 1927–Mai 1928*. Edited and annotated by Bärbel Dusik (Munich: Saur, 1992), doc. 258.

[33] Ibid., p. 785. Andreas Hofer led resistance in the Tyrol against Napoleon and was shot for this.

[34] See the *VB* of April 27–30, 1928, and Gustav Stresemann, *Vermächtnis*, Vol. III: *Von Thoiry bis zum Ausklang* (Berlin: Ullstein, 1933), pp. 281ff.

[35] Vol. II/2, doc. 261, 263, 265, 267-272, 274, 276, 277.

[36] See the *VB* of May 22, 1928.

[37] See *Hitler: Reden, Schriften, Anordnungen. Februar 1925 bis Januar 1933*, Vol. III: *Zwischen den Reichstagswahlen, Juli 1928–Februar 1929*, part 2: *März 1929–Dezember 1929*. Edited and annotated by Klaus A. Lankheit (Munich: Saur, 1994) doc. 34, 35, as well as part 3: *Januar 1930–September 1930*. Edited and annotated by Christian Hartmann (Munich: Saur, 1995), doc. 13. Also further reading indicated there.

[38] Text in: Vol. II/2, doc. 278.

[39] Ibid., doc. 280. The following allusion to Japan refers to the fighting between Japanese and Chinese nationalist troops on the Shandong peninsula in May 1928. In early June, the Japanese murdered Marshal Chang Tso-lin in Manchuria. See Paul S. Dull, "The Assassination of Chang Tso-lin," *Far Eastern Quarterly* 11 (1952), pp. 453–463; Seki Hiroharu, "The Manchurian Incident, 1931" in James W. Morely (ed.), *Japan Erupts: The London Naval Confer-*

ence and the Manchurian Incident, 1928–1932 (New York: Columbia Univ. Press, 1984), pp. 139–230.

[40] In this speech, Hitler also mentioned the destruction of the Bismarck Tower in Bromberg; a similar reference is found also in this manuscript.

[41] See the *VB* of July 6, 1928. Also the *VB* of July 13, 1928.

[42] See the *VB* of July 21, 1928.

[43] See Vol. II/2 and Vol. III/1.

[44] Text in: Vol. III/1, doc. 1.

[45] See the translation in Appendix II for parts of the speech of July 13.

[46] See Hitler's speech on May 20, 1928, in Munich. Text in: Vol. II/2, doc. 279.

[47] During this time, the decision was also made not to hold a Party rally in 1928, but instead to hold a general membership meeting together with a meeting of Party leaders. See Vol. III/1, doc. 3, 12–22.

[48] The entire complex is impressively described by Andreas Hillgruber, "Die 'Endlösung' und das deutsche Ostimperium als Kernstück des rasseideologischen Programms des Nationalsozialismus" in Hillgruber, *Deutsche Grossmacht- und Weltpolitik im 19. und 20. Jahrhundert* (Düsseldorf: Droste, 1977), pp. 252–275.

[49] In the subject index of Jäckel and Kuhn's *Hitler*, the Jewish question takes up more space than any other topic.

[50] The relevant sources are cited in Weinberg, *The Foreign Policy of Hitler's Germany 1933–1936*, pp. 26f.

[51] In the political testament and in the afterword to this testament; text in Max Domarus *Hitler: Reden und Proklamationen 1932-1945* (Neustadt: Schmidt, 1963), Vol. II, pp. 2236–39.

[52] Compare Gerhard L. Weinberg, *World in the Balance: Behind the Scenes of World War II* (Hanover, NH Univ. Press of New England, 1981), pp. 53–95, and Weinberg, "Why Hitler Declared War on the United States," *MHQ: The Quarterly Journal of Military History* (Spring 1992), pp. 18–23.

[53] Gerhard L. Weinberg, *The Foreign Policy of Hitler's Germany: Starting World War II, 1937–1939* (Chicago: Univ. of Chicago Press, 1980), pp. 270f., 286f.

[54] See Alexander Dallin, *German Rule in Russia 1941–1945: A Study of Occupation Policies* (London: St. Martin's, 1957), pp. 255ff. and the sources cited there.

[55] Excerpts from Hitler's address of July 1, 1943, are included in Helmut Krausnick, "Zu Hitlers Ostpolitik im Sommer 1943," *Vierteljahrshefte für Zeitgeschichte* 2 (1954), p. 311.

[56] One exception was a section from chapter VIII which appeared—without reference to the original manuscript—as an essay by Hitler in the June 1930 *Nationalsozialistischen Monatshefte* [National Socialist Monthly]. See chapter VIII, and notes 13, 40.

[57] Royalty register of the Eher-Verlag. See Hale, *Adolf Hitler: Taxpayer*.

[58] See the table talks, Trevor-Roper edition, pp. 329ff., 346f., 464f., 479; Ritter edition pp. 280f.; Jochmann edition, pp. 146, 292, 305f.; Schramm edition,

pp. 317, 343; also Walter Petwaidic, *Die autoritäre Anarchie: Streiflichter des deutschen Zusammenbruchs* (Hamburg: Hoffmann und Campe, 1946), p. 45; Hale, *The Captive Press*, p. 22.

59 See Hermann Hammer, "Die deutschen Ausgaben von Hitlers *Mein Kampf*," *Vierteljahrshefte für Zeitgeschichte* 4 (1956) pp. 161–178, especially p. 175. Hitler's statements on the South Tyrolean question were introduced in *Mein Kampf*, Vol. II (p. 283), and in the already mentioned special reproduction of the thirteenth chapter (see Vol. I, doc. 100, p. 284) as follows: "Yes, indeed, South Tyrol. Who among our bourgeois does not immediately have the bright flame of outrage burning on his clever face! If I take up this particular question here…" In the editions of *Mein Kampf* that appeared after 1930, the sentence "Who among our bourgeois…face" is omitted. The first English edition (New York: Reynal & Hitchcock, 1939) follows the old text (p. 911); the translation by Ralph Mannheim (Boston: Houghton Mifflin, 1943) follows the later version (p. 626). Konrad Heiden reports that in 1929 or 1930 Hitler was working on a manuscript about the relationship between art and race. Many of the ideas resemble the theses presented by Rosenberg in October 1930 in *The Myth of the Twentieth Century*. Because of the controversy ignited by Rosenberg, Hitler decided not to publish his manuscript (Konrad Heiden, *Der Führer: Hitler's Rise to Power* (Boston: Houghton Mifflin, 1944), pp. 363 and 365).

60 Speer made this comment before Hans Rothfels's foreword had been published. However, because it is not certain what report about the forthcoming publication Speer had received or could see in prison, the possibility of some sort of influence must remain open.

61 It is therefore not at all surprising that books such as Eberhard Jäckel, *Hitler's Weltanschauung: A Blueprint for Power* (Middletown, CT: Wesleyan Univ. Press, 1972) and Jäckel, *Hitlers Herrschaft: Vollzug einer Weltanschauung* (Stuttgart: Deutsche Verlags-Anstalt, 1991), frequently cite the *Second Book*.

62 Adolf Hitler, *Mein Kampf*, Vol. I: *Eine Abrechnung* (Munich: Eher, 1925), Vol. II: *Die nationalsozialistische Bewegung* (Munich: Eher, 1927). Here Vol. II, chapter 13: "Deutsche Bündnispolitik nach dem Kriege," pp. 261–300, and chapter 14: "Ostorientierung oder Ostpolitik," pp. 301–331.

63 Adolf Hitler, *Die Südtiroler Frage und das deutsche Bündnisproblem* (Munich: Eher, 1926). Text in: *Hitler: Reden, Schriften, Anordnungen. Februar 1925 bis Januar 1933*, Vol. I: *Die Wiedergründung der NSDAP, Februar 1925–Juni 1926*. Edited and annotated by Clemens Vollnhals (Munich: Saur, 1992), doc. 100. (The individual volumes of this series will again be cited once in their entirety and thereafter only by volume and document number.)

64 Allusion to the revolutionary events in the German Reich in November 1918.

65 On Hitler's view of Italy at that time, see Hans Woller, "Machtpolitisches Kalkül oder ideologische Affinität? Zur Frage des Verhältnisses zwischen Mussolini

und Hitler vor 1933," in: *Der Nationalsozialismus: Studien zur Ideologie und Herrschaft*. Edited by Wolfgang Benz, Hans Buchheim, and Hans Mommsen (Frankfurt a. M.: Fischer, 1993), pp. 42–63.

[66] Hitler also employed this "loss mathematics" during World War II. Fritz Todt, Reich Minister for Armaments and Ammunition, and Field Marshal General Wilhelm Keitel, Chief of the Armed Forces High Command, explained Hitler's view of the upcoming attack on the Soviet Union as follows to Major General Georg Thomas, head of the War Economy Office at the Armed Forces High Command: "The course of the war shows that we went too far in our autarkic endeavors…We must follow a different path and conquer that which we need and do not have. The manpower necessary to do that once will not be as great as the ongoing manpower needed to carry out synthetic production." Note by General Thomas, June 20, 1941 (text in: *Trial of the Major War Criminals before the International Military Tribunal*, Vol. XXVII (Nuremberg: The Tribunal, 1948), doc. 1456-PS, pp. 220–21.

[67] This refers to the advance guard of the mercenary formations, which in case of emergency also had to fight alone.

[68] Originally "must" instead of "may"; this was the only handwritten alteration in the original.

[69] The typist obviously heard or typed the word incorrectly; it should be "grow" instead of "be fed."

[70] Article 10 of the April 28, 1919, Covenant of the League of Nations guaranteed all member states "territorial integrity" and "political independence." The text of the Covenant of the League may be found in *Foreign Relations of the United States: The Paris Peace Conference 1919*, Vol. XIII (Washington DC: Govt. Printing Office, 1947), pp. 69–106. Germany was admitted with a permanent seat on the Council of the League in 1926; Hitler as chancellor withdrew Germany in 1933; the Nazi Party had opposed Germany's joining.

[71] See *Mein Kampf*, Vol. I, pp. 137ff.

[72] The practice of abandoning children, as well as that of selling children, was widespread in the ancient Greek and Roman world. It was carried out not only for medical reasons, but also for economic, inheritance, moral, or religious/superstitious reasons. See the entry for "Infanticide" in *The Oxford Classical Dictionary* (Oxford: Oxford Univ. Press, 1995), p. 757.

[73] Although there are relatively reliable numbers available for the Spartans—male full citizens—there are no corresponding verified figures for the social group of the Helots. At the end of the fifth century BCE, there were approximately 8,000 full Spartan citizens—a number that fell to about 3,500 by 420 BCE and to 1,500 by 371 BCE. Irrespective of the sharp (and quantitatively out of proportion) contrast between full citizens and Helots, Hitler's statements about the Helots appear greatly exaggerated. See the entry "Helots" in ibid. p. 680.

[74] Regarding Hitler's and the Nazi leadership's view of Sparta see, Karl Christ, "Spartaforschung und Spartabild" in. Christ (ed.), *Sparta* (Darmstadt: Wissenschafliche Buchgemeinschaft, 1986).

[75] Abortions were estimated at 200,000 to 400,000 per year during the time of the Weimar Republic; several estimates run as high as 1,000,000.

[76] See *Mein Kampf*, Vol. I, pp. 139ff.

[77] Interestingly, Alfred Hugenberg, the leader of the German Nationalist Party, also rejected internal colonization and saw foreign "agricultural colonies" as the key to solving the German food shortage. See Alfred Hugenberg, *Innere Colonisation im Nordwesten Deutschlands* (Strasbourg: Trübner, 1891), p. 452.

[78] The population density of the German Reich (including the Saar area) in June 1925 was 134.23 persons per square kilometer. See *Statistisches Jahrbuch für das Deutsche Reich 1929*, p. 5.

[79] See point 17 of the NSDAP party platform of February 24, 1920: "We demand land reform suitable to our national requirements, the passing of a law for the expropriation of land for communal purposes without compensation; the abolition of ground rent and the prohibition of all speculation in land." Text in: Jeremy Noakes and Geoffrey Pridham (eds.), *Nazism 1919–1945: A History in Documents and Eyewitness Accounts* (New York: Schocken, 1983), Vol. I, p. 15. In the present text, a departure from this point is recognizable. Hitler had declared already on April 13, 1928, that this demand was directed "primarily against the Jewish land-speculation companies." See Hitler: *Reden, Schriften, Anordnungen. Februar 1925 bis Januar 1933*, Vol. II: *Vom Weimarer Parteitag bis zur Reichstagwahl, Juli 1926–May 1928*, part 2: *August 1927–May 1928*. Edited and annotated by Bärbel Dusik (Munich: Saur, 1992), doc. 254.

[80] In April 1933 Hitler intended to pursue, at the international economic conference in London in the summer of 1933, an agreement against the industrialization of non-European areas. See records on the conference in the Reich Chancellery on April 24, 1933. Text in: *Documents on German Foreign Policy, 1918–1945*, Series C, Vol. I (Washington: Govt. Printing Office, 1957), p. 337. This was also one of the motives behind later plans to completely dismantle industry in the occupied Soviet Union. See Dallin, pp. 305–307.

[81] Carl von Clausewitz, *On War*, Vol. I, p. xxiii, "War is only the continuation of state policy by other means."

[82] See *Mein Kampf*, Vol. I, pp. 157ff.

[83] A brief survey of National Socialist efforts to counter "excessive urbanization" in Arthur Schweitzer, "On Depression and War: Nazi Phrase," *Political Science Quarterly*, LXII (1947), pp. 321–53; see also Jost Dülffer, "NS-Herrschaftssystem und Stadtgestaltung: Das Gesetz zur Neugestaltung deutscher Städte vom 4.10.1937," *German Studies Review* 12 (1989), pp. 69–89.

[84] Germany was required to turn over very substantial quantities of weapons by the terms of the Armistice of November 11, 1918. Text in: Harry R.

Rudin, *Armistice 1918* (New Haven: Yale Univ. Press, 1944), pp. 426–32; a fine recent treatment in Bullitt Lowry, *Armistice 1918* (Kent, Ohio: Kent State Univ. Press, 1996).

[85] See Michael Salewski, *Entwaffnung und Militärkontrolle in Deutschland 1919–1927* (Munich: Oldenbourg, 1966).

[86] Regarding the military service of German Jews, see Rolf Vogel, *Ein Stück von uns: Deutsche Juden in deutschen Armeen 1813–1976* (Mainz: Hase & Kochler, 1977), pp. 37 ff.

[87] Regarding the recruitment practices of the Prussian-German officer corps, see Karl Demeter, *The German Officer Corps in Society and State* (London: Weidenfeld & Nicolson, 1965); Martin Kitchen, *The German Officer Corps, 1890–1914* (Oxford: Clarendon, 1968).

[88] Wilhelm I (1787–1888), 1858 regent for Friedrich Wilhelm IV, 1861 Prussian king, 1871 German Emperor.

[89] Regarding the dominance of military behavior patterns in imperial Prussian-German society, see Emilio Willems, *A Way of Life and Death: Three Centuries of Prussian-German Militarism, An Anthropological Approach* (Nashville: Vanderbilt Univ. Press, 1986).

[90] Here Hitler is referring to the pseudo-science that ascribed a soul to every race. See, for example, Ludwig Ferdinand Clauss, *Rasse und Seele: Eine Einführung in die Gegenwart* (Munich: Lehmanns, 1926). During World War II a speaker for the Southeast-Europe Society gave talks accompanied by slides on the "Dinaric Racial Soul." Unfortunately the slides of the "Dinaric Racial Soul" have not survived.

[91] On the German revolution of 1918–1919, see Gerhard L. Weinberg, *Germany, Hitler and World War II* (New York: Cambridge Univ. Press, 1995), pp. 58–59.

[92] The phrase "Freedom and Bread" was one of the oldest slogans of the NSDAP; it was written over the masthead of the *Völkischer Beobachter* until 1945.

[93] Here Hitler is probably referring to Heinrich Class (1868–1953), 1901 member of the central leadership of the Pan-German League, 1908–1939 chairman of the Pan-German League, and author of the books *Bilanz des Neuen Kurses* (1903), *Deutsche Geschichte* (1908, under the pseudonym Einhart), *Wenn ich der Kaiser wär* (1912, under the pseudonym Fryman), and *Zum deutschen Kriegsziel* (1914). In 1933 Class was elected to the Reichstag as a member of the German Nationalist Party; he was a member of the Reichstag until 1945 (after November 1933 as a "guest" of the NSDAP faction). On the pan-German League, see Roger Chickering, *We Men Who Feel Most German: A Cultural Study of the Pan-German League, 1886–1914* (Boston: Allen & Unwin, 1984).

[94] Allusion to Benito Mussolini's march on Rome on October 27–28, 1922, which he used to force his appointment as Italian prime minister.

95 See Hans W. Gatzke, *Germany's Drive to the West* (Baltimore: Johns Hopkins Univ. Press, 1950), especially chapter V, which shows how the advocates of extreme annexationist war aims won over the German government just as Germany was defeated at the front.

96 Evidently the word was misheard or mistyped; "uncovered" is most likely what was meant.

97 Though numerically inferior, the Prussian army under the leadership of Frederick II, the Great, crushingly defeated Austrian units and imperial troops under the leadership of Prince Karl of Lorraine at Leuthen in Lower Silesia on December 5, 1757.

98 Text breaks off.

99 Otto von Bismarck-Schönhausen (1815–1898), 1862–1890 Prussian prime minister, 1871–1890 German chancellor.

100 By 1681 significant portions of the left-Rhine area in the southwest of the German Reich had come under French rule as "province allemande." The May 10, 1871, Treaty of Frankfurt stipulated that France was to cede this area, now designated Alsace-Lorraine, to Germany. See Dan P. Silverman, *Reluctant Union: Alsace-Lorraine and Imperial Germany, 1871–1918* (University Park: Pennsylvania State Univ. Press 1972).

101 Omission in the original. Hitler evidently did not know the necessary numbers offhand during the dictation; neither in this nor in other similar passages in the document were such numbers later inserted.

102 More than three million Poles lived in Germany before World War I. How many Germans in Alsace-Lorraine Hitler would have considered turned into French people cannot be determined.

103 Regarding the Prussian Polish policy, see Richard Blanke, *Prussian Poland in the German Empire (1871–1900)* (New York: Columbia Univ. Press, 1981).

104 The accumulation of negatives is a peculiarity of Hitler's style.

105 The German constitution of 1871 provided civic equality of Jews, but legal civic inequality of Jews in the German states continued until 1919.

106 The reference is to Italian irredentism, which after 1870 asserted a claim to Italian-populated areas in Austria-Hungary.

107 Designation for the southeastern bay of the North Sea within the German border area.

108 Evidence for this has not been identified. After 1871 Bismarck did not rule out a defensive war to secure the gains achieved, but he rejected further conquests.

109 Refers to the war of the German Confederation against Denmark (January 16 to October 30, 1864), the Prussian war against the German Confederation (June 21 to July 26, 1866), and the German-French war (July 19, 1870, to February 26, 1871).

110 Article 55 of the July 26, 1867, constitution of the North German Confederation designated the horizontally striped black, white, and red flag as the

flag of the navy and merchant marine, as did Article 55 of the April 16, 1871, constitution of the German Reich. Bismarck, who was indifferent about the heraldic question, justified this solution later with the fact that it combined the Prussian black and white with the red and white of the Hanseatic cities.

[111] Meaning Otto von Bismarck.

[112] On January 18, 1871, in the Hall of Mirrors at Versailles, the Prussian king Wilhelm I was proclaimed German emperor, while hostilities continued. The armistice was not signed until January 28, 1871.

[113] The origin of the black, red, and yellow color combination was supposedly the uniform of the Lützow Freikorps during the wars of liberation. After 1815 this color combination was taken up by the fraternities as a symbol of freedom and German unity, until the German national assembly made it the German war and commerce flag with the law of July 31, 1848. The August 11, 1919, constitution of the German Reich attempted, at least to some degree, to tie in with this tradition; Article 3 stated: "The Reich colors are black, red, and gold. The merchant flag is black, white, and red with the Reich colors in the upper left-hand corner." Text in: *Reichsgesetzblatt 1919*, p. 1383.

[114] The annual rate of population growth in the German Reich increased, with limited fluctuations, from 0.47% in 1871 to 1.57% in 1902 and flattened out only slightly until 1914. See *Sozialgeschichtliches Arbeitsbuch*, Vol. 2: *Materialien zur Statistik des Kaiserreichs 1870–1914*, by Gerd Hohorst, Jürgen Kocka, and Gerhard A. Ritter (Munich: Bech, 1975), pp. 29f.

[115] Between 1871 and 1914, the number of German emigrants reached its peak in the years 1881 and 1882, with 220,902 and 203,585 persons per year, respectively. The rest of the time the number was well under 200,000 per year. See ibid. pp. 38ff.

[116] During the nineteenth century, the food situation of the German population improved continuously. This is clear, as food expenditures made up a decreasing share of total household expenditures. If approximately 70% of the average family income was still spent on food in 1800, in 1900 it was only about 45%. Per capita meat consumption in Germany doubled between 1850 and 1913. See Hans J. Teuteberg, "Der Verzehr von Nahrungsmitteln in Deutschland pro Kopf und Jahr seit Beginn der Industrialisierung (1850–1975): Versuch einer Langzeitanalyse," *Archiv für Sozialgeschichte* XIX (1979), pp. 331–388.

[117] "Politics is the art of the possible." Bismarck in a conversation with Friedrich Meyer von Waldeck on August 11, 1867. See *Bismarck-Worte*, p. 19.

[118] Gustav Stresemann (1878–1929), 1918 cofounder and chairman of the German People's Party, 1919 member of the National Assembly and Reichstag until 1929, August 1923 to November 1923 Reich chancellor and foreign

minister, November 1923 to October 1923 foreign minister, 1926 Nobel Peace Prize (together with Aristide Briand).

[119] "The great questions of the day are not decided by speeches and majority resolutions—that was the mistake of 1848 and 1849—but by iron and blood." Bismarck in his first speech as prime minister before the Prussian Landtag on September 30, 1862. See *Bismarck-Worte,* p. 18.

[120] Refers to the Prussian constitutional conflict of 1861–1866 (in which Bismarck, prime minister since 1862, represented the interests of the royal government against the liberal majority of the assembly), the Kulturkampf against the Catholic Church and the Center in 1871–1887, and the conflict with the Social Democrats, which culminated in the 1878–1890 Anti-Socialist Law.

[121] German-Danish war, 1864; Prussian-Austrian war, 1866; and German-French war, 1870–71.

[122] Bismarck, who after 1852 belonged to the Seventh Heavy Landwehr Cavalry Regiment as a second lieutenant, often wore his uniform; however, political considerations always retained their primacy as the most decisive factor in his political activities.

[123] Regarding the internal structure of Germany after the establishment of the Reich, see Otto Pflanze, *Bismarck and the Development of Germany* (Princeton: Princeton Univ. Press, 1990).

[124] Ninth-century designation for the areas between the rivers Enns and Leitha, used for Austria.

[125] The Center Party's support for Austria arose from its confessional bond and the traditional Greater German position of political Catholicism, but also from opposition against Prussian hegemony and in some individual cases a complete rejection of the German nation state. See Wilfried Loth, *Katholiken im Kaiserreich: Der politische Katholizismus in der Krise des wilhelminischen Deutschlands* (Düsseldorf: Droste, 1984).

[126] After the establishment of the Reich, the Polish representatives, the Bavarian Patriots Party, the Protestant Hannoverian Party, and after 1875 also the representatives from Alsace-Lorraine affiliated themselves closely with the Center Party; to some degree they even entered into a "guest" relationship. This cooperation was based not only on clerical motives but also on particularist interests and anti-Prussian resentments. In the Kulturkampf, which broke out in 1871–72, these splinter groups were initially the only allies of the Center; these were soon attacked by the government as "Reich enemies." See Hajo Holborn, *A History of Modern Germany, 1840–1945* (New York: Knopf, 1969), pp. 258–66.

[127] The Center faction in the Reichstag voted in 1889 against the extension (sought by Bismarck) of the Anti-Socialist Law and even rejected the prison bill aimed against the unions and Social Democrats. Despite the politically

and socially heterogeneous character of the Center, the party leadership insisted on a fundamental rejection of socialism, which it tried to displace by developing its own Christian social doctrine and the establishment of specifically Christian labor unions.

[128] The left wing of the Social Democratic Party resolutely rejected the unconditional support for Germany's ally Austria-Hungary, which Reich Chancellor Bethmann Hollweg announced before the Reichstag in December 1912, in view of the increasing tensions in the Balkans. Georg Ledebour accused the Reich chancellor of encouraging the Austrian war faction to adopt a more aggressive policy with this unilateral expansion of a purely defensive alliance. The alliance itself, however, was not questioned by the Social Democratic Party, which had a Greater-Germany orientation. See Dieter Groh, *Negative Integration und revolutionärer Attentismus: Die deutsche Sozialdemokratie am Vorabend des Ersten Weltkrieges* (Frankfurt: Suhrkamp, 1973), pp. 374ff.

[129] Reference to the Triple Alliance pact concluded in 1882 between Germany, Austria-Hungary, and Italy—a secret defensive alliance in which the parties agreed to support each other in the event of a French attack and guaranteed neutrality in other cases. Holborn, p. 243.

[130] The three-year secret Reinsurance Treaty concluded between Russia and Germany in 1887 established reciprocal neutrality in the event of an attack by a third party against one of the treaty partners and recognized Russian claims in the Balkans and Turkish straits. Ibid. pp. 249–50.

[131] Bismarck also based his resignation submission of March 18, 1890, in part on the fact that the change in foreign policy demanded by Emperor Wilhelm II endangered Germany's good relations with Russia.

[132] The formal annexation of Bosnia and Herzegovina by Austria-Hungary took place on October 7, 1908, after the Austrian government was granted the right to have troops there in the 1878 Congress of Berlin. This increased the tensions between Austria and Serbia.

[133] Hitler has the chronology upside down. Austria had been authorized to occupy Bosnia-Herzegovina by the Congress of Berlin under Bismarck's chairmanship in 1878; the German-Austrian Alliance was signed in 1879; the Reinsurance Treaty in 1887. The actual sequence of events demonstrates the opposite of Hitler's theory.

[134] The German Social Democrats' view of Russia was determined by anti-Russian sentiments that had already become visible in Germany by the revolution years 1848–49. In 1914 the fear of "Russian despotism" still ensured initially largely unchallenged support for the national political truce policy in large segments of the Social Democratic Party. Ibid. pp. 428–29

[135] Town on the Bistritz in Bohemia, where on the morning of July 3, 1866, the decisive Prussian-Austrian battle (later labeled by the Prussian side as the

battle of Königgrätz) began. Particularly in French terminology, this battle became known as the Battle of Sadowa. See Gordon A. Craig, *The Battle of Königgrätz: Prussia's Victory over Austria* (Philadelphia: Univ. of Pennsylvania Press, 2003).

[136] In the early phases of the German-French war, the allied German armies defeated French forces on August 4, 1870, at Weissenburg; on August 6, 1870, at Wörth; on August 16, 1870, at Vionville-Mars-la-Tour; and on August 18, 1870, at Gravelotte-St. Privat. On August 19, 1870, a large portion of the French army was encircled at Metz. After the battle of Sedan on September 1, 1870, in which Emperor Napoleon III was captured, the remainder of the imperial French army capitulated. See Michael E. Howard *The Franco-Prussian War: The German Invasion of France, 1870–1871* (New York: Macmillan, 1961).

[137] On November 3, 1918, Austria-Hungary signed an armistice agreement with the Allies. See Bullitt Lowry, *Armistce 1918* (Kent, Ohio: Kent State Univ. Press, 1996), chap. 6.

[138] In the spring of 1917, Emperor Charles I took up contact with the French government, via his brother-in-law Prince Sixtus von Bourbon-Parma, to initiate negotiations toward a general peace. In this context he also indicated his readiness to support France's claims to Alsace-Lorraine. See Holger H. Herwig, *The First World War: Germany and Austria-Hungary, 1848–1918* (London: Arnold, 1997), pp. 317, 369–70.

[139] See *Mein Kampf,* Vol. I, pp. 133ff.

[140] The election law of January 26, 1907, gave universal, equal, secret, and direct franchise to all male citizens in the Austrian portion of Austria-Hungary. The German and Italian nationalities both benefited, and the Germans, with a 35.8% share of the population (according to the 1900 census), received 45.15% of the seats at the next election to the assembly. See Berthold Sutter, "Die politische und rechtliche Stellung der Deutschen in Österreich 1848–1918." In: *Die Habsburgermonarchi,* Vol. III: *Die Völker des Reiches,* 1 (Vienna: Verlag der Östereichischen Akademie der Wissenschaften, 1980), pp. 290f.

[141] Allusion to the Austrian Social Democrats' 1899 Brünn nationalities manifesto, which demanded equality for all nationalities but also proclaimed the "reconciliation of the working classes with the idea of the Reich." See Helmut Konrad, *Nationalismus und Internationalismus: Die österreichische Arbeiterbewegung vor dem Ersten Weltkrieg* (Vienna: Europa-Verlag, 1976), pp. 65ff.

[142] Meaning the April 8, 1866, secret alliance between Italy and Prussia, aimed against Austria. See Holborn, p. 178.

[143] On June 23, 1866, at Custozza, the Italian army suffered a defeat at the hands of the numerically inferior Austrian southern army; on July 20, 1866, the Italian fleet was defeated off Lissa, ibid., p.183.

[144] On July 2, 1866, the Austrian government asked France to mediate an armistice agreement with Italy; however, with the Prussian victory at Königgrätz on July 3, 1866, this no longer had any influence on the outcome of the war.

[145] Allusion to the secret consultations between France and Austria before the war of 1866, agreeing in the case of an Austrian victory to make the Prussian Rhine province an independent state. See Michael Derndarsky, "Das Klischee von 'Ces Messieurs de Vienne...': Der österreichisch-französische Geheimvertrag vom 12. Juni 1866—Symptom für die Unfähigkeit der österreichischen Aussenpolitik?" *Historische Zeitschrift* 235 (1982), pp. 289–353.

[146] See *Mein Kampf*, Vol. I, p. 148, where Hitler claims that an alliance can only be sustained on the basis of a "reciprocal transaction." In accordance with this theory, Reich Foreign Minister Joachim von Ribbentrop said to the Soviet People's Commissar for Foreign Affairs, Vyacheslav Molotov, on November 12, 1940, "Both partners of the German-Russian Pact had done some good business together." See *Documents on German Foreign Policy 1918–1945* Series D, Vol. XI, No. 325, p. 537.

[147] Actually "protective arms." Wilhelm II on May 7, 1908, in an address in Vienna.

[148] The term "Niebelungstreue," referring to Germany's relationship to Austria-Hungary, was coined by Reich Chancellor Bernhard von Bülow on March 29, 1909, before the Reichstag. The term denotes absolute and unquestioning loyalty.

[149] Based on the census of 1910, the Italian-speaking population in Austria-Hungary at that time can be estimated at about 795,000. See Umberto Corsini, "Die Italiener," in: *Die Habsburgermonarchie*, Vol. III/2, p. 852.

[150] See *Mein Kampf*, Vol. I, p. 136.

[151] Italy used the internal weakness of the Ottoman Empire, called forth by the revolution of the Young Turks, in order to initiate on September 25, 1911, the conquest of Tripoli, Cyrenaica, and the Dodecanese islands—a conquest for which the diplomatic groundwork had already been laid. Italy was able to secure its conquests in the Peace of Lausanne on October 18, 1912. See Cedric J. Low and F. Marzari, *Italian Foreign Policy 1870-1940* (London: Routledge & Paul, 1975), pp. 114ff.

[152] Before World War I, France had by far the lowest average annual population increase (0.18%) of all the European great powers. The population growth in Italy (0.63%), Austria-Hungary (0.87%), Great Britain (0.87%), Germany (1.36%), and Russia (1.37%) was significantly higher. In some years between 1890 and 1911 in France, the death rate exceeded the birth rate. See *Statistisches Jahrbuch für das Deutsche Reich 1913*, p. 3*; also *Histoire de la Population Française*, Vol. 4: *De 1914 à nous jours*. Edited by Jacques Dupâquier (Paris: Presses Universitaires, 1988), pp. 8f.

[153] Contrary to the claim in *Mein Kampf* (Vol. 1, p. 132), Hitler was still living in Vienna at the time of the Tripolitan War. He moved to Munich in May 1913 to avoid arrest for his failure to report for military service. See Ian Kershaw, *Hitler: 1889–1936 Hubris* (New York: Norton, 1999), p. 68.

[154] After the mid-nineteenth century, Germany no longer produced any agricultural surpluses. Only in the case of rye production was an exportable surplus achieved again after 1900. Between 1870 and 1910, the share of total imports represented by foodstuffs doubled from 13.9% to 26.7%; the share of raw-material imports fluctuated during this same time between 45% and 48.5%. See Karl Erich Born, *Wirtschafts- und Sozialgeschichte des Deutschen Kaiserreichs (1867/71–1914)* (Stuttgart: Steiner, 1985), pp. 27f., 73.

[155] In 1913 there were 22,386 Germans living in the colonies and protectorates of the German Reich. See *Statistisches Jahrbuch für das Deutsche Reich 1913*, p. 442. Regarding the significance of the colonies as potential settlement areas, see Francesca Schinzinger, *Die Kolonien und das Deutsche Reich: Die wirtschaftliche Bedeutung der deutschen Besitzungen in Übersee* (Stuttgart: Steiner, 1984), pp. 128ff.

[156] On December 6, 1897, Secretary of State in the Foreign Ministry Bernhard von Bülow justified before the Reichstag the seizure of Kiaochow from China: "We do not wish to put anyone in the shade, but we also demand our own place in the sun."

[157] Compare the almost identical statements in *Mein Kampf*, Vol. I, pp. 149ff.

[158] In the process of extending its sphere of influence in East Asia, Russia collided with Japanese expansion. Japan, which was not ready to withdraw from Korea, broke off diplomatic relations with Russia on February 6, 1904, destroyed the Russian fleet at Port Arthur on February 8, 1904, and declared war on February 10, 1904. After numerous defeats on land and at sea, Russia was forced in the September 5, 1905, Peace of Portsmouth (NH) to recognize Japanese hegemony in Korea and South Manchuria and to cede the southern part of Sakhalin to Japan.

[159] It is revealing to compare Hitler's figures with the size of the following states (1928 status): France: 551,000 km²; Poland: 388,000 km²; Italy: 310,000 km²; Yugoslavia: 249,000 km²; Czechoslovakia: 140,000 km²; Austria: 84,000 km². Germany lost just over 70,000 km² (in Europe) with the Treaty of Versailles. Hitler's rejection of the borders of 1914 as a goal can thus be understood easily. On May 2, 1928, Hitler declared in his speech directed against Stresemann: "We National Socialists take the view that all German foreign policy must steer clear of the ludicrous idea that the fate of Germany can be better shaped through so-called border corrections in terms of the 1914 borders. That does not matter to Germany at all anymore. *The borders of 1914 in no way satisfy our living requirements.* They could at best satisfy our romantic memories, but not the future of these 70 to 80 million people; this will not

be brought to life with an additional 50,000 or 60,000 km² of land. Either we will become an industrial power again (i.e., we again build all of our strength on the foundation of the international economy) *or we seek to win land and territory, and then we need not 60,000 km² but 300,000 or 400,000 km².*" See *Hitler: Reden, Schriften, Anordnungen,* Vol. II/2, doc. 268, p. 815.

160 By "sparsely populated" areas Hitler means areas which appeared advantageous to him for settlement purposes and which would qualify as sparsely populated after the deportation of the majority of inhabitants. See also Manfred Weissbecker, "'Wenn Hier Deutsche wohnten...': Beharrung und Veränderung im Russlandbild Hitlers und der NSDAP" in: Hans-Erich Volkmann (ed.), *Das Russlandbild im Dritten Reich* (Cologne: Böhlau, 1994), pp. 9–54.

161 See note 129.

162 The reference is probably to Georg Friedrich Baron (after 1914 Count) von Hertling (1843–1919), 1880 professor of philosophy in Bonn, after 1882 in Munich, 1875–1890 and 1896–1912 member of the Reichstag (Center Party), 1909-1912 chairman of the Center Party, Bavarian Prime Minister and Foreign Minister, November 1917 to September 1918 Reich Chancellor and Prussian Prime Minister.

163 Regarding the circumstances of the armistice negotiations of November 8 to 11, 1918, see Bullitt Lowry, *Armistice 1918* (Kent, Ohio: Kent State Univ. Press, 1996).

164 Matthias Erzberger (1875–1921), 1903–1921 member of the Reichstag (Center Party), 1918 secretary of state and member of the armistice commission, November 11, 1918, signatory of the armistice agreement, June 1919 to October 1919 vice chancellor, June 1919 to March 1920 Reich finance minister (resigned), murdered on August 26, 1921.

165 This claim was untrue, but it was persistently spread by Erzberger's opponents. See Klaus Epstein, *Matthias Erzberger and the Dilemma of German Democracy* (Princeton: Princeton Univ. Press, 1959).

166 From the fall of 1914 until the fall of 1916, the government of the Reich forbade all public discussion of war aims. See Peter Graf Kielmansegg, *Deutschland und der Erste Weltkrieg* (Frankfurt a. M.: Athenaion, 1968), p. 247.

167 Regarding the German war aims discussion, see Fritz Fischer, *Germany's Aims in the First World War* (New York: Norton, 1967).

168 On November 5, 1916, Austria-Hungary and Germany publicly declared their intent to create an independent kingdom of Poland after the war. Germany suggested the princes of Bavaria, Saxony, or Württemberg as possibilities for the regency of this state, which was dependent on the Central Powers. See Heinz Lemke, *Allianz und Rivalität: Die Mittelmächte und Polen im ersten Weltkrieg (Bis zur Februarrevolution)* (Berlin: Akademie, 1977), pp. 406ff.

¹⁶⁹ During World War I, the following states found themselves at war with Germany: as of 1914, Russia, France, Great Britain, Belgium, Serbia, Montenegro, Japan; as of 1916, Portugal, Italy, Romania; as of 1917, U.S.A., Cuba, Panama, Greece, Siam, Liberia, China, Brazil; and as of 1918, Guatemala, Nicaragua, Costa Rica, Haiti, Honduras. In addition, the following states broke off diplomatic relations with Germany in 1917: Bolivia, Peru, Uruguay, Ecuador.

¹⁷⁰ Village on the former German-Belgian border, between Eupen and Aachen.

¹⁷¹ In a September 9, 1917, memorandum from the Army High Command regarding the German national and military strength, the following was stipulated, along with numerous other measures: "Creation of new settlement land (territorial expansion through the war). Land distribution to peasants who participated in the war, farmers, gardeners, craftsmen, laborers who are agriculturally skilled and from whose families the state obtains the physically best and most numerous offspring." Text in: *Urkunden der Obersten Heeresleitung über ihre Tätigkeit 1916–18.* Edited by Erich Ludendorff (Berlin: Mittler, 1921), p. 227. Regarding the settlement plans for the Eastern European areas occupied by German troops, advocated primarily by the then quartermaster general Erich Ludendorff, see Fischer, chap. 17.

¹⁷² In World War I, 1,885,291 German soldiers were killed and 4,248,158 were wounded. See *Statistisches Jahrbuch für das Deutsche Reich 1924–25*, Berlin 1925, p. 25. For purposes of comparison, it may be noted that in World War II, German soldiers who died numbered 5,318,000. Rüdiger Overmans, *Deutsche militärische Verluste im Zweiten Weltkrieg* (Munich: Oldenbourg, 1999), p. 265.

¹⁷³ Hitler characterized the domestic policy task of his government in a similar way in a speech before the army and navy commanders on February 2, 1933: "1. Internally. Complete reversal of the current domestic policy situation in Germany. No toleration for the exercise of any ideas that are in opposition to that goal (pacifism!). Anyone who does not let himself be converted must be forced to yield. Eradication of Marxism—root and branch. Instilling in the youth and the entire people the idea that only fighting can save us, and that everything else is secondary to this idea. (Realized in the millions in the Nazi movement. It will grow.) Toughening up the youth and strengthening the will to defend with all possible means. Death penalty for treason. Firmest authoritarian state leadership. Elimination of the cancer of democracy!" See Thilo Vogelsang, "Neue Dokumente zur Geschichte der Reichswehr 1930–1933" *Vierteljahrshefte für Zeitgeschichte* 2 (1954), pp. 434f.

¹⁷⁴ A revised version of the following section appeared as an essay by Hitler (though without any reference to the underlying manuscript) in June 1930 in the *Nationalsozialistischen Monatshefte*. Text in: *Hitler: Reden, Schriften, Anordnungen, Februar, 1925 bis Januar 1933*, Vol. III: *Zwischen den Reichstagswahlen,*

Juli 1928-Februar 1929, Part 3: *Januar 1930-September 1930*. Edited and annotated by Christian Hartmann (Munich: Saur, 1995), doc. 68.

[175] At the outbreak of World War I, the initial warring states possessed the following measures of strength:

	Population (in millions)	Wartime size of Army	Total number trained men
Germany	67.0	3,823,000	4,900,000
Austria-Hungary	51.3	2,500,000	3,034,000
Central Powers	118.3	6,323,000	7,934,000
France	39.6	3,580,000	4,980,000
Russia	173.3	4,800,000	6,300,000
England	45.3	350,000	1,000,000
Serbia	4.0	300,000	400,000
Montenegro	0.3	40,000	60,000
Entente	262.5	9,070,000	12,740,000

See *Der Weltkrieg 1914 bis 1918. Bearbeitet im Reichsarchiv. Kriegsrüstung und Kriegswirtschaft*, Vol. I: *Die militärische, wirtschaftliche und finanzielle Rüstung Deutschlands von der Reichsgründung bis zum Ausbruch des Weltkrieges* (Berlin: Mittler, 1930), p. 221.

[176] Regarding the relationship between society and army in the German Reich at that time, see Gerhard Ritter, *The Sword and the Sceptre: The Problem of Militarism in Germany*, Vol. II: *The European Powers and the Wilhelminian Empire, 1890–1914* (Coral Gables, FL: Univ. of Miami Press, 1969).

[177] Article 173 of the June 28, 1919, Treaty of Versailles specified: "Universal compulsory military service shall be abolished in Germany. The German Army may only be constituted and recruited by means of voluntary enlistment." Text in: *Foreign Relations of the United States 1919; The Paris Peace Conference*, Vol. XIII, pp. 329–30.

[178] Article 160 of the June 28, 1919, Treaty of Versailles specified, among other things: "The Army shall be devoted exclusively to the maintenance of order within the territory and to the control of the frontiers." Text in: Ibid. p. 319.

[179] Regarding the organization and sociology of the British armed forces, see Correlli Barnett, *Britain and Her Army 1509–1970: A Military, Political and Social Survey* (New York: Morrow, 1970).

[180] On January 27, 1916, with the Military Service Act, Great Britain introduced universal compulsory military service for unmarried or widowed men between the ages of 18 and 41. See Ralph J. Q. Adams and Philip P. Poirier, *The Conscription Controversy in Great Britain, 1900-18* (Columbus: Ohio State Univ. Press, 1987).

181   See *Mein Kampf*, Vol. I, pp. 151.

182   The proposed two-power standard was aimed against the French and Russian navies. See Elmar B. Potter and Chester W. Nimitz, *Sea Power: A Naval History* (Englewood Cliffs, NJ: Prentice-Hall, 1960), p. 378.

183   Allusion to the army bill of 1913, which did not conform to the demands of the General Staff for a considerable increase in the strength of the peacetime presence. See Stig Förster, *Der doppelte Militarismus: Die deutsche Heeresrüstungspolitik zwischen Status-quo-Sicherung und Aggression 1890-1913* (Stuttgart: Steiner, 1985), pp. 266ff.

184   With regard to preventive wars, Bismarck said in retrospect that he had always opposed the idea "in the conviction that even victorious wars can only be justified when they are forced, and that one cannot see destiny in the cards enough to anticipate the historical development according to one's own calculations." Otto Fürst von Bismarck, *Gedanken und Erinnerungen*. Vol. 2 (Stuttgart: Cotta, 1922), p. 105.

185   Vincent Comte de Benedetti (1817–1900), French diplomat, 1864–1870 ambassador in Berlin. In July 1870 he delivered to Wilhelm I, who was staying in Bad Ems, the French demands regarding the succession to the Spanish throne.

186   Allusion to the Prussian-Austrian war of 1866.

187   Adolphe Niel (1802–1869), marshal, after 1867 French Minister of War, reorganizer of the French army. There is not the slightest evidence that Bismarck's decision for war with France had anything to do with Niel's reforms.

188   Regarding the outbreak of the German-French war, see Eberhard Kolb, *Europa vor dem Krieg von 1870: Mächtekonstellation, Konfliktfelder, Kriegsausbruch* (Munich: Oldenbourg, 1987).

189   On March 16, 1866, to the Austrian envoy in Berlin, Alois Graf von Károlyi. See Robert von Roosbroeck, "Die politisch-diplomatische Vorgeschichte." In Wolfgang von Groote and Ursula von Gersdorff (eds.), *Entscheidung 1866* (Stuttgart: Deutsche Verlags-Anstalt, 1966), p.70.

190   Possibly an allusion to the bribed Saxon chancellery secretary Friedrich Wilhelm Mentzel, who after 1753 obtained copies of the diplomatic reports from Vienna and St. Petersburg for Frederick II, the Great. Also possible are Maximilian von Weingarten, secretary of the Austrian envoy de la Puebla, or the Prussian envoy in the Hague, Heller; a report by Heller, in turn based on a report from the Dutch envoy in St. Petersburg, was decisive in Frederick's 1756 initiation of war (later known as the Seven Years' War) against the anti-Prussian coalition.

191   Misheard or mistyped; "on land" is what was meant (see the same formulation on p. 119 above).

192   Due to the Russo-Japanese War of 1904–05.

193 See note 17. Regarding the conception and operational planning of the Reichswehr leadership, see Michael Geyer, *Aufrüstung oder Sicherheit: Die Reichswehr in der Krise der Machtpolitik 1924–1936* (Wiesbaden: Steiner, 1980), pp. 188ff.

194 Presumably an allusion to the allegedly nonpolitical attitude of the German army in the Weimar Republic.

195 Allusion to those officers and soldiers who were discharged from the Reichswehr because of their participation in the Kapp Putsch in 1920 and the Hitler Putsch in 1923. See Francis L. Carsten, *The Reichswehr and Politics 1918–1933* (Berkeley: Univ. of California Press, 1973), pp. 93–99, 184–85; Harold J. Gordon, *The Reichswehr and the German Republic, 1919-1926* (Princeton: Princeton Univ. Press, 1957), pp. 249–50.

196 Hans von Seeckt (1866–1936) 1920–1926 Chief of the Reichswehr Army Command, 1933–1935 military advisor to Chiang Kai-shek.

197 Seeckt had allowed Prince Wilhelm of Prussia to participate in a military exercise in early September 1926. Pressured by the Reich Defense Minister, Otto Gessler, Seeckt thereupon submitted his resignation, which was accepted on October 8, 1926. Carsten, pp. 245–48.

198 End of the essay published in the *Nationalsozialistischen Monatsheften*. See note 174.

199 Further evidence that the text originated in 1928.

200 See *Mein Kampf*, Vol. II, p. 312.

201 Allusion to the internal reorganization of the Prussian state between the Peace of Tilsit on July 9, 1807 (preceded by the crushing defeat of the Prussian troops in the double battle of Jena and Auerstädt on October 14, 1806), and the official beginning of Prussia's revolt against the French occupation through the Russian-Prussian military alliance of Kalisz on February 26, 1813.

202 At the conference of Locarno (October 5–16, 1925)—in which Germany, Great Britain, France, Belgium, Italy, Poland, and Czechoslovakia took part— in addition to various arbitration agreements, the so-called Rhine Pact or Security Pact was negotiated. By this treaty Germany accepted its western border but also received a guarantee of it from Great Britain and Italy. See Jon Jacobson, *Locarno Diplomacy: Germany and the West, 1925–1929* (Princeton: Princeton Univ. Press, 1972).

203 Stresemann justified his policy repeatedly with the example of Bismarck, not least in order to rebut his critics from the right—for example, in the speech at the German People's Party congress in Hannover on March 30, 1924: "But precisely because we endorse the Bismarckian idea of realpolitik, we must demand that the others who also wish to avow Bismarck must conduct realpolitik and not adopt a policy of illusion." Text in: *Stresemann: Reden und Schriften. Politik, Geschichte, Literatur 1897–1926*, Vol. 2 (Dresden, 1926), p. 167.

204 See *Mein Kampf*, Vol. II, pp. 310f.

205 Article 51 of the June 28, 1919, Treaty of Versailles revoked the transfer of Alsace-Lorraine to the German Reich (agreed in the Frankfurt peace treaty of May 10, 1871), effective November 11, 1918. Text in: *Foreign Relations of the United States 1919, The Paris Peace Conference*, Vol. XIII, p. 183.

206 Refers to the parts of the industrial area of eastern Upper Silesia given to Poland by the Geneva arbitration of 1922 after the plebiscite. See ibid., pp. 212–16.

207 Article 27 of the September 10, 1919, peace treaty of Saint-Germain-en-Laye established the borders of the Republic of Austria in such a way that the areas of South Tyrol south of the Brenner fell to Italy. Text in: Carnegie Endowment for International Peace, *The Treaties of Peace 1919-1923 (New York: The Carnegie Endowment, 1924)*, Vol. I, p. 273.

208 Allusion to Article 231 of the Treaty of Versailles, which declared that "The Allied and Associated Governments affirm and Germany accepts the responsibility of Germany and her allies for causing all the loss and damage to which the Allied and Associated Governments have been subjected as a consequence of the war imposed upon them by the aggression of Germany and her allies." Text in: *Foreign Relations*, p. 413. See also Fritz Dickman, "Die Kriegsschuldfrage auf der Friedenskonferenz von Paris 1919." *Historische Zeitschrift* 197 (1963), pp. 1–101.

209 Omissions in the original. At the end of 1925, in all states throughout the world, Germans numbered 94,428,430; of those, 62,500,000 formed the German Reich. See Wilhelm Winkler, *Statistisches Handbuch, Handbuch des gesamten Deutschtums* (Berlin: Verlag Deutsche Rundschau, 1927), pp. 18ff. with specification of the underlying criteria for the definitions.

210 These are the last words on page 124 of the original; more than half the page is blank. Hitler probably resumed dictation after a short interruption and then replaced these last lines with the first words on page 125 of the original (here see the following chapter).

211 Omissions in the original. On the basis of the figures given here, 66.19% of the 94,428,430 Germans referred to lived in the German Reich.

212 In the original, ten lines were left blank here.

213 Here Hitler likely intended to quote the number of Germans living in several non-European countries such as Canada, the United States, and possibly South America. That is the only context in which the following thoughts make sense.

214 In 1921, a total of 6,372,177 people lived in the areas that the German Reich had to surrender, according to the terms of the June 28, 1919, Treaty of Versailles; of that number, 2,797,024 were of German nationality. If there were a total of 94,428,430 Germans, the incorporation of these areas would have raised the percentage of Germans living in the German Reich from 66.19% to 69.15%. See Winkler, *Statistisches Handbuch*, p. 24.

215   In the Weimar Republic there were a large number of private as well as state organizations whose goal was the cultural, political, and economic support of Germans living abroad. Their work was largely coordinated and financially supported through the German Foreign Ministry. See John Hiden, "The Weimar Republic and the Problem of the Auslandsdeutsche," *Journal of Contemporary History* 12 (1977), pp. 273-289.

216   Allusion to South Tyrol, where according to the census of 1921 there were 195,650 German speakers. See Winkler, *Statistisches Handbuch*, p. 19.

217   The use of the word "peace" for the time before World War I was still widespread ten years after the end of the war.

218   See *Mein Kampf*, Vol. I, pp. 139f.

219   Regarding Hitler's picture of America, see Gerhard L. Weinberg, "Hitler's Image of the United States," *The American Historical Review* LXIX (1963–64), pp. 1006–1021; also in Gerhard L. Weinberg, *World in the Balance: Behind the Scenes of World War II* (Hanover, NH: University Press of New England, 1981), pp. 53–74.

220   Reference to the British declaration of war against Germany.

221   Regarding the status of research into the outbreak of World War I, see, for example, John W. Langdon, *July 1914: The Long Debate 1918–1990* (Providence, RI: Berg, 1991).

222   In 1927, 35,686,000 RM worth of motorcycles and motor vehicles were exported from the U.S.A. to the German Reich. At that time, equivalent German goods valued at 693,000 RM were sold in the U.S.A. See *Statistisches Jahrbuch für das Deutsche Reich 1928*, pp. 327f.

223   Hitler made similar remarks in a speech on December 3, 1928, in Nuremberg: "The German automobile industry, for example, has its potential already limited, so that, for example, the American automobile industry can from the start already add production methods on a scale that allows them to appear competitive even here." This speech had until recently been mistakenly dated December 8, 1928. Text in: *Hitler: Reden, Schriften, Anordnungen. Februar 1925 bis Januar 1933*, Vol. III: *Zwischen den Reichstagwahlen, Juli 1928–Februar 1929*, part 1: *Juli 1928–Februar 1929*. Edited and annotated by Bärbel Dusik and Klaus A. Lankheit, with the collaboration of Christian Hartmann (Munich: Saur, 1994), doc. 61.

224   Clearly misheard or mistyped; "that" is likely what was meant.

225   Hitler spoke differently in World War II. See Gerhard L. Weinberg, *World in the Balance: Behind the Scenes of World War II*, pp. 53ff.

226   Allusion to the May 26, 1924, Immigration Act of 1924 to limit the Immigration of aliens into the United States, which regulated immigration into the U.S.A. much more tightly. The First Quota Act of May 19, 1921, had already established maximum limits for individual ethnic groups. Text in: *Laws Applicable to Immigration and Nationality: Embracing Statutes of a Permanent*

Character, and Treaties, Proclamations, Executive Orders, and Reorganization Plans Affecting the Immigration and Naturalization Service. Edited by the United States Department of Justice (Washington: Government Printing Office, 1953), pp. 397ff, 408ff.

[227] The law of differentiation is part of the genetic theory of Gregor Mendel (1822–1884): If genetically different individuals are crossbred, their offspring will not all be alike; in addition to genetically mixed individuals, genetically pure individuals like the father or the mother will appear as well.

[228] Clearly misheard or mistyped; "at least" is likely what was meant.

[229] Here Hitler is attacking the pan-European movement of Count Richard Coudenhove-Kalergi. Attacks on Coudenhove-Kalergi appeared in the Nazi newspaper the *Völkischer Beobachter (VB)* at approximately the time of the dictation of these lines. See the *VB* of July 5, 1928, "Der paneuropäische Schwindel," as well as July 17, 1928, "Der aufdringliche Coudenhove-Kalergi." Regarding the political objectives of the pan-Europe movement, see Ralph White, "The Europeanism of Coudenhove-Kalergi" in: Peter M. R. Stirk (ed.), *European Unity in Context: The Interwar Period* (New York: Pinter, 1989), pp. 23–40.

[230] Omissions in the original. In 1920 the U.S.A. encompassed an area of 9,371,749 km^2 with a population of 105,765,656 inhabitants. See *Statistisches Jahrbuch für das Deutsche Reich 1928*, p. 4*.

[231] Omissions in the original. In 1926 the USSR encompassed a total area of 21,342,872 km^2 with a population of 146,989,460 inhabitants. See ibid., p. 1*f.

[232] In 1920 China encompassed an area of 11,081,111 km^2 with a population of 433,000,000 inhabitants. See *Statistisches Jahrbuch für das Deutsche Reich 1928*, p. 2*.

[233] Regarding Hitler's notions of a European polity, see Paul Kluke, "National-sozialistische Europaideologie," *Vierteljahrshefte für Zeitgeschichte* 3 (1955), pp. 240–275.

[234] The assertion that one of the duties of the Nazi government must be preparing the German people to stand up to the United States is one of the significant new concepts in Hitler's second book.

[235] Count Richard Coudenhove-Kalergi (1894–1972), 1923 founder of the Pan-Europe Union (PEU), September 1929 president of the Pan-Europe Union, after March 1938 in exile, 1941 teaching position at New York University, 1944 draft constitution for the "United States of Europe."

[236] With the First Quota Act of May 19, 1921, the government of the U.S.A. attempted to establish individual upper limits for immigration into the U.S.A. Per year, a maximum of 3% of those nationality groups whose members had lived in the U.S.A. as of 1910 (but who were born outside the U.S.A.) were allowed to immigrate. Exclusions to this arrangement included those

from the so-called Asiatic barred zone. See Michael C. Le May, *From Open Door to Dutch Door: An Analysis of U.S. Immigration Policy since 1820* (New York: Praeger, 1987), pp. 74ff. Text of the law: *Laws Applicable to Immigration and Nationality*, pp. 397ff.

[237] Of the 4,107,209 people who immigrated to the U.S.A. in 1921–30, 58% were from southern and eastern Europe, 23% from northern and western Europe, 11% from North America, 5% from Latin America, and 3% from Asia. See Le May, *Open Door*, pp. 5, 76. It is worth noting that Hitler subsequently reversed his analysis of the United States. Instead of the gathering place of the so-called Nordics, it became a hopelessly weak mixture.

[238] Coudenhove-Kalergi lived in Vienna at that time.

[239] Clearly misheard or mistyped; "natural and comprehensible" was likely meant.

[240] Loose political alignment between Great Britain, France, and Russia after the British-Russian settlement in Asia in 1907; supplemented with military agreements in 1911–12.

[241] On September 8, 1926, the League of Nations assembly admitted Germany into the League of Nations with a permanent seat on the League Council.

[242] The German national assembly, which met in Frankfurt from May 18, 1848, until May 30, 1849, did not succeed in achieving its goal of creating a German nation state.

[243] Allusion to the support that the Greek war of independence against Turkey (1821–1829) found in Germany. See Christoph Hauser, *Anfänge bürgerlicher Organisation: Philhellenismus und Frühliberalismus in Südwestdeutschland* (Göttingen: Vandenhoeck & Ruprecht, 1990).

[244] During the Crimean War (1853–1856) and the Russo-Turkish War (1877–1878).

[245] Meaning the Tripolitan War.

[246] The Polish uprisings against Russian domination (1830–31 and 1863) found great sympathy among the German liberals. See Peter Ehlen (ed.), *Der polnische Freiheitskampf 1830–31 und die liberale deutsche Polenfreundschaft* (Munich: J. Bermans, 1982).

[247] The goodwill with which many Germans followed the Boers' fight against Great Britain found its most consequential expression in the telegram of Wilhelm II, dated January 3, 1896, in which he congratulated the president of the Transvaal, Paul "Ohm" Krüger, on safeguarding "the independence of the land against attacks from the outside." The already tense German-British relationship was further strained by this statement. See Paul M. Kennedy, *The Rise of the Anglo-German Antagonism 1860–1914* (London: Allen & Unwin, 1980), pp. 219ff.

[248] Clearly misheard or mistyped in the original; "daferne" should have been "sofern" in the original; also "Partei" instead of "Partie."

[249] Collective designation for the three wars fought by the Prussian king Frederick II, the Great, between 1740 and 1763 against the German empress Maria Theresa and her allies over the possession of Silesia.

[250] Refers to the British-French colonial wars that culminated in the Seven Years' War (French and Indian War) of 1756–1763.

[251] Refers to the Franco-Prussian War of 1870–1871.

[252] On October 14, 1806, in the double battle of Jena and Auerstädt, two Prussian corps were devastatingly defeated by the troops of Napoleon I. French occupation, a reduction in the size of the Prussian state by about half, and extensive contributions to France were the most significant provisions of the peace agreement concluded in Tilsit on July 9, 1807.

[253] Karl Reichsfreiherr vom und zum Stein (1757–1831), 1807–08 leading state minister, 1812–13 advisor to Czar Alexander I, 1813–14 head of the Central Administrative Council.

[254] On April 6, 1917, the United States declared war on Germany as a result of Germany's unrestricted submarine warfare; on December 7, 1917, the declaration of war against Austria-Hungary followed.

[255] Carl von Clausewitz (1780–1831), 1795 Prussian lieutenant, 1810 major in the general staff, 1818 major general, author of military history works and the book *On War*.

[256] Hitler's summary interpretation of Clausewitz's 1812 *Bekenntnisschrift*. Text in: *Carl von Clausewitz: Politische Schriften und Briefe*. Edited by Hans Rothfels (Munich, 1922), pp. 80–119. See also Norbert Krüger, "Adolf Hitlers Clausewitzkenntnis," *Wehrwissenschaftliche Rundschau* 18 (1968), pp. 467–471.

[257] See *Mein Kampf*, Vol. I, p. 98: "If a people is being led to its destruction by means of governmental power, then the rebellion of every member of such a community is no longer a right but a duty."

[258] Evidence of the document's year of origin.

[259] August Neidhart (after 1814 Count) von Gneisenau (1760–1831), 1809 Prussian colonel, member of the military reorganization commission, 1813 major general, quartermaster general of the Silesian army as successor to Scharnhorst, 1816 retired as general.

[260] Gerhard (after 1804 von) Scharnhorst (1755–1813), 1778 Hanoverian ensign, 1801 Prussian lieutenant colonel, 1807 director of the war department, chair of the military reorganization commission, chief of general staff, 1813 lieutenant general, quartermaster general of the Silesian army.

[261] Gebhard Leberecht (after 1814 Prince Blücher von Wahlstatt) von Blücher (1742–1819), 1801 Prussian lieutenant general, 1813 commander of the Silesian army, field marshal.

[262] Allusion to the alliance concluded by France and Poland on February 19, 1921. The agreement included mutual consultation on common foreign policy questions, promotion of economic relations, and, above all, mutual military support in the case of an unprovoked defensive war. The technical and operational details were specified more precisely in a secret military convention on February 21, 1921. The improvement in German-French rela-

tions through the Locarno Pact of October 16, 1925, and the extensive po-
litical isolation of Poland, however, compromised the value of this alliance.
See Piotr S. Wandycz, *The Twilight of French Eastern Alliances, 1926–1936: French-
Czechoslovak-Polish Relations from Locarno to the Remilitarization of the Rhineland*
(Princeton: Princeton Univ. Press, 1988).

263   Referring to the "Little Entente," a system, supported by France, of bilat-
eral defensive treaties between Czechoslovakia, Romania, and the Kingdom
of Serbs, Croats, and Slovenes (1929: Yugoslavia) to secure the status quo
in the Danube region, as established in the 1919–20 Paris-suburb treaties.
See Magda Adám, *Richtung Selbstvernichtung: Die Kleine Entente 1920–1938*
(Vienna: Österreichischer Bundesverlag, 1988).

264   Article 180 of the June 28, 1919, Treaty of Versailles stipulated that "all
fortified works, fortresses, and field works situated in German territory to
the west of a line drawn fifty kilometers to the east of the Rhine shall be
disarmed and dismantled." Articles 42 and 43 forbade the new construction of any kind of military fortification as well as the maintenance of German armed forces in this zone. Text in: *The Paris Peace Conference 1919*, Vol.
XIII, pp. 159, 333.

265   Article 190 of the Treaty of Versailles authorized replacement construction
for the warships permitted to the German Reich. The cruisers built according to the guidelines established in the treaty—the *Emden* (launched 1925),
the *Königsberg* (launched 1927), the *Karlsruhe* (launched 1927), and the *Köln*
(launched 1928)—each had a displacement of 6,000 tons and a speed of 32
nautical miles per hour (except the *Emden*, whose speed was 29 nautical miles
per hour). Text in: Ibid., p. 348.

266   Here Hitler does not address the then highly topical question of the new
warships usually called "pocket battleships." In Wolfgang Wacker's study, *Der
Bau des Panzerschiffes "A" und der Reichstag* (Tübingen: J.C.B. Mohr, 1959), the
attitude of the NSDAP also plays a limited role (see p. 32, note 82, and p.
69). The Reichstag representatives of the NSDAP voted for the new construction, but in his speech at an NSDAP meeting in Munich on October
10, 1928, Hitler said the following about this type of ship: "A 10,000-ton
ship means nothing today when compared to the up to 38,000-ton battle
cruisers of the world powers." Text in: *Völkischer Beobachter*, 12 Oct. 1928.
This assessment of the warship clarifies the present passage.

267   Not until the adoption of the Young Plan by the Reichstag on March 12,
1930, was the early evacuation of the Rhineland guaranteed (by July 1, 1930).

268   The first attempts to use warships as takeoff and landing areas for aircraft
were made by the American navy in 1910. In 1928 Great Britain had at its
command six aircraft carriers standing by with up to 36 aircraft per carrier.
The United States had four aircraft carriers with a maximum of 72 aircraft,
France had one large carrier (maximum 30 aircraft) and two small carriers,

and Japan had four aircraft carriers with a maximum of 50 aircraft. See Hans-Joachim Mau and Charles E. Schrell, *Flugzeugträger, Trägerflugzeuge* (Berlin: Transpress, 1991).

[269] Articles 164–172 of the June 28, 1919, Treaty of Versailles precisely stipulated the number and type of weapons for the German armed forces. Text in: *The Paris Peace Conference 1919*, Vol. XIII, pp. 323–29.

[270] Multifaceted cooperation between Germany and the Soviet Union was supported by German industrialists in particular, but also by some senior representatives of the Reichswehr and diplomacy. See Rolf Dieter Müller, *Das Tor zur Weltmacht: Die Bedeutung der Sowjetunion für die deutsche Wirtschafts- und Rüstungspolitik zwischen den Weltkriegen* (Boppard a. Rh.: H. Boldt, 1984).

[271] Regarding Hitler's view of France, see Eberhard Jäckel, *Frankreich in Hitlers Europa: Die deutsche Frankreichpolitik im Zweiten Weltkrieg* (Stuttgart: Deutsche Verlags-Anstalt, 1966), pp. 13ff.

[272] See Thilo Vogelsang, "Hitlers Brief an Reichenau vom 4. Dezember 1932," *Vierteljahrshefte für Zeitgeschichte* 7 (1959), p. 434.

[273] Clearly misheard or mistyped; "change" is likely what was meant ["endet" vs. "ändert"].

[274] The conversation between Bismarck and the French general Emanuel Felix Baron von Wimpffen took place on September 1, 1870, during the capitulation negotiations of the German-French war of 1870–71. See Heinrich Poschinger (ed.), *Bismarck-Portefeuille*, Vol. II (Stuttgart: Deutsche Verlags-Anstalt, 1898), pp. 42ff.

[275] "The other parts of the world have monkeys; Europe has the French. It all balances out." See *Aus Arthur Schopenhauers Handschriftlichem Nachlass.* Edited by Julius Frauenstädt (Leipzig, 1864), p. 386.

[276] See *Mein Kampf*, Vol. II, pp 321 ff.

[277] The German Communist Party espoused a close connection between Germany and the Soviet Union and voted in the Reichstag for the German-Soviet neutrality accord of April 24, 1926. See Heinric August Winkler, *Der Schein der Normalität: Arbeiter und Arbeiterbewegung in der Weimarer Republik 1924–1930* (Berlin: J. H. W. Dietz, 1985), pp. 191, 290f.

[278] The courting of foreign investors was part of the so-called New Economic Policy with which the Soviet Russian leadership attempted after 1921 to cope with the economic disasters left behind by World War I, civil war, and war communism. These concesions to the mechanisms of a free market economy contributed to a limited economic recovery for he USSR and molded its economy until the end of the twenties. See Christine A. White, *British and American Commercial Relations with Soviet Russia, 1918–1924* (Chapel Hill: Univ. of North Carolina Press, 1992).

[279] Clearly misheard or mistyped; "the" is likely what was meant.

[280] The *Berliner Tagblatt* was established in 1872 as a liberal local Berlin newspaper and was soon considered one of the most important newspapers in Ger-

many, not least because of its widespread news service: Wolff's Telegraphic Bureau. In 1906 Theodor Wolff became editor in chief of the paper, which supported the German Democratic Party during the Weimar Republic. See Gotthart Schwartz, *Theodor Wolff und das* Berliner Tageblatt: *Eine liberale Stimme in der deutschen Poitik 1906–1933* (Tübigen: Mohr, 1968).

281 The *Frankfurter Zeitung* traces its history back to the *Frankfurter Handelszeitung*, which appeared after 1856, after 1866 as the *Frankfurter Zeitung und Handelsblatt*. Appealing for political and economic independence, the *Frankfurter Zeitung* had already developed into one of the leading liberal newspapers in Germany before 1914, with increasing international significance. In 1934 the *Frankfurter Zeitung*, whose management had been taken over by the brothers Heinrich and Kurt Simon in 1910, reached a peak circulation of more than 100,000 copies. See Günther Gillessen, *Auf verlorenem Posten: Die* Frankfurter Zeitung *im Dritten Reich* (Berlin: Siedler, 1986).

282 The reference is clearly to the periodicals *Berliner Illustrierte Zeitung* and *Das Illustrierte Blatt*, Frankfurt a. M., which were published by the publishing companies of the *Berliner Tageblatt* and *Frankfurter Zeitung*, respectively.

283 Clear allusion to the then strictly secret military cooperation between the Reichswehr and the Red Army, centered after 1921 on air and tank warfare as well as the use of poison gas. Through reports in the *Manchester Guardian* of December 3 and 6, 1926, the public was for the first time informed of the existence of German secret weapons schools and armament factories in the Soviet Union. This revelation resulted in a debate in the Reichstag on December 16, 1926. See Manfred Zeidler, *Reichswehr und Rote Armee 1920–1933: Wege und Stationen einer ungewöhnlichen Zusammenarbeit* (Munich: R. Oldenbourg, 1993), pp. 143ff.

284 Meaning not the geographic area of White Russia (Belorussia) but the enemies of the Bolsheviks (who were identified by the color red) during the civil war. They were referred to as "Whites," although they did not form a unit either politically or organizationally.

285 Presumably an allusion to the Soviet defeat in the Polish-Soviet war of 1918–1920. Although the Red Army advanced to immediately outside Warsaw, it found itself in retreat from the beginning of the Polish counteroffensive on August 16, 1920, to the armistice on October 12, 1920. The Treaty of Riga, on March 18, 1921, awarded large areas of Belorussia and the Ukraine to Poland.

286 The addition in parenthesis was like this in the original.

287 In the original, consistently "upper classes," "intelligentsia," etc., in the text that follows.

288 The term "nihilism" incorporates every position involving the absolute negation of moral concepts or articles of faith. In 1861 Ivan Sergeyevich Turgenev, in his novel *Fathers and Sons*, named the Russian revolutionary anarchists "Nihilists," whereupon they began to identify themselves in this way.

[289] Regarding Germany's pro-Russian neutrality during the Russo-Japanese War of 1904–05, and the tensions that arose with Great Britain as a result, see Jonathan Steinberg, "Germany and the Russo-Japanese War," *The American Historical Review* LXXV (1970), pp. 1965–1986.

[290] According to Theodor Mommsen: "In the old world as well, Jewry was an effective ferment of cosmopolitanism and national decomposition and in this respect a preferentially entitled member of that Caesarean state whose polity was actually nothing but cosmopolitanism, whose national character was basically nothing but humanity." See Theodor Mommsen, *Römische Geschichte*. Complete edition in eight volumes, Vol. V: *Die Begründung der Militärmonarchie*, part 2: *Der letzte Kampf der römischen Republik* (Munich, 1976), p. 216.

[291] Clearly misheard or mistyped; "see" is likely what was meant ["bestehen" vs. "sehen"].

[292] A detailed view of the stance of the NSDAP on the colonial issue in Klaus Hildebrand, *Vom Reich zum Weltreich: Hitler, NSDAP und kolonliale Frage 1919–1945* (Munich: Fink, 1969, pp. 122ff. A brief survey in Gerhard L. Weinberg, *World in the Balance: Behind the Scenes of World War II* (Hanover, NH: Univ. Press of New England, 1981), pp. 96–136.

[293] Helmuth (after 1870 Count) von Moltke (1800–1891), 1858 chief of the Prussian army general staff, 1871 field marshal.

[294] "...usually only the competent have luck in the long run." In Helmut von Moltke's 1871 essay "Über Strategie." Text in: *Moltke: Vom Kabinettskrieg zum Volkskrieg. Selected Works*. Edited by Stig Förster (Bonn: Bouvier, 1992), p. 631.

[295] Between 1902 and 1912, Great Britain, as the protectorate power in Egypt and Sudan, carried out numerous dam projects in order to improve agricultural production, which had been declining since the end of the nineteenth century. In 1925 a new dam was completed near the city of Sennar in the Sudan, and others were planned in the years that followed. See *The Cambridge History of Africa*, Vol. 7: *From 1905 to 1940*. Edited by A. D. Roberts (Cambridge: Cambridge Univ. Press, 1986), pp. 750f, 776.

[296] Refers to the wars against Spain in 1587–1604 and 1654–1659, against the Netherlands in 1652–1654, 1665–1667, and 1672–1674, and the numerous conflicts with France during the period between 1701 and 1815, in which England or Great Britain asserted itself as a naval and world power.

[297] The phrase "God punish England," was widespread in the German Reich during World War I, in the form of adhesive labels for letters, posters, plaques over house doors, or headings for magazines and newspapers (information kindly contributed by the archive of the Bibliothek für Zeitgeschichte [Library of Contemporary History] in Stuttgart).

[298] In the War of the Austrian Succession (1740–1748), Prussia and Great Britain belonged to opposing alliances. With the Treaty of Westminster in 1756,

Prussia took over the protection of Hanover and fought on Great Britain's side during the Seven Years War (1756–1763).

299 Friedrich Wilhelm 1640–1688, Elector of Brandenburg.

300 In 1683 Brandenburg acquired some territory on the Gulf of Guinea, and Arguin on the Mauritanian coast. It had rights of use on the Antillean island of St. Thomas. The Brandenburg fleet arose from letters of marque that the Great Elector issued against France and Sweden. In 1675 this fleet was formally taken over into Brandenburg service, and in 1684 possession was transferred to the state. Due to the decline of Brandenburg's colonial trade, however, no usable ships remained at the end of the century.

301 Friedrich Wilhelm I (1688–1740), 1714 king in Prussia.

302 Regarding the maritime notions and naval strategies of Wilhelm II and Hitler, see Jost Dülffer, "Wilhelm II. und Adolf Hitler: Ein Vergleich ihrer Marinekonzeptionen." In: Jürgen Elvert (ed.), *Kiel, die Deutschen und die See* (Stuttgart, 1992), pp. 49–69.

303 Refers to the Hanseatic League, an association of north German trading cities, centered on Lübeck, that was in control of much of the trade in the Baltic area from the 14th to the 17th centuries.

304 Wilhelm II, in an address on the occasion of the opening of the free port of Stettin on September 23, 1898. Regarding the expansion of German naval forces in the era of Wilhelm II, see Holger H. Herwig, *"Luxury Fleet": The Imperial German Navy, 1888–1918* (Boston: Allen & Unwin, 1980).

305 See on this topic Thomas Schaarschmidt, *Aussenpolitik und Öffentliche Meinung in Grossbritannien während des deutsch-französischen Kriegs von 1870/71* (Frankfurt a. M.: Lang, 1993).

306 For domestic policy reasons, Bismarck had propagated the legend that he had come into conflict with the chief of general staff, Helmuth von Moltke, over the bombardment of Paris. See Rudolf Stadelmann, *Moltke und der Staat* (Krefeld: Scherpe-Verlag 1950), pp. 232ff.

307 The preliminary peace treaty concluded in 1878 between Russia and the Ottoman Empire was revised that same year at the Congress of Berlin (March 16 to July 13, 1878).

308 On the development of German-British relations after the establishment of the Reich, see Paul M. Kennedy, *The Rise of the Anglo-German Antagonism, 1860–1914* (London: Allen & Unwin, 1980).

309 In the 1913 budget, for example, the land forces were to receive 775 million marks for ongoing expenses and 580 million marks for one-time expenses. The navy received 197 million marks for ongoing and 233 million marks for one-time expenses. See *Statistisches Jahrbuch für das Deutsche Reich 1913*, pp. 336ff.

310 The ships of the German high-seas fleet that were surrendered according to the armistice agreement of November 11, 1918, were interned at the Brit-

ish Scapa Flow naval base and scuttled by their German crews on June 21, 1919, the day the armistice agreement expired.

[311] Allusion to the British alliance offers between 1898 and 1901. See Kennedy, *Anglo-German Antagonism*, pp. 234ff.

[312] Meaning the British-Japanese alliance of January 30, 1902, which established the neutrality of both partners in a war with a single third power, but made assistance obligatory in a war with more than one other power; the agreement also provided for an adjustment of the colonial interests of both powers in Southeast Asia.

[313] It is noteworthy that Hitler here expresses very different views about the leading minds of a democratic system than in his general remarks about democracy.

[314] The United States declared war against Germany on April 6, 1917, and against Austria-Hungary on December 7, 1917.

[315] Allusion to the so-called stab-in-the-back myth. Regarding its exploitation in the contemporary political conflict, see Ulrich Heinemann, "Die Last der Vergangenheit: Zur politischen Bedeutung der Kriegsschuld- und Dolchstossdiskussion" in: Karl Dietrich Bracher, Manfred Funke, and Hans-Adolf Jacobsen (eds.): *Die Weimarer Republik 1918–1933: Politik, Wirtschaft, Gesellschaft* (Düsseldorf: Droste, 1987), pp. 371–386.

[316] Possible allusion to the so-called Paris Gun of the German army, a 38 cm railroad gun calibrated down to 21 cm, with a firing range of nearly 132 km. In use in 1918, the shelling of Paris from 90 km away had a greater propaganda than military value. See John Batchelor and Ian Hogg, *Die Geschichte der Artillerie* (Munich, 1977), pp. 29, 42. In World War II, London was supposed to be shelled by the German V-3. See Olaf Groehler, "Die 'Hochdruckpumpe' (V3): Entwicklung und Misere einer 'Wunderwaffe,'" *Militärgeschichte* 5 (1977), pp. 738-744. Regarding German-English relations in general, see Gerhard L. Weinberg, "Hitler and England, 1933–1945: Pretense and Reality," *German Studies Review* 8 (1985), pp. 299-309.

[317] See chap. VI, note 109.

[318] The Dawes Plan, accepted by the Reichstag on August 29, 1924, represented a provisional settlement of German reparations payments. These payments were to total 1 to 1.75 billion RM annually until 1927–28 and 2.5 billion RM thereafter. They were to be financed from the Reich budget as well as from payments by the Reich railroad and industry. To secure the claims, the Reich railroad and Reich central bank were placed under international supervision. Most of the money paid came from American investors. Text in: *Reichsgesetzblatt 1924*, II, pp. 289ff. See Werner Link, *Die amerikanische Stabilisierungspolitik in Deutschland 1921–1932* (Düsseldorf: Droste, 1970), pp. 201ff; Stephen A. Schuker, *American "Reparations" to Germany, 1919–1933* (Princeton: Department of Economics, Princeton University, 1988).

[319] These last lines are on the same page as the first lines of the following chapter.

[320] Although Mussolini attempted to integrate Germany into his revisionist foreign policy concept, German-Italian relations were, until the death of Stresemann on October 3, 1929, determined by his consideration toward France. Stresemann's ideological aversion to the fascist state, as well as the Italian policy in South Tyrol (which was not accepted by Stresemann), also contributed to a worsening of German-Italian relations. See Vera Torunsky, *Entente der Revisionisten? Mussolini und Stresemann 1922–1929* (Cologne: Böhlau, 1986).

[321] After the 1858–59 war between Sardinia-Piedmont and France on one side and Austria-Hungary on the other, the majority of the Italian principalities were united into the kingdom of Italy by March 14, 1861, under the leadership of the kingdom of Piedmont and Sardinia. After the war against Austria, Italy was enlarged by the addition of Venetia in 1866, and during the German-French war in 1870 by the addition of the Papal States.

[322] Camillo Benso Conte di Cavour (1810–1861), Italian statesman, 1847 co-publisher of the newspaper *Risorgimento*, 1850–1852 Sardinian trade and naval minister, after 1851 also finance minister, 1852–1859 and again 1860–1861 premier, after March 14, 1861, first Italian premier.

[323] Meaning the Kingdom of the Serbs, Croats, and Slovenes (Yugoslavia as of October 1929).

[324] The great Italian emigration wave at the end of the nineteenth century focused primarily on the United States, Argentina, and Brazil; between 1876 and 1914, Italian immigration to these states totaled 871,221, 370,254, and 249,504 persons, respectively. 92,762 Italians immigrated into other South and Central American states, bringing the total to 1,583,741. See Herbert S. Klein, "The Integration of Italian Immigrants into the United States and Argentina: A Comparative Analysis," *The American Historical Review* LXXXVIII (1983), p. 308.

[325] After the consolidation of Mussolini's rule, Italian foreign policy appeared initially to orient itself according to prior historical, geopolitical, and economic indicators. However, new tendencies soon began to emerge: an ideologically motivated claim to great-power status, consideration for the nationalistically incited expectations of the nation, and an attempt to exert a subversive influence abroad. These changes in the style and objectives of Italian diplomacy caused conflicts with the neighbors—for example, with Greece (1923, the Corfu crisis); with the Kingdom of the Serbs, Croats, and Slovenes (1924, the annexation of Fiume); with Austria and Germany (regarding the forced Italianization in South Tyrol); and with France (regarding Italian colonial policy in North Africa). See Alan Cassels, *Mussolini's Early Diplomacy* (Princeton: Princeton Univ. Press, 1970).

[326] By the outbreak of World War I, Italy had succeeded in extending its influence to parts of Africa as well as parts of the Mediterranean area. In 1928 Italian Somaliland was an Italian colony, and Eritrea, Libya, and the Dodecanese island group were under Italian administration. See Denis Mack Smith, *Mussolini's Roman Empire* (London: Longman, 1976), pp. 32ff.

[327] The idea of a French-Italian war had engaged Hitler for years. It clearly stemmed from his preconceived idea of the "Italian policy of space"; similar ideas are present in the Hossbach report on Hitler's November 5, 1937, conference. (*Trial of the Major War Criminals before the International Military Tribunal Nuremberg*, Vol. XXV, doc. 386-PS, pp. 409, 411.) At approximately the time Hitler was dictating this text, the "Der deutsche Frontsoldat" supplement to the *VB* (part 1: *VB* of June 3-4, 1928, part 2: *VB* of June 23, 1928, as well as a commentary in the *VB* of July 3, 1928, "Italiens Zweifrontenkrieg!") published a lengthy article by Konstantin Hierl, "Italiens kommender Zweifrontenkrieg!" which outlined the scenario of an Italian military conflict with France and Yugoslavia.

[328] Page 240 of the original begins here. Pages 240–324 are carbon copies (see the introduction, note 13).

[329] With regard to Bismarck's estimation of Italy as an alliance partner, reserved or negative examples are more likely to be found. In response to a report from the German ambassador in Vienna, Heinrich VII, Prince of Reuss, dated October 17, 1880, he remarked: "One cannot pursue Italy if one wants something from it; in addition, promises have no guarantee if Italy has no interest in keeping them." See *Die Grosse Politik der Europäischen Kabinette 1871– 1914* (ed. by Johannes Lepsius et al.), Vol. 3: *Das Bismarcksche Bündnissystem* (Berlin: Deutsche Verlagsgesellschaft, 1922), p. 185. From that same year, the following remark by Bismarck has been passed on: "Italy is the spoiled child that receives everything from others without ever having to make the effort or have the merit to work for it itself; its slogan 'farà da se' is the most impudent untruth that I know. French blood procured Lombardy for it, German blood Venetia, the cosmopolitan gangs of the revolution gave it Naples and the Roman states; what has it done itself?...Italy is not a serious military power." See *Bismarck selbst: Tausend Gedanken des Fürsten Otto von Bismarck.* Compiled and introduced by Robert Ingrim (Stuttgart: Deutsche Verlags-Anstalt, 1950), p. 263.

[330] Theobald von Bethmann Hollweg (1856–1921), 1905 Prussian interior minister, 1909 to July 1917 Reich chancellor and Prussian premier.

[331] Allusion to the "Little Entente."

[332] In their concluding communiqué at the conference in Bucharest from June 20 to 22, 1928, the representatives of the Little Entente identified their relations with Austria as friendly and declared their intention to develop these relations further. The plans to incorporate Austria economically into the Little

Entente system sparked a debate in the Austrian national council, in the course of which federal chancellor Ignaz Seipel declared that Austria had no reason "to be integrated economically into a system in which, as a second-class member, as it were, it would have no political say. Austria will never be available for a solution that does not also include the great German Reich." See *Schulthess' europäischer Geschichtskalender 1928* (Munich: Beck, 1929), pp. 225, 377.

[333] In 1920 approximately 1,866,000 people lived in Vienna. With a total of 6,534,481 Austrians, this represented 28.56% of the Austrian population. See *Statistisches Jahrbuch für das Deutsche Reich 1929*, pp. 1*, 9*.

[334] Term for one who commits crimes to obtain fame; from the Greek Herostratus, who in 356 BCE set fire to the temple of Artemis in Ephesus in order to become famous.

[335] See, for example, Hitler's August 1, 1920, speech. Text in: Eberhard Jäckel and Axel Kuhn (eds.), *Hitler: Sämtliche Aufzeichnungen 1905–1924* (Stuttgart: Deutsche Verlags-Anstalt, 1980), p. 168.

[336] Benito Mussolini (1883–1945), teacher, 1910 secretary of the socialist provincial federation of Forlì, 1912 director of the party organ *l'Avanti!*, 1914 expelled from the party, 1914 founder of the daily newspaper *Il Popolo d'Italia*, 1919 founder and leader (Duce) of the Fasci di combattimento (after 1921: Partito Nazionale Fascista), 1922–1943 Italian premier, 1938 commander-in-chief of the Italian armed forces, 1943–1945 head of state of the Republic of Salò (Repubblica Sociale Italiana), shot on April 28, 1945.

[337] The Italianization policy in South Tyrol was radicalized only after Mussolini's seizure of power in 1922. See Leopold Steurer, *Südtirol zwischen Rom und Berlin 1919–1939* (Vienna: Europaverlag, 1980), pp. 61f., 100.

[338] Italy was unable to assert its extensive claims from the London treaty of 1915 at the Paris Peace Conference. After its conclusion, the phrase "vittoria mutilata" took root in Italy. See C. J. Lowe and F. Marzari, *Italian Foreign Policy. 1870–1940* (London: Routledge & Paul, 1975), pp. 160ff.

[339] In a speech to officers at the St. Cyr military school, Clemenceau declared: "The peace that we have just made ensures you ten years of conflict in central Europe." See Hellmuth Rössler (ed.), *Ideologie und Machtpolitik 1919: Plan und Werk der Pariser Friedenskonferenz 1919* (Göttingen: Musterschmidt, 1966), p. 56.

[340] Georges Benjamin Clemenceau (1841–1929), 1871–1893 member of the French national assembly, 1902 senator, 1906–1909 and 1917–1920 French premier, 1919 president of the Paris Peace Conference.

[341] These issues have been most recently reviewed in John W. Langdon, *July 1914: The Long Debate, 1918–1990* (Providence, RI: Berg, 1991).

[342] When Italy entered the war on May 23, 1915, the Italian army consisted of 35 infantry divisions, 4 cavalry divisions, and 52 Alpini battalions, totaling

approximately 850,000 men. See *Der Weltkrieg 1914 bis 1918.* Bearbeitet im Reichsarchiv, Vol. VIII: *Die Operationen des Jahres 1915: Die Ereignisse im Westen im Frühjahr und Sommer, im Osten vom Frühjahr bis zum Jahresende* (Berlin: Mittler, 1932), pp. 26ff.

[343] The issue of nationalities was of central importance to the organization and self-conception of the Austro-Hungarian army. The relatively liberal nationalities policy, which attempted to take into consideration the ethnic composition of the individual regiments, was nevertheless unable to prevent desertion from developing into a serious problem from the beginning of World War I. After entire units had defected to the enemy—six companies of the (Czech) 36th Infantry Regiment, for example, on October 20, 1914—the Austro-Hungarian army high command began deploying ethnically mixed units; this, however, did not solve the desertion problem. See Manfred Rauchensteiner, *Der Tod des Doppeladlers: Österreich-Ungarn und der Erste Weltkrieg* (Graz: Styria, 1993), pp. 205f., 267ff., 282, 348ff., 480ff.

[344] The attempts of the Allies during World War I to take advantage of national independence efforts (aimed against the Central Powers) to form military units were most successful with the Haller Army—named after its commander, Colonel Józef Haller de Hallenburg—stationed in France and Italy. The Haller Army recruited Poles living abroad and also prisoners of war of Polish nationality; in October 1918 it consisted of approximately 25,000 to 30,000 men. Another example was the Czechoslovak Legion, which initially fought in Russia, France, and Italy. It was made up of two-thirds Austro-Hungarian prisoners of war and one-third Russian citizens; it numbered approximately 35,000 men at the end of 197. See Rainer Schumacher, *Die preussischen Ostprovinzen und die Politik des Deutschen Reiches 1918–1919: Die Geschichte der östlichen Gebietsverluste Deutschlands im politischen Spannungsfeld zwischen Nationalstaatsprinzip und Machtanspruch*, Ph.D. diss., Cologne 1985, p. 83; John F. N. Bradley, *The Czechslovak Legion in Russia 1914–1920* (New York: Columbia Univ. Press, 1991).

[345] A brief recent summary of peace efforts during the war in Roger Chickering, *Imperial Germany and the Great War, 1914–1918* (Cambridge: Cambridge Univ. Press, 1988), pp.168–72.

[346] In 1900, the German-speaking population of the western part of Austria-Hungary (Cisleithania) was 9,170,939; by 1910 that number had increased to 9,950,266. See Peter Urbanitsch, "Die Deutschen in Österreich: Statistisch-deskriptiver Überblick." In: *Die Habsburgermonarchie*, Vol. III/1, pp. 38f.

[347] Meaning the ore basin of Longwy-Briey. See Fritz Fischer, *Germany's Aims in the First World War* (New York: Norton, 1967).

[348] Hitler does not mention Erich Ludendorff's decisive role in these plans. In World War II, when the German military leadership suggested the formation and integration of Russian volunteer units, Hitler justified his (on prin-

ciple) negative attitude with Ludendorff's unrealized hope of obtaining Polish divisions through the proclamation of a Polish state, as in the conference on June 8, 1943, see George Fischer, "Vlasow and Hitler," *Journal of Modern History* XXIII (1951), pp. 58–71; also Hitler's speech to the army group commanders of the eastern army on July 1, 1943, see Helmut Krausnick, "Zu Hitlers Ostpolitik im Sommer 1943," *Vierteljahrshefte für Zeitgeschichte* 2 (1954), pp. 305–312.

[349]   After November 1918, fighting broke out between Austrian and Slovenian–South Slavic troops over the Slovenian-populated border areas of Carinthia. On June 5, 1919, an armistice was concluded, with an Italian army corps enforcing its observance. In the October 10, 1920, plebiscite, 22,025 votes were cast for affiliation with Austria and 15,279 for the Kingdom of the Serbs, Croats, and Slovenes. Italy took a pro-Austrian stance on the Carinthian border issue. See Erwin Steinböck, "Kärnten" in: Erika Weinzierl and Kurt Skalnik (eds.), *Österreich 1918–1938: Geschichte der Ersten Republik*, Vol. 2 (Graz: Styria, 1983) pp. 802ff.

[350]   During the Polish uprising in Upper Silesia, the Reich government had the impression that the Italian occupation troops opposed the insurgents, whereas the French were passive or assisted them. See Peter Wulf (ed.), *Akten der Reichskanzlei: Weimarer Republik, Das Kabinett Fehrenbach, 25. Juni bis 4. Mai 1921* (Boppard a. Rh.: Boldt, 1972), pp. 158f.

[351]   Connecting with the ancient Roman symbol for the state's power over life and death, the fasci di combattimento selected the fasces as the emblem of their political struggle. With the decree of December 12, 1926, it became the official symbol of the Italian state.

[352]   In 1921, there were 3,218,005 German-speakers (23.6% of the total population) living in Czechoslovakia. In Romania there were 715,902 German-speakers (4.6%) in 1920, and in the Kingdom of the Serbs, Croats, and Slovenes there were 513,472 German-speakers (4.3%) in 1921. See Winkler, *Statistisches Handbuch*, pp. 140, 145f.

[353]   Compare the almost identical statements in Hitler's July 13, 1928, speech, in Appendix II.

[354]   See, for example, Hitler's August 1, 1920, speech, in: Jäckel/Kuhn, *Hitler*, p. 168.

[355]   Refers to the protest rally held in front of the Feldherrnhalle on February 6, 1921, by the patriotic associations against the German reparations obligations agreed upon at the Paris conference (January 24–30, 1921). According to police reports, "the well-known anti-Semitic leader Hitler attempted to bring his party-political tendencies to bear, but could not gain acceptance." See ibid., p. 312.

[356]   Article 78 of the August 11, 1919, constitution of the German Reich stated that fostering foreign relations was "exclusively the concern of the Reich."

Nevertheless, plans to disband the Bavarian foreign ministry were not realized. The ministry, led *ex officio* by the Bavarian premier, instead repeatedly took on tasks from other departments. In 1928 the free state of Bavaria had only one embassy, at the Holy See, along with diplomatic representation in Berlin and Stuttgart. France, after 1920, was the only foreign power represented by an envoy in Munich. See Wilhelm Volkert (ed.), *Handbuch der bayerischen Ämter: Gemeinden und Gerichte 1799–1980* (Munich: Beck, 1983), pp. 23ff.

[357] Andreas Hofer (1767–1810), on February 20, 1810, tried according to martial law and shot in Mantua.

[358] All the omissions are in the original. According to the census of December 1, 1921, in South Tyrol 193,271 people indicated German as the language they commonly used, and 27,048 indicated Italian. See Walter Freiberg, *Südtirol und der italienische Nationalismus* (Innsbruck: Wagner, 1989), p. 155. The underlying criteria of the definitions are given there as well.

[359] Reincorporation of the predominantly Italian-populated Trentino was not seriously under discussion.

[360] Hitler would ignore such considerations in 1943 with his de facto annexation of South Tyrol and additional large parts of northern Italy. See Karl Stuhlpfarrer, *Die Operationszonen "Alpenvorland" und "Adriatisches Küstenland" 1943–1945* (Vienna: Hollinek, 1969).

[361] Omission in the original. 8,691 km^2. See Winkler, *Statistisches Handbuch*, p. 24.

[362] Omissions in the original. According to Winkler's estimation, 20,362,800 German-speakers in Europe lived outside the German Reich at that time; of those, 9,160,000 lived in Austria and Switzerland. See Winkler, *Statistisches Handbuch*, pp. 18ff.

[363] Perhaps what Hitler meant by this strange wording was that in several of these other situations the number of Germans was very much higher.

[364] This was meant to be taken seriously. In the Polish territories annexed in 1939, the Germans established a special court for the determination of the supposed racial value of individuals (Oberste Prüfungshof für Volkszugehörigkeitsfragen in den eingegliederten Ostgebieten).

[365] Hitler apparently expected that a German-Italian victory over France would enable the seizure of land in the east. This remark also supports the view that Hitler conceived of his foreign policy program as a sequence of steps. See also *Mein Kampf*, Vol. II, pp. 338ff.

[366] To defend himself from criticism (appearing in the Social Democratic and conservative right-wing press) that his position on the South Tyrolean question was attributable to Italian money, Hitler sued for libel against the articles "Mussolini, Südtirol und die Nationalsozialisten" (Mussolini, South Tyrol, and the National Socialists) and "Streiflichter aus dem Wahlkampf" (Notes from the Election Campaign) in the *Deutsche Tageblatt* of March 13, 1928, and Au-

gust 8, 1928, respectively; "Redendes Schweigen" (Silence That Speaks) in the *Bayerische Kurier* of May 16, 1928; an SPD (a German Social Democratic Party) poster, "Adolf Hitler entlarvt!" (Adolf Hitler Exposed!) (Central Bavarian State Archive, 8167); and an article in the *Münchener Post* of May 21, 1928, "Die entlarvten Verräter Südtirols" (The Exposed Betrayers of South Tyrol). The original case was heard in May 1929 and the appeal in February 1930. See *Hitler: Reden, Schriften, Anordnungen. Februar 1925 bis Januar 1933*, vol. III: *Zwischen den Reichstagwahlen, Juli 1928–Februar 1929*, Part 2: *März 1929–Dezember 1929*. Edited and annotated by Klaus A. Lankheit (Munich: Saur, 1994), doc. 34, 35; Vol. III/3, doc. 13.

[367] Hitler enlisted at Recruiting Station VI of the 2nd Bavarian Infantry Regiment on August 16, 1914; on September 1, 1914, he was transferred to Reserve Infantry Regiment 16 (List) and deployed on the western front from October 22, 1914, until October 14, 1918. He was promoted to private first class on November 3, 1914, and was discharged from military service on March 31, 1920. Hitler was decorated on December 2, 1914, with the Iron Cross 2nd Class, on May 18, 1918, with the black insignia for the wounded, and on August 4, 1918, with the Iron Cross 1st Class. See Anton Joachimsthaler, *Korrektur einer Biographie* (Munich: Herbig, 1989), pp. 99ff.

[368] For example, in the speeches in Munich on November 13, 1919, "Brest-Litowsk und Versailles" (Brest-Litovsk and Versailles); on December 10, 1919, "Deutschland vor seiner tiefsten Erniedrigung" (Germany Before Its Deepest Humiliation); on January 31, 1920, "Der Friede von Versailles" (The Peace of Versailles); on the same topic on February 14, 1920; on February 28, 1920, and March 4, 1920, "Die Wahrheit über den 'Gewaltfrieden von Brest-Litowsk?' und den sogenannten 'Frieden der Versöhnung und Verständigung von Versailles'" (The Truth about the 'Forced Peace of Brest-Litovsk?' and the So-Called 'Peace of Reconciliation and Understanding of Versailles'); on May 7, 1920, in Stuttgart on the same topic; on June 19, 1920, in Kolbermoor, "Der Schandfriede von Brest-Litowsk und der Versöhnungsfriede von Versailles" (The Shameful Peace of Brest-Litovsk and the Reconciliation Peace of Versailles); and on July 15, 1920, in Munich, "Brest-Litowsk—Versailles" (Brest-Litovsk—Versailles). See Jäckel/Kuhn, *Hitler*, pp. 92ff., 96ff., 107, 109, 111, 113ff., 130, 149, 162.

[369] The peace treaty between Austria, the Allies, and the successor states of Austria-Hungary was signed on September 10, 1919, in Saint-Germain-en-Laye. Text in: *The Treaties of Peace 1919-1923*, Vol. II, pp. 250–385.

[370] A war with Italy over South Tyrol was never under discussion.

[371] Similar to Hitler's words in his May 23, 1928, speech. Text in: Vol. II/2, doc. 280.

[372] Meaning Benito Mussolini.

[373] See also Hitler's extensive comments on cultural policy in his speeches of April 3 and 9, 1929. Text in: Vol. III/2, doc. 17, 21.

[374] The Viennese composer Ernst Krenek (1900–1991) achieved an international success with his *Jonny spielt auf* (Jonny Strikes up the Band). After its world premiere in Leipzig on February 10, 1927, the opera, which incorporated jazz elements, was performed on more than a hundred stages over the course of the next two years. It was performed for the first time in Munich on June 16, 1928. The modern stylistic elements, along with the main character, the colorful Negro jazz violinist Jonny, caused furious protests and demonstrations in the right-wing camp—as can be traced, for example, in the *VB* during 1928, especially for the same time as the dictation of this book. Krenek emigrated to the United States in 1938. See Jost Hermand and Frank Trommler, *Die Kultur der Weimarer Republik* (Munich: Nymphenburg, 1978), pp. 317f.

[375] A comparison with Hitler's speech of July 13, 1928 (see Appendix II), and the reference to the five months elapsed that year are further evidence that the book was dictated at the end of June or beginning of July 1928. In this speech he says, among other things: "We have had nine dead and 670 wounded by the German 'terror' in the first five months of this year." The *Völkische Beobachter* of November 9, 1928, however, lists five allegedly murdered political opponents in 1928.

[376] Probably an allusion to the dramatic war crimes trial of the naval officers Ludwig Dithmar and John Bold in 1921. On June 27, 1918, as commander of the German submarine *U 86*, Helmut Patzig had the British hospital ship *Llandovery Castle* sunk and its lifeboats subsequently fired upon with the intent of killing all British witnesses. Patzig, designated by the Allies as a war criminal, was a fugitive since the end of 1919. The other two officers were charged with complicity by the state prosecutor and sentenced to four years in prison for aiding and abetting homicide. See Walter Schwengler, *Völkerrecht, Versailler Vertrag und Auslieferungsfrage: Die Strafverfolgung wegen Kriegsverbrechen als Problem des Friedensschlusses 1919/20* (Stuttgart: Deutsche Verlags-Anstalt, 1982), p. 347.

[377] Probably meaning the political murders committed in 1920–21 by the members of the Upper Silesian self-defense force. But investigations by the authorities can be verified in only eight cases, and proceedings were not initiated in a single one. However, in April/May 1928, Lieutenant Edmund Heines (ret.)—in the meantime commander of the SA regiment in Munich—was, among others, tried by the Stettin jury court for his involvement in a political murder in July 1920 in Pomerania. In this trial, a witness declared that between 1920 and 1922 approximately two hundred political murders had been committed in Silesia and reported to a government agency, which organized the Upper Silesian self-defense force. Although Heines was sentenced to fifteen years in prison for homicide, the state prosecutor prevented the complex of Upper Silesian political murders—which caused a great public

stir—from being further unraveled. See Irmela Nagel, *Fememorde und Fememordprozesse in der Weimarer Republik* (Cologne: Böhlau, 1991), pp. 33ff., 60ff., 244ff.

378 Among those about whom Hitler was so enthusiastic was Rudolf Höss, later the commandant of Auschwitz; see Martin Broszat (ed.), *Kommandant in Auschwitz: Autobiographische Aufzeichnungen von Rudolf Höss* (Stuttgart: Deutsche Verlags-Anstalt, 1958), pp. 35-37.

379 The basic rights established in the August 11, 1919, constitution of the German Reich guaranteed the individual political freedoms without precluding measures to defend the democratic constitution. The first law in defense of the republic, passed on July 21, 1922, and still valid in 1928, did not contradict either in theory or in execution the general legal conditions established by the constitution. In the late twenties, however, the will of the executive fully to exhaust the possibilities intended in the law in defense of the republic weakened, partly due to structural/organizational reasons, but above all due to the decreasing willingness of the responsible state organs to defend the constitution. Text of the law in defense of the republic: *Reichsgesetzblatt 1922*, I, pp. 585ff. Renewal on June 2, 1927: *Reichsgesetzblatt 1927*, I, p. 125. See Christoph Gusy, *Weimar: Die wehrlose Republik? Verfassungsschutzrecht und Verfassungsschutz in der Weimarer Republik* (Tübingen: Mohr, 1991), pp. 43ff., 128ff., 245ff.; Gusy, "Die Grundrechte in der Weimarer Republik," *Zeitschrift für Neuere Rechtsgeschichte* 15 (1993), pp. 163–183.

380 Dietrich Eckart (1868–1923), writer and translator, 1918–1923 publisher of the weekly *Auf gut Deutsch*, 1921–1923 editor-in-chief of the *VB*.

381 After the failure of the Hitler putsch, Eckart was arrested on November 15, 1923, and incarcerated in Stadelheim, then in Landsberg. His November 22, 1923, request to be released because of his "creeping heart disease"—caused by his alcoholism—was granted on December 20, 1923. Eckart died on December 26, 1923. See Margarete Plewnia, *Auf dem Weg zu Hitler: Der "Völkische" Publizist Dietrich Eckart* (Bremen: Schünemann, 1970), pp. 92f.

382 The Bavarian government had attempted to deport Hitler to Austria in 1924. The Austrian government insisted, however, that Hitler had lost his Austrian citizenship by serving in the German military. When Hitler expressed his readiness to renounce this citizenship himself, the Austrian government granted this request on April 30, 1925, in conjunction with a general prohibition of entry into Austria. See Donald Cameron Watt, "Die bayerischen Bemühungen um Ausweisung Hitlers 1924," *Vierteljahrshefte für Zeitgeschichte* 6 (1958), pp. 270–280.

383 The National Socialists were subject to numerous legal actions for libel, blasphemy, or abuse of religion, based on §§ 166ff. and 185ff. of the penal code. See Manfred Krohn, *Die deutsche Justiz im Urteil der Nationalsozialisten 1920–1933* (Frankfurt a. M.: P. Lang, 1991), pp. 137ff.

384 Clearly misheard or mistyped; "esaltato," Italian for (political) "enthusiast," is likely what was meant.

385 In Bromberg in early May 1928, the Bismarck tower was demolished. See the *Deutsche Allgemeine Zeitung* of May 10, 1928; also the *VB* of May 23, 1928, "Starke Erregung über die Sprengung des Bismarck-Turms" (Uproar over the Demolition of the Bismarck Tower). Hitler spoke that same day in the Bürgerbräukeller on the topic of South Tyrol. Among the statements resembling those made here is the sentence: "In Bromberg they calmly demolished a Bismarck tower—the German press ignores it placidly." See Vol. II/2, doc. 280.

386 After World War I, approximately 150,000 persons were expelled from Alsace-Lorraine or emigrated to the German Reich under the option provision of the peace treaty. See Karl-Heinz Rothenberger, *Heimat- und Autonomiebewegung* (Frankfurt/M.: P. Lang, 1975), p. 37.

387 Although little reliable information exists on the situation of the German minority in Poland at the time, it is certain that the number of victims was not this high. After December 1918, there were numerous Polish uprisings in the provinces of Posen and Upper Silesia, in which presumably hundreds of combatants died on both the German and Polish sides. In addition, there were also frequent smaller individual riots against the German minority, the last on May 15, 1927, in Rybnik. See Thomas Urban, *Deutsche in Polen: Geschichte und Gegenwart einer Minderheit* (Munich: Beck, 1993), pp. 27ff.

388 Clearly misheard or mistyped; "many" is likely what was meant ("endliche" vs. "etliche").

389 Regarding the Polish government's policy toward German-speaking residents, see Stephan Horak, *Poland and Her National Minorities, 1919–1939: A Case Study* (New York: Columbia Univ. Press, 1961), pp. 37ff., 94ff.

390 Use of the term "concentration camp" can be traced back to 1895. During the Cuban revolution, Spanish troops interned civilians in defined camps called "Campos de concentración." The term became popular with an explicitly negative meaning during the Boer War (1899–1902), when terrible conditions caused numerous victims among the civilian Boers interned in the concentration camps. After 1918, not only the phenomenon but also the term appeared during the civil wars or was used by the totalitarian regimes then forming. The goal remained the control and suppression of supposed or actual opponents, now also in peacetime. Hitler mentioned the British concentration camps of the Boer War as early as September 20, 1920, and demanded for the first time on March 13, 1921, that the German Jews be "secured" in concentration camps. The other NSDAP propagandists, even before 1933, were not afraid to blatantly threaten the establishment of concentration camps either. See Klaus Drobisch and Günther Wieland, *System der NS-Konzentrationslager 1933–1939* (Berlin: Akademie Verlag, 1993), pp. 13ff.; Jäcker Kuhn, *Hitler*, pp. 233, 348.

391 Refers to the Ruhr conflict of 1923.

392 The *Statistische Jahrbuch für das Deutsche Reich 1929* (p. 45) indicates that 15,974 suicides took place in 1927. Although the German statistical annual is not entirely reliable in this regard, suicides in Germany increased rather than decreased after Hitler became chancellor in 1933.

393 Hitler often addressed the question of national as well as individual suicide. He discussed the topic at length in his speeches of May 2, 8, and 19, 1928, and in the speech of July 13, 1928 (Appendix II). The suicide issue was also mentioned frequently at that time in the *VB*, for example on January 5 and August 21, 1928. An NSDAP campaign poster for the Reichstag election of May 20, 1928, contained a reference to "everyone's freedom to die by suicide." (Reproduction: Adolf Dresler and Fritz Maier-Hartmann, *Dokumente der Zeitgeschichte: Die Sammlung Rehse*, Vol., I (Munich, 1938, p. 195). On May 17, 1933, in his first speech on foreign policy after he came to power, Hitler also lamented the "224,000 people" who had committed suicide since the signing of the Versailles Treaty. Text in: Max Domarus, *Hitler: Reden und Proklamationen 1932–1945. Kommentiert von einem deutschen Zeitgenossen.* Vol. 1 *1932–1934 Triumph* (Neustadt: Schmidt, 1962), p. 279; English edition (Wauconda, IL: Bolchazy-Carducci, 1990), p. 333. Hitler's remarks on February 1, 1943, on the occasion of the capitulation of the German Sixth Army in Stalingrad, likewise center on the question of suicide. He referred to the "eighteen or twenty thousand" suicides in the peacetime years and regretted that the commander of the Sixth Army had not shot himself. See Helmut Heiber (ed.), *Hitler and His Generals: Military Conferences 1942–1945* (New York: Enigma Books, 2003), pp. 59–67.

394 The colors black and yellow symbolized the Austrian monarchy and were derived from the black Reich eagle on a gold or yellow background, which the Habsburgs adopted as their coat of arms.

395 District capital in the Polish region of Poznañ, part of the German Reich until 1920.

396 Regarding Stresemann's perceptions of war aims, see Annelise Thimme, *Gustav Stresemann: Eine politische Biographie zur Geschichte der Weimarer Republik* (Hannover: Goedel, 1957), pp. 21ff.

397 According to the December 1, 1921, census, Italy had a population of 38,710,576. See *Statistisches Jahrbuch für das Deutsche Reich 1928*, p. 1*.

398 The Andreas Hofer League, which arose from the *Bund Heimat* (Homeland League) in 1919, was, along with the Bavarian branch of the Society for Germans Abroad, one of the most radical associations for South Tyrol. The proclaimed goal was the revision of the Brenner border and the integration of South Tyrol into a future Greater Germany. See Isolde von Mersi, *Ziele und Praxis der Öffentlichkeitsarbeit der österreichischen Schutzvereine für Südtirol 1918–1939, 1945–1976*, Ph.D. diss, Vienna 1979, pp. 60ff.

[399] In his May 23, 1928, speech, Hitler also spoke of the South Tyroleans as serving as a bridge between Italy and Germany until the two countries could go to war together against France. Text in: Vol. II/2, doc. 280.

[400] Not known to whom Hitler is referring.

[401] In the *VB* of March 6, 1928, Alfred Rosenberg wrote something similar in his article "Mussolinis Südtirolrede" (Mussolini's South Tyrol Speech): Mussolini had been "very poorly advised" on the South Tyrolean question, because he had played into the hands of Italy's German enemies with his speech on March 4, 1928.

[402] After World War I, Italy initially did not categorically reject the incorporation of German Austria into the German Reich; long-term security for the Brenner border remained much more decisive for Italian foreign policy. At the Paris peace conference, however, the Italian representatives accepted the Allied position and agreed to the annexation prohibition in the peace treaties. See Josef Muhr, *Die deutsch-italienischen Beziehungen in der Ära des Ersten Weltkrieges (1914–1922)* (Göttingen: Musterschmidt, 1977), pp. 147ff.

[403] This possibility was discussed publicly in 1928.

[404] Omissions in the original. In 1923 Austria encompassed an area of 83,838 km² with a population of 6,534,481. See *Statistisches Jahrbuch für das Deutsche Reich 1929*, p. 1*.

[405] One reason for Hitler's misunderstanding of Italy's stance on the annexation issue is discernable here; in 1933–34 this nearly led to a rupture between Germany and Italy.

[406] In the original these words begin a new page, separated from the previous text by a line—which otherwise served to indicate a chapter break. The cohesiveness of the content, however, and the use of the term "chapter" imply that the sections identified in this edition as A–C were originally conceived as belonging together.

[407] If there really was an "introduction," it has not been preserved. Because this document is paginated consecutively, the "preface" could be what is meant. However, the topic addressed here is not mentioned in the preface; the relevant comments are, in fact, on pages 121–130 of the original (here pp. 188–201)

[408] The president of the United States, Woodrow Wilson, declared before the Senate on January 22, 1917: "They imply, first of all, that it must be a peace without victory." See Arthur S. Link, *Wilson: Campaigns for Progressivism and Peace. 1916–1917* (Princeton: Princeton Univ. Press, 1965), p. 265.

[409] Passed by the Reichstag on July 19, 1917. Text in: Erich Matthias and Rudolf Morsey (eds.) *Der Interfraktionelle Ausschuss 1917/18, Quellen zur Geschichte des Parlamentarismus und der Politischen Parteien, Von der konstitutionellen Monarchie zur parlamentarischen Republik*, Vol. 1/I (Düsseldorf: Droste, 1959), pp. 114f.

[410] Refers to the January 8, 1918, peace program (the Fourteen Points) of the U.S. president. Text in: *Foreign Relations of the United States, 1918, Supplement 1*,

Vol. I pp. 12–17. See also Klaus Schwabe, *Woodrow Wilson, Revolutionary Germany and Peacemaking, 1918–1919* (Chapel Hill: Univ. of North Carolina Press, 1985), pp. 11–20. Woodrow Wilson (1856–1924), historian, 1890 professor at Princeton University, 1902–1910 president of Princeton University, 1911–12 governor of New Jersey, 1913–1921 president of the United States, 1919 Nobel Peace Prize.

411   Allusion to the wave of strikes in Berlin and other cities in the German Reich from January 28 to February 4, 1918. See Holger H. Herwig *The First World War: Germany and Austria-Hungary 1914–1918* (London: Arnold, 1997), pp. 378–81.

412   Meaning the peace treaties of Versailles (June 28, 1919) and Saint-Germain-en-Laye (September 10, 1919).

413   The article, inserted below, appeared on June 26, 1928. This confirms that the book was dictated at the end of June, beginning of July, even if the word "today" in the text right after the article is not to be taken literally.

414   William James Flynn (1867–1928), 1897 entry into the U.S. Secret Service, 1910–1911 reorganized the New York criminal investigation department, 1912-1917 head of the U.S. Secret Service, 1919–1921 head of the Bureau of Investigation in the Department of Justice (as of July 1, 1935: Federal Bureau of Investigation). The recollections referred to are Flynn's article "Tapped Wires," which appeared in the New York weekly *Liberty* on June 2, 1928. The article reported on the—politically relatively unimportant—telephone conversations of the German embassy in Washington, which were tapped by the American Secret Service (the agency responsible for the security of the president) during World War I.

415   The text of the article from the June 26, 1928, issue of the *Münchner Neuesten Nachtrichten* is missing in the original but was to have been inserted later; the rest of the page remained blank. This article, which distorts the meaning of the American source, is included here. The *VB* reported on the same matter on August 18, 1928, in an article entitled "Graf Bernstorff deutscher Botschafter in USA" (Count Bernstorff German Ambassador in the USA), which evidently used the *Münchner Neuesten Nachrichten* as its only source. The *VB* demanded: "Enough of this scandal. May a future state court save the Flynn publications as material for an indictment. But the dignified ambassador [*Johann Heinrich Graf von Bernstorff*] is one of the foreign policy aces of the Democratic Party, a member of the Reichstag, of course, and German representative to the League of Nations for disarmament issues." For a serious study of the ambassador, see Reinhard R. Doerries, *Imperial Challenge: Ambassador Count Bernsdorff and German-American Relations, 1908–1917* (Chapel Hill: Univ. of North Carolina Press, 1989).

416   Friedrich Wilhelm Elven, 1919–1941 publisher of the *Cincinnati Freie Presse*, reported since 1923 for the *Münchner Neuesten Nachrichten.* See *Documents on German Foreign Policy 1918–1945*, Series C, Vol. III, p. 1114.

[417] Johann Heinrich Count von Bernstorff (1862–1939), after 1890 in the German diplomatic service, from 1908 to May 1917 German ambassador in Washington, September 1917 to 1919 ambassador in Constantinople, 1921–1928 member of the Reichstag (German Democratic Party), 1922 president of the German league for the League of Nations, 1926–1931 German representative on the preliminary disarmament commission of the League of Nations, after 1933 in exile.

[418] Bernard Baruch (1870–1965), American financier, 1916 member of the "Advisory Commission of the National Defense Council," 1917 head of the raw materials and metals commission, 1918 chairman of the War Industries Board, 1919 participated in the Paris Peace Conference.

[419] Harry Elmer Barnes (1889–1968), 1918 Ph.D. from Columbia University, 1917 to 1948 taught history at various American universities. The text referred to here is *The Genesis of the World War* (New York: Knopf, 1929).

[420] Robert Lansing (1864–1928), after 1892 advisor to the American government, 1915–1920 U.S. Secretary of State.

[421] On December 30, 1915, the lightly armed British mail steamer *Persia* was sunk south of Crete by the German submarine *U 38*, costing the lives of 334 people, including two Americans. This further strained German-American relations. See Paul G. Halpern, *The Naval War in the Mediterranean 1914–1918* (Annapolis: Naval Institute Press, 1987), pp. 200f.

[422] Thomas Pryor Gore (1870–1949), 1907–1921 and 1931–1937 senator from Oklahoma (Democratic Party).

[423] On February 25, 1916, Senator Gore proposed a resolution that the Senate warn against travel on armed ships and recommend that no passports be issued to American citizens for such trips. See Arthur S. Link, *Wilson: Confusion and Crises 1915–1916* (Princeton: Princeton Univ. Press, 1964), pp. 177ff.

[424] Edward Mandell House (1856–1938), American diplomat, 1912 personal advisor to President Woodrow Wilson, 1914–1916 special representative of the president in Europe, 1917 U.S. representative on the Allied Supreme War Council, 1918–1919 U.S. representative at the Versailles peace conference.

[425] Meaning Boris A. Bakhmetev (1880-1951), Russian professor of engineering, Menshevik sympathizer, 1916 chairman of a Russian trade commission for the acquisition of war matériel from the United States, 1917–1922 ambassador in Washington for the Provisional Russian Government, subsequently founder and chairman of the Bakhmetev Foundation in the United States.

[426] In accordance with this view, during World War II Hitler initially wanted to leave the war in the Mediterranean entirely in Mussolini's hands. See Gerhard Schreiber, "Die politische und militärische Entwicklung im Mittelmeerraum 1939/40," in: *Das Deutsche Reich und der Zweite Weltkrieg*, Vol. 3: *Der*

Mittelmeerraum und Südosteuropa: Von der "non belligeranza" Italiens bis zum Kriegseintritt der Vereinigten Staaten (Stuttgart: Deutsche Verlags-Anstalt, 1984), pp. 4–277.

[427] Regarding British-Italian relations at the time, see P. G. Edwards, "Britain, Mussolini and the 'Locarno-Geneva System,'" *European Studies Review* 10 (1980), pp. 1–16.

[428] The Rif-Kabylie rebellion, which broke out in 1920, was put down in late May 1926 through the close cooperation of Spain and France. On July 13, 1926, an accord was signed regarding Morocco, and on August 15, 1926, a trade agreement was concluded between Spain and France. See Stanley G. Payne, *Politics and the Military in Modern Spain* (Stanford: Stanford Univ. Press, 1967), pp. 216ff.

[429] Regarding Hungarian-Yugoslavian relations at the time, see Ignác Romsics, "István Bethlens Aussenpolitik in den Jahren 1921–1931," *Südost Forschungen* II (1990), pp. 243–291.

[430] Hitler had already polemicized in *Mein Kampf* against a "league of the oppressed" and named in this context the Balkan states, Egypt, and India. See *Mein Kampf*, Vol. II, pp. 318ff.

[431] Here Hitler hints at ideas that would later be further developed, particularly by Werner Daitz; see Werner Daitz, *Der Weg zur völkischen Wirtschaft und zur europäischen Grossraumwirtschaft* (Dresden: Meinhold, 1938 and 1943).

[432] The actual conclusion of the book begins here; the topic of Jewry is taken up quite arbitrarily and abruptly, much as it is in Hitler's political testament.

[433] As is generally known, the situation was precisely the opposite. To the extent that one can even speak of a "Jewish" position in World War I, it was—due to the pogroms in Russia—more pro- than anti-German.

[434] Precise data on the casualties caused in the territory of the Soviet Union by World War I, the civil war, the peasant uprisings, and the accompanying catastrophes of starvation and disease are unavailable today. Cautious estimates suggest a total loss of nine million people, broken down as follows: approximately two million deaths in World War I and three hundred thousand to one million deaths in the civil war; if one estimates a million refugees, then the remaining losses would result from the disease epidemics of 1918–1923 (presumably less than three million dead), the famine in 1920–21, and the peasant uprisings. See Robert Conquest, *The Harvest of Sorrow: Soviet Collectivization and the Terror-Famine* (New York: Oxford Univ. Press, 1986), pp. 53f. For a critique of the figures presented by Conquest, see Stephan Merl, "Wie viele Opfer forderte die 'Liquidierung der Kulaken als Klasse'? Anmerkungen zu einem Buch von Robert Conquest," *Geschichte und Gesellschaft* 14 (1988), pp. 534–540.

[435] In World War I, 1,885,291 German soldiers were killed and 4,248,158 wounded. See *Statistisches Jahrbuch für das Deutsche Reich 1924/25*, p. 25.

436 In December 1917 the Soviet government issued a decree on civil marriage ceremonies, and in April 1918 the first code of law concerning marriage. This code permitted civil marriages as well as divorce, and emphasized the equality of husband and wife as well as the voluntary nature of marriage. On January 1, 1927, a new legal regulation came into effect, equalizing officially registered and nonregistered marriages and facilitating divorce. See Beatrice Brodsky Farnsworth, "Bolshevik Alternatives and the Soviet Family: The 1926 Marriage Law Debate," in Dorothy Atkinson, et al. (eds.), *Women in Russia* (Stanford: Stanford Univ. Press, 1977), pp. 139–165.

437 In Italian fascism—quite in contrast to National Socialism—anti-Semitism initially played only a marginal role; when it existed at all, it was usually politically rather than racially based. Mussolini, who maintained friendly relations with Italians of Jewish descent, referred to the anti-Semitism of the NSDAP at that time as absurd and unscientific. See Meir Michaelis, *Mussolini and the Jews: German-Italian Relations and the Jewish Question in Italy 1922–1945* (Oxford: Oxford Univ. Press, 1978); and also Renzo De Felice, *The Jews in Fascist Italy. A History* (New York: Enigma, 2001).

438 The *Deutschvölkische Freiheitsbewegung* (Ethnic German Liberation Movement) did not obtain a mandate in the Reichstag election of May 20, 1928.

439 The wording of the final pages and a line at the end permit the assumption that this was to be the conclusion of the book and that no pages are missing.

440 The figure may have been misheard; the correct number is likely 16,000. This passage of the speech (including the error) was included in Karl Richard Ganzer's book *Vom Ringen Hitlers um das Reich 1924–1933* (Berlin: Zeitgeschichteverlag, 1935),

INDEX

A

Abel, Werner xix
Abrahamsohn, Itzig Veitel 208
Adám, Magda 267
Adams, Ralf J. Q. 259
Alexander I 266
Amann, Max xii, xxiv, 242
Atkinson, Dorothy 288
Attanasio, Salvator 242
Auriti, Giacinto xvii

B

Bakhmetev, Boris 222, 286
Bakmateff, see Bakhmetev
Barnes, Harry Elmer 220, 286
Baruch, Bernard 220, 286
Batchelor, John 272
Beethoven, Ludwig van 162
Benedetti, Vincent Comte de 89, 260
Benz, Wolfgang 247
Berg, Josef xii–xiv, 235, 263, 275
Bernstorff, Johann Heinrich, Count 220–22, 285–86
Bethmann Hollweg, Theobald von 180, 184, 253, 274
Bismarck-Schönhausen, Otto von xxii, 52, 54–5, 58–61, 64, 68–70, 74, 83, 89–90, 95, 120, 128, 130, 136, 146, 153–54, 171–74, 184, 211, 254, 261, 267–70, 276, 278, 284, 287–88
Blanke, Richard 250
Blücher, Gebhard Leberecht von 135, 266
Bold, John 280
Born, Karl Erich 256
Bourbon-Parma, Sixtus von 254
Bracher, Karl Dietrich 272
Bradley, John F. N. 276
Briand, Aristide 252

Brière, Francis 242
Brodsky, Beatrice 288
Broszat, Martin 243, 281
Buchheim, Hans 247
Bülow 255
Bülow, Bernhard von 255–56

C

Cameron, Norman 241
Carsten, Francis L. 261
Cassels, Alan 273
Cavour, Camillo Benso Conte di 176, 237, 273
Chang Tso-lin 244
Chiang Kai-shek 261
Chickering, Roger 249, 276
Christ, Karl 248
Class, Heinrich 249
Clausewitz, Carl von 131, 135, 248, 266
Clauss, Ludwig Ferdinand 249
Clemenceau, Georges Benjamin 184, 192, 275
Collotti, Enzo 243
Conquest, Robert 287
Corsini, Umberto 255
Coudenhove-Kalegri, Richard Nicolas Count 117, 264–65
Craig, Gordon A. 254

D

Dacre of Glanton, Lord xii
Daitz, Werner 287
Dallin, Alexander 245, 248
De Felice, Renzo 288
Demeter, Karl 249
Derndarsky, Michael 255
Dickman, Fritz 262
Dithmar, Ludwig 280
Doerries, Reinhard R. 285
Domarus, Max 245, 283

Dresler, Adolf 235, 242, 283
Drobisch, Klaus 282
Dülffer, Jost 248, 271
Dull, Paul S. 244
Dusik, Bärbel 243–44, 248, 263

E
East, Sherrod E. 243
Eckart, Dietrich 204, 291
Edwards, P. G. 287
Ehlen, Peter 265
Elizabeth, Empress 205
Elven, Friedrich Wilhelm 219, 285
Elvert, Jürgen 271
Epp, Franz Ritter von xix
Epstein, Klaus 257
Erzberger, Matthias 83, 209, 257

F
Fischer, Fritz 257–58, 276
Fischer, George 277
Flynn, William James 219–22, 285
Förster, Stig 260, 270
Frank, Hans 243
Frauenstädt, Julius 268
Frederick the Great 11, 46, 90, 127, 130, 165, 170, 260, 265
Freiberg, Walter 278
Friedrich Wilhelm I 166, 271
Friedrich Wilhelm IV 249
Funke, Manfred 272

G
Ganzer, Karl Richard 288
Gatzke, Hans W. 250
Gersdorff, Ursula von 260
Gessler, Otto 261
Geyer, Michael 261
Gillessen, Günther 269
Gneisenau, August Neidhart von 135, 266
Gordon, Harold J. 261
Gore, Thomas Pryor 221–22, 286

Groehler, Olaf 272
Groh, Dieter 253
Groote, Wolfgang von 260
Gusy, Christoph 281

H
Hale 242, 245–46
Halem Oron J. 242
Haller de Hallenburg, Józef 276
Halpern, Paul G. 286
Hammer, Hermann 246
Harris, Robert 241
Hartmann, Christian ix, 243–44, 259, 263
Hauser, Christoph 265
Heiber, Helmut 283
Heiden, Konrad 246
Heims, Heinrich 241
Heinemann, Ulrich 272
Heines, Edmund 280
Heinrich VII, Prince of Reuss 274
Heller 260
Hermand, Jost 280
Herostratus 182, 275
Hertling, Georg Friedrich Baron von 257
Herwig, Holger H. 254, 271, 285
Hess, Rudolf xiv–xv, xx, xxiii, 243
Hiden, John 263
Hierl, Konstantin 274
Hildebrand, Klaus 270
Hillgruber, Andreas 245
Hiroharu, Seki 244
Hofer, Andreas xix, 194–95, 210, 244, 278, 283
Hogg, Ian 272
Hohorst, Gerd 251
Holborn, Hajo 252–54
Horak, Stephan 282
Höss, Rudolf 281
House, Edward Mandell 222, 286
Howard, Michael E. 254
Hugenberg, Alfred xxiv, 248

I

Ingrim, Robert   274

J

Jäckel, Eberhard   241, 243, 245–46,
    268, 275, 277, 279
Jäcker   282
Jacobsen, Hans-Adolf   272
Jacobson, Jon   261
Joachimsthaler, Anton   241–42, 29
Jochmann   245
Jochmann, Werner   241

K

Karl of Lorraine, Prince   250
Károlyi, Alois, Count   260
Kater, Michael   241
Keitel, Wilhelm   247
Kennedy, Paul M.   265, 271–72
Kershaw, Ian   244, 256
Kielmansegg, Peter Count   257
Kitchen, Martin   249
Klein, Herbert S.   273
Kluke, Paul   264
Kocka, Jürgen   251
Krenek, Ernst   280
Kolb, Eberhard   260
Konrad, Helmut   254
Krause, Karl Wilhelm   242
Krausnick, Helmut   245, 277
Krohn, Manfred   281
Krüger, Norbert   266
Krüger, Paul   265
Kuhn, Axel   241, 243, 245, 275, 277,
    279, 282

L

Langdon, John W.   263, 275
Lankheit, Klaus A.   ix, 243–44, 263, 279
Lansing, Robert   221, 286
Lauer, Erich   xii
Le May, Michael C.   265
Leake, Paul M.   235

Ledebour, Georg   253
Lemke, Heinz   257
Lepsius, Johannes   274
Lindemann   244
Link, Arthur S.   272, 284, 286
Loth, Wilfried   252
Low, Cedric J.   255
Lowe, C. J.   275
Lowry, Bullitt   249, 254, 257
Lüdecke, Kurt G. W.   243–44
Ludendorff, Erich   258, 276–77

M

Maier-Hartmann, Fritz   283
Mannheim, Ralph   246
Maria Theresa   265
Marzari, F.   255, 275
Matthias, Erich   284
Mau, Hans-Joachim   268
Melkus, Eduard   xviii
Mendel, Gregor   110, 264
Mentzel, Friedrich Wilhelm   260
Merl, Stephan   287
Mersi, Isolde von   283
Michaelis, Meir   288
Molotov, Vyacheslav   255
Moltke, Helmuth von   161, 270–71
Mommsen, Hans   247
Mommsen, Theodor   270
Morely, James W.   244
Morsey, Rudolf   284
Muhr, Josef   284
Müller, Rolf Dieter   268
Mussolini, Benito   xvi–xix, 182, 194,
    239, 243, 246, 249, 273, 275, 278–
    79, 284, 286–88

N

Nachfolger, Franz Eher   xii
Nagel, Irmela   281
Napoleon I   11, 89, 128, 164, 244, 254,
    266–67
Napoleon III   89, 254

Niel, Adolphe 89, 260
Nimitz, Chester W. 260
Noakes, Jeremy 248

O
Overmans, Rüdiger 258

P
Patzig, Helmut 280
Payne, Stanley G. 287
Pese, Walter Werner 243
Peter the Great 148
Petwaidic, Walter 246
Pflanze, Otto 252
Phelps, Reginald H. 242
Picker, Henry 241
Plewnia, Margarete 281
Poirier, Philip P. 259
Poschinger, Heinrich 268
Potter, Elmar B. 260
Price, Billy F. 241
Pridham, Geoffrey 248
Puebla, de la 260

R
Rauchensteiner, Manfred 276
Ribbentrop, Joachim von 255
Ritschel, Karl Heinz 243
Ritter, Gerhard xii, 241, 245, 251, 259
Roberts, A. D. 270
Romsics, Ignác 287
Roosbroeck, Robert von 260
Rosen, Edgar R. 243
Rosenberg, Alfred xvi, xviii, 246, 284
Rössler, Hellmuth 275
Rothenberger, Karl-Heinz 282
Rothfels, Hans xxv, 246, 266
Rudin, Harry R. 248
Rust, Bernhard xiv

S
Salewski, Michael 249
Schaarschmidt, Thomas 271
Scharnhorst, Gerhard Johann David von 135, 266
Schinzinger, Francesca 256
Schirach, Baldur von xiii
Schopenhauer, Arthur 143
Schramm, Percy Ernst 241, 245
Schreiber, Gerhard 286
Schrell, Charles E. 268
Schroeder 241–42
Schubert, Günter 243
Schuker, Stephen A. 272
Schumacher, Rainer 243, 276
Schwabe, Klaus 285
Schwartz, Gotthart 269
Schweitzer, Arthur 248
Schwengler, Walter 280
Seeckt, Hans von 92–3, 261
Seipel, Ignaz xvii–xviii, xx, 275
Shakespeare, William xxvi
Silverman, Dan P. 250
Simon, Heinrich 269
Simon, Kurt 269
Skalnik, Kurt 277
Smith, Denis Mack 274
Smith, Krista xxx
Speer, Albert xiii, xxv, 243, 246
Stadelmann, Rudolf 271
Stein, Karl Reichfreiherr von 128, 135, 266
Steinberg, Jonathan 270
Steinböck, Erwin 277
Steurer, Leopold 275
Stevens, R. H. 241
Stirk, Peter M. R. 264
Stresemann, Gustav xv, xviii–xix, xxiv, 58, 95, 122, 230–31, 256, 260, 268, 272, 277, 279, 288
Stuhlpfarrer, Karl 278
Sutter, Berthold 254

T

Taylor, Telford 242–43
Teuteberg, Hans J. 251
Thomas, Georg 247
Todt, Fritz 247
Torunsky, Vera 273
Trevor-Roper, Hugh R. xii, 245
Trommler, Frank 280
Turgenev, Ivan S. 269
Tyrell, Albrecht ix, xiv

U

Urban, Thomas 282
Urbanitsch, Peter 276

V

Vogel, Rolf 249
Vogelsang, Thilo 258, 268
Volkert, Wilhelm 278
Volkmann, Hans-Erich 257
Vollnhals, Clemens 241, 246

W

Wacker, Wolfgang 267
Waldeck, Friedrich Meyer von 251
Wandycz, Piotr S. 267

Watt, Donald Cameron 281
Weinberg, Gerhard L. xiii, 241–43,
245, 249, 263, 270, 272
Weingarten, Maximilian von 260
Weinzierl, Erika 277
Weissbecker, Manfred 257
White, Christine A. 268
White, Ralph 264
Wieland, Günther 282
Wilhelm I 31, 249, 251, 260
Wilhelm II 255, 265, 271
Wilhelm, Prince of Prussia 261
Willems, Emilio 249
Wilson, Woodrow 218, 220–22, 284–
86
Winkler, Heinric August 262–63, 268,
277–78
Winkler, Wilhelm 262
Wolff, Theodor 269
Woller, Hans 246
Wulf, Peter 277

Z

Zeidler, Manfred 269
Zoller, Albert xi, 241–42